D0000926

GETTING
FROM
COLLEGE
TO CAREER

Discarded from
Garfield County Public
Library System

Garfield County Libraries
Gordon Cooper Branch Library
76 South 4ᵗʰ Street
Carbondale, CO 81623
(970) 963-2889 • Fax (970) 963-8573
www.GCPLD.org

GETTING FROM COLLEGE TO CAREER

Your Essential Guide to
Succeeding in the
Real World

Revised Edition

Lindsey Pollak

HARPER
BUSINESS

NEW YORK • LONDON • TORONTO • SYDNEY

HARPER

BUSINESS

A previous edition of this book was published in 2007 by Collins, an imprint of HarperCollins Publishers.

GETTING FROM COLLEGE TO CAREER. Copyright © 2007, 2012 by Lindsey Pollak. All rights reserved. Printed in the United States of America. No part of this book may be used or reproduced in any manner whatsoever without written permission except in the case of brief quotations embodied in critical articles and reviews. For information address HarperCollins Publishers, 10 East 53rd Street, New York, NY 10022.

HarperCollins books may be purchased for educational, business, or sales promotional use. For information please write: Special Markets Department, HarperCollins Publishers, 10 East 53rd Street, New York, NY 10022.

FIRST REVISED EDITION

Designed by Nancy Singer Olaguera/ISPN Publishing Services

The Library of Congress has catalogued the previous edition as follows:
Pollak, Lindsey.
  Getting from college to career : 90 things to do before you join the real world / by Lindsey Pollak.
     p. cm.
  ISBN 978-0-06-114259-8
  1. College students—Vocational guidance—United States. 2. College students—United States—Life skills guides. I. Title.
  LB2343.P57 2007
  378.1'98—dc22

                                                              2006051822

ISBN 978-0-06-206927-6 (revised edition)

12 13 14 15 16   OV/RRD   10 9 8 7 6 5 4 3 2

To Evan and Chloe

TO EVAN AND CHLOE

CONTENTS

INTRODUCTION xi

HOW TO GET THE MOST OUT OF THIS BOOK xix

1 **Get Started** 1
  1. Start Wherever You Are
  2. Know the Numbers
  3. Avoid the Biggest Mistake in Career Prep and Job Hunting
  4. Embrace Your Stereotype
  5. Overcome Your Stereotype
  6. Get Organized
  7. Don't Ignore the Obvious
  8. Subscribe to a Daily News Source
  9. Set Yourself Up for Success
  10. Use Your Helicopter

2 **Stop Being a Student and Start Being a Professional** 29
  11. Upgrade to Grown-up Contact Methods
  12. E-mail Like a Professional
  13. Get Carded
  14. Clean Up Your Internet Image
  15. Shine Online
  16. Become an Industry Expert

3 Figure Out What You Want . . . and What You Don't   49

17. Start a Really Big List
18. Get Rid of the "Shoulds"
19. Don't Be Caught "Hitchhiking": Assess Yourself
20. Explore a Passion
21. Put Money into Perspective
22. Declare a Take Yourself to Work Day: Job Shadow
23. Tweet
24. Consider a Coach
25. Hero Worship
26. Seek a Mentor
27. Relax—A Job Is Not a Soul Mate

4 Talk. Listen. Repeat. (i.e., Network)   89

28. Talk. Listen. Repeat.
29. Be Able to Introduce Yourself
30. Network with Your Neighbors
31. Set Up Informational Interviews
32. Make the Most of Informational Interviews
33. Become an Active Alum . . . Even Before You Graduate
34. Associate
35. Connect with Diversity
36. Work Some New Rooms
37. Make Every Networking Event a Success
38. Nix These Networking Event No-Nos
39. Be the First to Follow Up
40. Keep in Touch

5 Gain Real World Experience   137

41. Be a Leader
42. Be a Joiner
43. Intern . . . Early and Often
44. Practice the Eight Essentials of Internship Achievement
45. Temp

46. Volunteer
47. Skip South Beach
48. Be Superstrategic About Part-Time Work
49. Put Out Your Own Shingle
50. GOTV
51. Go Global
52. Fail

6 Give Yourself an Edge   **182**
53. Minor in Something Majorly Helpful
54. Keep Learning
55. Become BRIC Savvy
56. Be a Winner
57. Take a Physical Challenge
58. Present
59. Perform Five Minutes of Stand-Up
60. Have a Hobby
61. Blog
62. Open Your Mouth and Say "Om"

7 Market Yourself on Paper and Online   **209**
63. Make Over Your Résumé
64. Put Your Résumé Through the Wringer
65. Craft Impressive Cover Letters
66. Create a Brag Book
67. Become Professional Friends with Facebook

8 Find Opportunities   **233**
68. Follow Every Rainbow
69. Take Candy from Strangers
70. Start Small
71. Look Up the Best
72. Consider You.gov
73. Work to Change the World

74. Tackle a Project
75. Look Online
76. Think "And," Not "Or"

9 Overprepare for Interviews 263
77. Conduct Company Research
78. Know Your Value
79. Figure In Work-Life Fit
80. Buy a Dark Suit
81. Take Your Elbows Off the Table
82. Mock Interview
83. Never, Ever, Ever Arrive Late to a Job Interview
84. Be Nice to Receptionists
85. Go with the Flow
86. Be Available
87. Persist (Without Being a Pest)

10 Before You Head Off into the Real World . . . 306
88. Ask for Help When You Need It
89. Become a Lifelong Expert on Finding Your Own Bliss
90. *Don't* Curb Your Enthusiasm

RESOURCES 311
AUTHOR'S NOTE 323
ACKNOWLEDGMENTS 325

INTRODUCTION

It's not easy to figure out what to be when you grow up.

In college I was pretty sure I was going to be a lawyer. Before that I wanted to be a high school teacher or a college professor. When I was five I wanted to be a toll collector.

So, how did I end up being a writer and career expert? I'll give you the short version, because otherwise my story, like most people's career tales, could take up this entire book.

Around my sophomore year of college I started to realize that I would eventually graduate and have to find something else to do with my life besides being a student. Law school seemed like the best option for an American Studies major with a concentration in literature and no experience in anything—and that's what a lot of people said I should do, so I signed up for a free practice LSAT exam and bought a study guide. But all of the legal stuff in the guide bored me so much that I gave up and just took the test cold. "I'm smart," I rationalized. "Everyone thinks I should go to law school. Maybe I'm a natural. How hard could this be?"

Ha!

I never told anyone that I took that practice test. I thought the questions seemed impossible. Every answer seemed plausible. I guessed on half the choices and couldn't finish in the time allotted. I never picked up my scores because I was too scared of having the lowest practice LSAT score in history.

If the fact that I wasn't even interested enough in law to get through the study guide hadn't been enough of a sign, the LSAT experience was. Being a lawyer was out.

After that, I turned to my parents for help, and my mom introduced me to a nonprofit women's business organization where she had trained to start and manage her small business. She thought it would be a good place for me to meet a lot of different businesspeople from a lot of different industries. It turned out the organization was looking for an intern, so I offered myself for the (unpaid) job and got my first dose of work experience that summer. It was fun. I did research, filed stuff, got the three other staff people salads with dressing on the side for lunch, and enjoyed one major perk: the staff often went to business networking events in the community, and they brought me along with them.

One day, one of the staffers brought me to a local Rotary Club meeting, where a kind older gentleman sat next to me and chatted with me for a while. "So, what are you going to do after college, Lindsey?" he asked eventually, as people always do.

"I have no idea," I said. "I've thought about law school, but I'm not sure."

"Have you ever thought about going abroad? Rotary offers international graduate school scholarships and I think you'd be a good candidate."

In Tip #68, "Follow Every Rainbow," you'll see that I recommend exploring a wide variety of options to find the right career path, because you never know which one will lead to your pot of gold. That man, that moment at the Rotary Club meeting, turned out to be mine.

Once I learned about the Rotary Ambassadorial Scholarship program, through which you can attend graduate school in the country of your choice, I applied immediately. For two weeks straight all I did was write essays, gather transcripts, request reference letters, and think about spending a few years as a glamorous expat. I decided I wanted to continue learning more about women in business, so I applied to women's studies master's degree programs. And I wanted to live someplace fun and warmer than the East Coast of the United States, where I had spent my whole life, so I chose Australia.

Somehow, and I really can't explain it, something just clicked deep in my gut that going abroad was the exact thing I wanted to do after college. Just a day earlier, I had absolutely no idea what I wanted. But when I heard about this opportunity, I knew it was right. And a year and a half later, when I found myself in Melbourne, Australia, interviewing women business owners, journaling every morning, volunteering as a reading series coordinator, and writing my master's thesis day and night, I was on my way to a career as a professional writer and career expert.

Was it fate that I met that man and he changed my life? Perhaps. But if I had been sick that morning and hadn't attended the Rotary meeting, I believe it would have happened some other way. The point is that I didn't know my right career path until I saw it, heard it, touched it. This is why throughout the book you'll notice my obsession with taking action, trying new things, meeting new people, and having a wide variety of experiences. You have to get out there and see what exists. What's possible. What's calling your name. I don't believe you can plan your career by sitting in your dorm room or bedroom and just thinking really hard.

I know that the sitting-in-your-room-and-thinking strategy doesn't work because, unfortunately, I tried it when I returned home from two and a half amazing years in Australia. Even though I had fallen in love with interviewing people and writing, and even though I had just enjoyed a unique international adventure, and even though I had earned a master's degree, I couldn't decide what kind of jobs to pursue back home in the United States. After all, I still hadn't had a Real Job yet. I was sad that my overseas adventure had ended, I felt like my friends back home were light-years ahead of me in the job market, and I felt overwhelmed by deciding what city to live in, what positions to apply for, and what direction to take. So I did the only natural thing: I froze.

For about four months I lived at home with my parents and spent hours on the computer typing phrases like "writer" and "international experience" into a jobs website and hoping my dream career would pop up on the screen. I'm sorry to report that didn't happen, and it never does. Jobs just don't come to you. Career plans don't grow on trees. And well-meaning parents and friends can only do so much to help.

In a nutshell, my scientific diagnosis of my post-Australia situation is that it totally sucked. There were some days when I wanted to move right back to Melbourne and find some additional graduate degree to pursue. There were some bad days when I sent one semiproductive e-mail in the morning and then watched TV all day and ate nothing but frozen yogurt. And there were some very bad days when I felt I was a miserable failure with my best years behind me, and I spent the entire day under the covers.

Eventually, at some point, perhaps from sheer boredom or a need to go out and buy more frozen yogurt, I began to leave the house, pick up the phone, and take little bits of action. I called a few people I'd worked with at the nonprofit organization where I had my summer internship in college. I called some people I had met through that local Rotary Club and asked to attend a meeting. I signed up for a few sessions with a career coach. I started to make lists of my interests and my contacts and my life goals. My mom took me to buy a suit. Every few days I did a little something more, and slowly, painfully slowly, momentum started to build.

Action always yields rewards.

My reward came in the form of a fax. One day I received a fax from Fran, my former boss at the nonprofit women's business organization. She sent me a one-page article from *BusinessWeek* magazine about the launch of a new website for businesswomen, started by the founders of *Working Woman* magazine. The head-line of the article was circled, and Fran had written, "Call them!"

And so I did.

I called New York City information and asked for the main number of *Working Woman* magazine. I dialed the number imme-diately and asked to speak to someone in human resources. The receptionist put me through and when the woman answered, I told her that I had seen the recent article in *BusinessWeek*, and I had just received a master's degree in women's studies, and my thesis was about businesswomen, and I would love to know if they were hiring. She asked me to fax my résumé, and the next day invited me in for an interview. A few weeks later, they offered me a job working at the new website.

So, to recap how I got my first job in the Real World: explor-ing things I didn't have a knack for (law), getting whatever kind of experience I could (internship), following my passion and gut instincts (Australia), making and maintaining relationships (Fran), getting involved with professional organizations (Rotary Club), following leads (the fax), and selling myself (the call to *Working Woman*). No one strategy would have done it. No to-do item was the magic bullet. Success came from a combination of factors, actions, and connections. The challenge is that you never know which combination will ultimately work, so you have to try them all.

That's what this book is all about: taking action and trying a variety of things to find your first job in the Real World. Most career books for college students and recent grads teach you how to write a résumé and tell you what to say on a job interview. That's great, but what they miss is all of the work you need to do *before* that point so you have impressive things to put on that résumé, experiences to talk about on those job interviews, and, perhaps most important, the confidence and preparedness to take advan-tage of the opportunities that arise.

Getting from College to Career is the book I wish had existed when I was in college. It's the book I wish my younger brother and sister had. It's a collection of all of the tips, ideas, advice, secrets, strategies, and warnings that I didn't even know I didn't know. It's the book that can help make this weird time—full of questions, transitions, and decisions—as painless and productive as possible.

According to the consulting firm Human Resource Executives, 85 percent of entry-level job candidates are poorly prepared for the job search process. That's a scary statistic, and it doesn't surprise me at all. I felt totally unprepared for the working world when I was a student. And now, working as a writer, consultant, and speaker specializing in entry-level career advice, I regularly speak to groups of college students from all over the country, who ask the same questions: How do I figure out what I should do with my life? Where do I get a job without experience? What if I make a mistake? Can you please help?!

My short answers are: You figure it out by asking a lot of questions and trying a lot of different things. You have a lot more experience than you think you do. You will make mistakes, and that's a good thing. And, yes, I want to help. In fact, I won't rest until I've given you 90 strategies to try.

In the spirit of being painless (and hopefully fun), the book's chapters are presented as easy-to-read tips. You'll notice that many of the tips include an exercise box called "Make This Work for You." The goal of these boxes is for you to customize the tip to your unique situation and to learn helpful tricks and shortcuts for staying motivated over time. You'll find "Done!" boxes at the end of each of these exercises so you can place a big, fat, satisfying check mark when you've completed the action.

You'll also come across "Extra Credit" boxes throughout the book, where I've asked various experts to provide you with even more detailed information about certain topics. "Proof It's Possible" boxes offer real stories about real young people whose early career efforts have paid off, such as Erin Berkery, who turned a temp job into a dream job in publishing, and Bobby Lopez, who wrote a fan letter to Stephen Sondheim in high school, worked as a temp at Pfizer for Viagra, and then cocreated the musicals *Avenue Q* and *The Book of Mormon* and won his first Tony Award in his twenties. And finally, "Reality Check" boxes share quotes from real people who've survived the postcollege job search and lived to tell about it.

I look forward to sharing this college-to-career journey with you. Welcome, in advance, to the Real World. I think you'll like it here.

HOW TO GET THE MOST OUT OF THIS BOOK

I have one simple instruction for applying the advice in this book: focus on the tips that you feel will have the most immediate impact for you. You can read every page or skip the tips that don't feel applicable to your situation. This book does not contain a step-by-step, all-inclusive guide to getting a job. Rather, it offers the very best tips I've gathered on a wide variety of topics to help you stand out from the crowd and make a successful transition from college student to career professional. I've attempted to give you the greatest variety and best advice available, but if a certain tip doesn't speak to you, skip it and move on to more relevant information. Or read the tip for inspiration and ideas, but apply the suggested actions in your own way. The most important thing is for you to find the resources and tools you need to get focused on what you want to do, get experience and connections, and get hired by the employer of your dreams.

Don't wait another minute to get started working on your transition from college to your career in the Real World: 90 tips are ready and waiting!

Make This Book Work for You

My favorite part of going to the movies is definitely the trailers. I could watch previews all day; I love to get a sense of a movie before I spend my money and time to see it. So, I'd like to give you that same opportunity. While all of the tips in this book can apply to anyone, here are some special instructions to readers in particular situations:

- If you have absolutely no idea what career path you want to pursue, pay special attention to Tips #19, 22, and 25. As you've already learned from my story, you probably won't know the perfect industry or job for you until you experience it. It's great to sit and think about what you might want to do, but you'll figure it out much faster if you leave the house and try things.

- If you are shy and feel that might get in the way of your job search, check out Tips #4, 26, 31, and 37. Meeting and talking to people is the single most effective action you can take to find the right career. But you don't have to be the most outgoing person in the world to do this.

- If you identify yourself as part of a minority group or you're a first-generation American, you may face additional challenges as you begin your postcollege job search. But you also have some advantages and opportunities. Check out Tips #26, 35, and 71 for special strategies.

- If you have a deep passion but you're not sure how to make a living with it, you'll want to pore over Tips #20, 21, and 76. Rest assured that I am 100 percent in favor of following your bliss, so all you'll get from me is encouragement.

GETTING
FROM
COLLEGE
TO CAREER

Chapter 1

GET STARTED

This first section is all about getting ready to discover and pursue your ideal career. I am entirely certain that you, no matter who you are, or what the economy is doing, can find a terrific, fulfilling, enjoyable job that will start you on the road to a career that will make you happy and successful. But first you have to believe that it's really possible. No matter what, don't let anything—including your own thoughts or fears—interfere with getting a head start on your bright future.

1. START WHEREVER YOU ARE

Between my own first job search and researching this book, I've read virtually every career-advice-for-college-students book, blog, and Twitter feed available. And every single one offers the same opening advice about finding a great postcollege job: start early.

Good advice, for sure, and I wholeheartedly agree. If you are reading this book as a college freshman, sophomore, or junior, then you are in great shape. But . . . .

What if you haven't started early? What if you have, in fact, started really, really late? What if you're a second-semester senior? What if—gasp!—you are reading this book when you're already a year or two out of college and you still haven't found a job or a career path?

I'm here to tell you that it's okay.

I agree with all of the other books that it is ideal to start thinking about your career plans as early in your life as possible, but I also know the reality is that many people don't do this, and it isn't very helpful to tell a college senior that she should have started doing internships her freshman year. I promise you that this book contains strategies for those who are starting early (Welcome, freshmen!) and those who are starting later.

It is never too early or too late. But one thing is essential: you must choose to start your planning and searching wherever you are *right now.* The smartest strategy for any job seeker is to accept and embrace your starting point. Your task will be to maximize the advantages of your particular situation and work hard to minimize the obstacles. Virtually every tip in this book applies to job seekers at every stage of the process.

But whether you are a freshman, sophomore, junior, senior, recent grad, or not-so-recent grad, there is one thing you must do as the first step of this book:

Starting this minute, commit to starting and having a great career. Therapists and self-help gurus will tell you that happiness is a choice; well, I think that having a great career is a choice, too. You can make it happen. And by taking action on the tips in this book, you will.

As you'll see in many of the stories ahead, if you're willing to do some work, take some risks, and apply some wise advice, you can and will get a terrific job and build a smart career path. Don't worry about what you could've done, would've done, or should've done up to this point. Just get started right now.

Your very first assignment: put a big, fat, satisfying check mark in the box below. The path to your dream career is waiting.

━━ ━━ ━━ ━━ ━━ ━━ ━━

Make This Work for You

Make a commitment to work on your career, starting today.

☐ Done!

━━ ━━ ━━ ━━ ━━ ━━ ━━

2. KNOW THE NUMBERS

When you're graduating and just starting out in the workforce, particularly in challenging economic times, it may seem that *everyone* is getting a job faster than you are or *no one* is moving back home to live with their parents. Well, it's time for a reality check. The truth is that over a million people graduate from college each year, so I promise that whatever your situation, lots and lots of other people are right there with you. Take this quick quiz to learn the real stats about college graduates and the job market.

1. How long does it take the average college graduate to get a job?
   a. Less than 3 months
   b. 3 to 9 months
   c. Over a year

Answer: b. According to the National Association of Colleges and Employers' 2011 Student Survey, the median time that seniors from the class of 2011 took to land a job was 7.74 months. In 2010 the median was 6.95 months. Be prepared not to find a position overnight.

2. What percentage of college graduates move back home after graduation?
   a. 30%
   b. 50%
   c. 80%

Answer: c. The number of grads moving back home has steadily increased, thanks in part to the global economic recession. According to CollegeGrad.com, among U.S. college graduates, 80 percent moved back home with their parents, up from 67 percent in 2006. The message? It's perfectly okay and totally normal to move back in with your parents or parent for a while to save money and get on your feet professionally.

3. How long do most recent college graduates plan to stay in their first jobs?
   a. 3 to 6 months
   b. 1 to 3 years
   c. At least 5 years

Answer: b. According to Right Management, 55 percent of 2010 college graduates said they planned to stay in their first jobs for one to three years. If you're an average American college graduate, it's highly unlikely that your first employer will be your last. While it's commendable to look for an employer you'll want to remain with for a long time, it's okay to make a decision based on where you want to be for the next few years only.

4. How much more money over a lifetime does a college graduate make than a high school graduate?
   a. 25% more
   b. 50% more
   c. 75% more

Answer: c. The U.S. Census Bureau reports that over a typical, forty-year working lifetime, the average college graduate earns about 75 percent more. So, yes, that degree is worth it!

5. About how many jobs will the average person have in his or her lifetime?
   a. 5 to 7
   b. 12 to 15
   c. 20 to 25

Answer: b. According to the Bureau of Labor Statistics, the average worker currently holds ten different jobs before age forty, and this number is projected to grow. Forrester Research predicts that today's youngest workers—that's you—will hold twelve to fifteen jobs in their lifetimes.

3. AVOID THE BIGGEST MISTAKE IN CAREER PREP AND JOB HUNTING

Remember how the nicest grade-school teachers always said, "There are no stupid questions." Well, I would add that there are no stupid ways to gain experience and look for a job. The only stupid thing you can do is to do nothing.

That's right—the worst mistake you can make is not to take any action at all. How do I know this? Because I did it. As you learned in the introduction, when I returned from graduate school in Australia and moved back into my old bedroom in my parents' house, I spent about a month under the covers. I did absolutely nothing, except sprain my ankle when I finally ventured out jogging one day. That led to another month of doing absolutely nothing.

By not taking any action at all, I pretty much guaranteed that I wouldn't find a job. Once I started making some phone calls, meeting some people for lunch, and sending out my résumé, I built momentum and began to find opportunities. The minute I took action—any action—things started happening.

Whenever you are stuck, frustrated, nervous, clueless, confused, discouraged, or overwhelmed, in my experience the answer is always action. Just do something. That's why this book is arranged in action-oriented tips. Every page includes a way for you to move forward, no matter where you are in the career planning process. And I recommend taking at least one career-related action every single day.

This is a great mind-set to keep with you at every stage of your career. As long as you're not standing still, you can rest assured that you're moving closer to your goals and dreams.

4. EMBRACE YOUR STEREOTYPE

I know that you're a special person with many unique qualities that we will explore and expand upon throughout the tips in this book. At the same time, you are also totally generic. What I mean by this is that you are in no way the first, the last, or even the fifty-millionth person to be in your current life stage.

Along with the burping baby, the blushing bride, and the midlife crisis man with a brand new sports car, the I-am-ready-to-take-on-the-world-just-as-soon-as-I-figure-out-what-I-am-going-to-do-next-year-and-for-the-rest-of-my-life graduating college student is a familiar American stereotype. Everyone knows it's challenging but also exciting to go from a campus environment to the Real World, but hopefully you can take comfort from the fact that almost everyone who has gone to college has experienced this in some form. You've probably already realized this from the number of times adults have said to you, sometimes in a good way and sometimes in a bad way, "Boy, I sure remember what it was like to be in your position!"

Instead of rolling your eyes every time someone says this, my advice is to take advantage of it. Whenever you're telling anyone, from a relative to a professor to a random stranger in line behind you at Subway, that you are looking for your first job and that person's response is something like, "Wow, I'm so glad I'm not in your shoes!" or "Wait until you have three kids and a mortgage, kid. You'll be dying to go back to this time in your life," don't just smirk. Instead, smile, take a deep breath, and then treat the situation as an opportunity. Ask for some free advice. I bet you'll be surprised at the responses you get and the detailed ideas or real job leads you might pick up. As long as you ask politely and with genuine interest, most people will take a few minutes to help an earnest young college student or recent grad.

What exactly should you ask in such situations? Here are some good, simple questions you can pose to anyone and everyone who seems to take an interest in your situation:

- What's your best job search tip?
- What was your first job, and do you think it was a good choice?
- Who do you think are the best employers in this area?
- Have you heard about any young people with really cool jobs during or after college?
- What do you wish you had known when you were my age?

By asking questions like the ones above, you'll start collecting tips, suggestions, and warnings that can really make a difference for you. For instance, if nine out of ten people tell you that they wish they had learned more about their career before jumping into it, then you might want to take that advice quite seriously. If your parents, your older brother, and your three cousins from Ohio practically cry when they talk about how much they regretted procrastinating finding a job after college, then you'll be much more likely to start as soon as possible.

Remember, no-cost research opportunities are literally everywhere, including on the phone that's probably sitting right next to you as you read this. There is an enormous amount of information, experience, and expertise out there that you can tap into at every stage of your first job search and for the rest of your life. So, start asking questions, listening to the answers, and taking copious notes.

Besides getting some good information, this exercise is important for another reason: you want to get into the habit of regularly talking about your career planning, job search, future goals, and networking needs so they become a more and more comfortable topic of discussion for you. This will come in handy later when we start to talk about the importance of networking.

To give you a head start, I surveyed a hundred professionals in a variety of fields and asked what they wish they had known at your life stage. Here are some of the most revealing answers, and you'll find more in sidebars throughout the book:

> "I wish I had known that I wasn't going to be an overnight success."
> *Derek Billings, creative director*

> "There are no mistakes, and even a job that seems to have been a mistake or a bad fit can lead you to the next step—the people you meet, the experience you had, etc."
> *Cali Williams Yost, author,* Work+Life, *and president and founder, Work+Life Fit, Inc.*

"As a journalist, I now know that what I enjoy as a reader doesn't have much bearing on what I'll like as an employee. Just because you love to read a certain magazine, it doesn't necessarily mean that you'll enjoy working there."

> *Julianne Pepitone, staff reporter, CNN*
> *Money*

"If you're patient, big dreams can come true. Success doesn't always come in lightning-fast ways and in ways that you could have predicted. Stay focused on your dreams, but be willing to bend."

> *Maggie Jackson, columnist and author,*
> Distracted: The Erosion of Attention and
> the Coming Dark Age

"I wish I knew earlier in my career that working hard would not contribute to my long-term success as much as building lifelong professional relationships based on trust and mutual respect."

> *Dr. Lois P. Frankel, author,* Nice Girls Don't
> Get the Corner Office *and* Nice Girls Just
> Don't Get It

Make This Work for You

This week, ask at least three people: What do you wish you'd known about your career when you were my age? Record the three pieces of advice you find most helpful:

1.

2.

3.

Now commit to incorporating this advice into the rest of your career planning and job search.

☐ **Done!**

- - - - - - - - - - - - - -

5. OVERCOME YOUR STEREOTYPE

Remember that positive, fresh-faced college grad stereotype from the last tip? Well, it has a dark side. Some people don't exactly have the best impression of college grads today. I like to think of this as the "Kids today!" grump syndrome (usually said while the person rolls his eyes). Just as your parents and grandparents will tell you that they walked uphill both ways to school, they will tell you that college graduates in their day were more polite, more respectful, and more hardworking than today's young people.

The thing is, well . . . it's kind of true.

Current young people—known as Generation Y or Millennials—don't exactly have the best reputation in the workplace.

Here are some of the comments I've heard from Baby Boomer and Generation X–aged human resources executives and other professionals who interview and hire entry-level employees. I asked the simple question, "What is your impression of recent college grads in the workforce today?" Some of the not-so-positive responses included:

- "They feel a sense of entitlement, but they don't have the skills to back up their confidence."
- "They don't seem to care about building a career."
- "They're lazy."
- "They want instant feedback and instant gratification."

Lots of people had good things to say as well, and no stereotype is ever 100 percent true, but it's important to know that this perception is out there. Why am I telling you this? Not to make you feel bad. It's because I believe that just as you can turn the more positive college grad stereotype to your advantage, you can turn the negative impression of your generation into a huge advantage as well. How? By *not* reinforcing this stereotype.

Think about it: If most people—job interviewers especially— believe that young people are lazy, entitled, and rude—then you can really stand out by being hardworking, respectful, and well mannered. If a corporate recruiter calls fifteen job candidates and you are the only one with a professional-sounding voice mail message, who do you think will get the interview? If you greet your interviewer as Ms. Stewart and everyone else jumps right to calling her Martha, who will make the best first impression? Courtesy and humility count. In fact, a vice-president of recruiting at Citigroup told me that the number one way entry-level candidates distinguish themselves is simply by being polite.

6. GET ORGANIZED

No matter when or where you start to work on your postcollege career planning, I recommend treating the process as if you're taking a class on the subject. There won't be any exams, but there will be plenty of reading, handouts, note taking, and studying. This means you need an organization system. Lucky for you, I'm a type A, Virgo, hyperorganized person who once had a dream about alphabetizing my bookshelf (embarrassing, but true). So, you're learning from a pro. Here are my suggestions for the tools you'll need to keep track of your career planning and job searching. You can implement this system no matter when you start this process.

1. First and foremost, you need a **notebook** to keep track of ideas, research, planning, and other information. You can use a computer document or smartphone app if you prefer, but I recommend buying a notebook with a cover that makes you feel happy and positive—the good energy can't hurt, right? From this point forward, keep your career planning notebook with you at all times. You never know when you might think of a new idea or hear about a company or program you want to look into. And by keeping all of your notes in one place, you're less likely to lose any ideas or information. If you're really hard core, you can even keep the notebook on your nightstand, in case you have any great career brainstorms while you're dozing off to sleep at night.

2. Next, develop a **filing system**, on your computer or in a file drawer, to keep track of documents, applications, brochures, newspaper clippings, résumés, event invitations, etc. Make a new folder for every single opportunity you're considering so information is easy to access when you need it. To be

even more organized, you can group your files into categories. Depending on your particular interests, categories could include: Internship Opportunities, Potential Employers, Study-Abroad Applications, Networking Contacts, Volunteer Organizations, Articles to Read, Events Attended, Associations, Cover Letters, Recommendation Letters, and Encouraging Notes from Mom.

3. Buy a **calendar** (or use a web-based version such as GCal) and plan to mark down every application deadline, networking event, informational interview, and anything else related to your job search. Keep all of your appointments, job search–related or not, on one calendar so you don't accidentally book an interview on the same day as lunch with your grandmother or a biology exam. If you're following the advice to take at least one action every day on behalf of your career planning or job search, mark each action on your calendar to keep track of your progress.

4. Once you get heavily into your job search, you'll also want to keep a **spreadsheet or notebook log** to keep track of every interaction you have with the companies to which you're applying. Note the date on which you send in a résumé, the date of any scheduled interviews, the date you send a thank-you note, the date you make a follow-up phone call, and any other interactions in person, online, or by phone. Jot down a few notes about each interaction as well. For instance, "Ms. Healy is on vacation—assistant said to call back in one week" (and then mark this on your calendar), or "E-mailed cover letter and résumé to XYZ Corp. human resources department. Also posted résumé in HR database." When you're applying to lots of jobs it's easy to lose track of who's who and what's what. Don't rely on your memory for information this important.

5. Create a **contact database system.** You need a way to keep track of every person you meet along your career planning path—from networking contacts to career counselors to friends to alumni to company recruiters. Your network is hugely important to your career, so you don't want to lose track of anyone you meet. Take your pick from Gmail contacts, Apple Address Book, Microsoft Outlook, or any other contact management software. An old-school address book is fine too. It doesn't matter what you use as long as you have a system that works for you. If you choose computer software, be sure to print out your contact list occasionally and have a backup method, in case your computer crashes or you lose your laptop. On that note, I also would advise against keeping contact information only in your cell phone, just in case the device breaks or gets misplaced.

According to Mary Carlomagno, the owner of order, the organization company (www.orderperiod.com), and author of *Give It Up! My Year of Learning to Live Better with Less*, an important aspect of staying organized is keeping your contacts up to date. "A good rule of thumb is this: if you are unable to place who the person is from his or her business card, chances are you won't reconnect," advises Mary. How can you keep people straight in your mind when you're meeting lots of recruiters and other new contacts during your job search? Mary recommends using a memory hook: "After you meet someone for

Reality Check

"What do I wish I had known when I graduated college that I know now? To keep the contact information of everyone you ever meet anywhere, with notes!"

Karlin Sloan,
CEO, Karlin Sloan & Company, leadership development consulting

the first time, make a note for each contact person, where you met or the topic of your conversation." That should help you with recall later on.

The most important message about being organized with your career planning and job searching is to develop a system that works for you. Determining your career path and searching for a job are hard enough as it is; don't let an overflowing desk drawer of Diet Coke–stained résumés or a lost Post-it note with a recruiter's phone number make it any harder.

Remember also that the research and organizing you do now is likely to come in handy later in your career. I'm pretty sure that this will not be the only job search you ever undertake, so think of the information you're collecting now as the beginnings of your personal, customized, superorganized career research library.

7. DON'T IGNORE THE OBVIOUS

Do not pass Go, do not collect $200, until you've visited your school's career services office.

Often students ignore this resource if they're not attracted to the companies that typically recruit on their campus, or they criticize their school's career services office for not doing enough. One respondent to my survey commented, "To be honest, I wish that my career services office had coddled us all a bit more." Another person said, "Career Services, at least at my school, was very focused on educating us only about the jobs that were recruiting on campus. And they gave much more attention to the business students. So if you were a liberal arts major, you were very much left to fend for yourself, which was hard."

Perhaps you have similar complaints, which may be entirely justified. According to a 2006 study by CareerDNA and Teenage Research Unlimited, 65 percent of graduating seniors say they've never bothered to use their college career center. And yet, according to the National Association of Colleges and Employers (NACE), students from the class of 2010 who visited their college career centers had a median salary $5,700 higher than those who never set foot in the career services office. I admit that I barely set foot in mine when I was an undergrad. And I can tell you that it's a decision I deeply regret. Now that I'm out here in the Real World, and especially because I work with people on building their careers, I know how much we could all benefit from what these offices have to offer—and if you're a current student or recent alum, most of the services are entirely free to you right now.

Even if you aren't interested in any of the companies actively recruiting on your campus, I guarantee you will benefit from taking advantage of at least one, if not all, of the following services:

- Assessment testing
- Résumé and online profile critiquing
- Databases of apprenticeship/job shadow/internship opportunities
- Interview training and mock interviewing (often with videotaping) in person or via phone or Skype
- Career counseling
- Career fairs and recruiting events
- Workshops, seminars, and lectures with expert speakers
- Networking with career services staff. Think about it: they know all the employers!

The thing is, all of these resources won't come to you; you have to meet your career services office halfway. You need to walk in and use the resource library. You need to sign up for e-mail alerts, Facebook updates, and Twitter feeds from the career services office to know when expert speakers are coming to campus. You need to sign up for mock interviews, career counseling, and résumé critiques. If nothing else, visit the website of your school's career center—most have online resources that can be very helpful during your planning and searching.

If I had it all to do over again, I would have walked into the career services center my freshman year. I would have taken advantage of all the free help I could get. The good news for me, and for you if you've already graduated, is that, according to the National Association of Colleges and Employers' 2005 survey of colleges and universities across the country, 96.3 percent of career centers report that they extend services to job-seeking alumni, often for no cost.

Career planning and job hunting are hard enough; don't miss out on the easy stuff.

8. SUBSCRIBE TO A DAILY NEWS SOURCE

This tip involves a homework assignment for the rest of your life (yes, there's still homework after graduation). I honestly consider this to be my number one job search and career development tip and share it with every audience I ever speak to: read the news every single day. In many cases, you don't even have to pay for a subscription, as most news sites are available for free online. I highly recommend a national news source, such as the *New York Times*, CNN.com, or the *Wall Street Journal*, but a local news outlet, particularly from a major metropolitan area, can be a good resource as well. This tip will change your life—personally and professionally.

Here's why:

You will be aware of new opportunities. You'll read about new companies forming, "hot" industries that are expanding, store openings, new management teams, events, and of course you'll find classified job listings. Any of these could lead to a real job prospect, and you want to be the first to know.

You'll never be tongue-tied at a recruiting function, networking event, alumni picnic—or even on a date. By keeping up with the news you can feel comfortable chatting with pretty much anyone about current events. "Have you seen the new vampire movie that got such great reviews?" "What do you think of the organic food trend?" "Did you read about that eighteen-year-old who was elected mayor of his town?" Chitchat is a serious part of the Real World, and those who read the news have a leg up in the small-talk department.

You'll avoid dangerous mistakes. By reading the news every day, particularly the business section if you're interested in a corporate career, you'll be sure to know if a company you're visiting for an interview appeared in an article that day. You'll never make the mistake of praising a CEO who was just indicted on fraud charges. And you'll be aware of any advertising campaigns the company is running, so you can comment on new products they may discuss when interviewing you. If you're interested in a career in politics or public relations, industries obsessed with current events, reading the news—especially twenty-four-hour news websites—is positively essential.

You can assess yourself if you're unsure of your career direction. As you're reading each day, see which articles you are naturally drawn to. Notice which sections or stories you skip and which ones you read from beginning to end. Which part do you read first? Which articles bore you to tears? Notice what most appeals to you and look for patterns in your interests. Perhaps you find yourself attracted to articles about science or philanthropy or criminal trials. This is a sign that these may be career avenues you should explore.

And finally, you can use the news for a shot of inspiration and ideas. Newspapers, news websites, news-based Twitter feeds, and current events blogs are chock-full of stories about successful people, heroic people, creative people, balanced people, and ambitious people. I urge you to file and share stories that motivate you and save them in an "I want to be like that!" folder that you can look through whenever your job search becomes frustrating or overwhelming. I know a woman who decided to adopt a baby from China because of an article she saw in a newspaper. I've donated to charities whose work has been featured on blogs I read. And some of the tips in this book have come from career strategies I've read about—you guessed it—in the news.

Make This Work for You

Reading the news daily may sound like a great idea today. And tomorrow. And the next day. And maybe even for a week or two. But what happens when you start to work the early shift at your part-time job and you no longer have time to sit for half an hour with a bagel and the morning news? What happens if you leave home and can't mooch off your parents' *Wall Street Journal* subscription any longer?

Here are some tips to make sure you keep up with your news reading habit:

- **Have news headlines delivered directly to your inbox.** Most news sources offer free e-newsletters that feature the top daily stories. It only takes a few minutes to scan down a list of headlines and read at least the first paragraph of each story to stay on top of the news. The first time you check your e-mail each morning, make this the first message you open to ensure you keep up with this habit. At the very least, make a national news website your home page, and scan the day's headlines when you open your Internet browser.

- **Combine newspaper reading with another daily activity.** If you prefer reading the real, live paper, the best way to stick with the practice is to combine your paper reading with something else you really enjoy, or something you do each day anyway. For example, if you go to the gym every morning, read the newspaper while you're riding the exercise bike or climbing on the StairMaster. (It takes some balance, but I promise you it's possible!) If you sit in the park and eat a sandwich during your thirty-minute lunch break every day, spend fifteen minutes of that time flipping through the paper while you eat. If you ride a train or bus to work, spend that time reading the paper instead of daydreaming or napping. All this works if you read the news on an iPad as well.

- **Bring the news to class.** This tip comes from Felice Nudelman, executive director of education initiatives for the *New York Times.* Felice advises students, particularly those who aren't used to reading a newspaper regularly, to scroll through the day's headlines and pick one that relates to a class they're taking. Ask the professor how his or her class relates to the current issue. For instance, if you see an article about global warming, you might bring it to a chemistry or biology professor for discussion. If you see an article about globalization in business, you might discuss the piece with an economics professor. According to Felice, reading the newspaper doesn't have to be a solitary activity. "In fact, it's one of the most social things you can do," she says. "Use the newspaper for discussion and debate. Make it part of your conversation."

- **Don't panic if you miss a day.** If you're cramming for an interview and worried because you skipped the previous day's news, check out the "Letters to the Editor" section, which offers feedback from that day's articles.

☐ Done!

9. SET YOURSELF UP FOR SUCCESS

One of the cool things about working in a professional office is all the stuff you get to use: scanners, color copiers, multiple-line phones, water coolers, those little single-serving flavored coffee packs, and, most important, IT and maintenance people who come and fix all that stuff when it breaks down.

When you're in college or you've just graduated, many of these professional machines and services are harder to come by. But if you want to win a job with a company, you'll need to access the same services they have at their fingertips. During your job search, you'll need to find ways to scan images, copy résumés, back up important documents, and much more. This tip is about setting yourself up to have access to all the services you'll need to land a great job. Depending on the size of your college or university, you may have easy access to some of these as a student; if not, you'll need to seek out local sources.

Here are the resources you should be sure to have at your fingertips:

- **File backup service.** Whether you choose Google Docs, Dropbox, Mozy, or a zip drive, you must back up all of your job search documents, including résumés and cover letters, in case something happens to your primary computer. Take it from someone who didn't back up the first paper she wrote in college and had to start over from scratch—always, always back up everything.

- **Tech support.** Who can you call if your computer crashes at 2:00 a.m.? Who can unjam your printer when an important cover letter gets stuck? If your school has twenty-four-hour tech support, be sure you know the phone number or e-mail address. If not, seek out a friend, family member, or other service (I'm a big fan of Best Buy's Geek Squad, which will provide phone or at-home support in many cities) just in case you experience any technical difficulties.

- **Superfast dry cleaner.** "In by 9, out by 5" will be music to your ears if you spill coffee on your best interview suit or get invited at the last minute to a networking function. There have been days when no relationship in my life was as important as having a dry cleaner I could beg to help me with special service. If this is not an option for you, then buy yourself a strong stain-stick product and brush up on your ironing skills.

- **Coffee shop that's good for meetings.** While you'll often meet at a professional contact's office (because this is most convenient for the contact), sometimes the person will ask you to recommend a meeting spot. It's a great idea to have a reliable location that you can always recommend in such situations. What makes a place "good for meetings"?

- It's open early and late. Find a place where you can meet people before work or after work.
- You can almost always get a table. There's nothing more awkward than standing around with a person you've just met with a steaming hot latte in your hand, waiting for a table to open up.
- It has free wi-fi. You and your contact may want to Google some information or look up a contact on LinkedIn, so make sure you're in a spot where your laptop or iPad can connect.
- It's relatively quiet. Obviously a library is not a good choice, since people will be shushing you the whole meeting. But you also want to avoid any place that has live music or a booming bass in the background.
- It's on the beaten path. Be careful to pick a spot that's easy for someone to find if he or she has never been there. Spots in the middle of a college quad or in a student building may be difficult for an outsider to find. You should know the exact address of your favorite coffee shop and easy directions by car or public transportation in case you need to provide that information.
- The coffee is good. Okay, this one is not essential, but it definitely helps.

Career planning and job hunting are stressful enough. While you can't account for every last-minute request or wardrobe emergency, you can be prepared for common situations, like the ones mentioned above. If other services or resources are important for your particular situation, be equipped for those too. You can never be too prepared.

10. USE YOUR HELICOPTER

Have you heard that the Millennial generation is sometimes referred to as the "helicopter" generation?

Why, you ask?

Because some parents of your generation "hover" over their kids. (And yes, really aggressive, superinvolved parents are nicknamed "Black Hawks.")

Whether your parents are very involved in your life or tend to be more hands-off, I believe that moms and dads (and stepmoms and stepdads) can play an important and useful role in the job searches of college students and recent grads. If you're comfortable asking your parents for help with your career, there is a lot they can do to support you at any stage. Why not use every resource you've got—especially one that loves you?

The thing is, there are some areas where it is totally appropriate and encouraged for your parents to help with your career planning and job search, and many of the tips in this book can involve your parents' help. At the same time, there are other situations where it is totally inappropriate for your parents to be involved. So be careful! When in doubt, ask someone outside of your family (such as a career services staff person, a professor, or a trusted professional friend) whether or not parental involvement would be kosher. Here are some basic guidelines:

When to green-light Mom and Dad's help:

Parents are most helpful and appropriately involved in your career planning and job search when they act as support and a sounding board. Here are some examples:

- **Reviewing your assessments together.** When you take any assessment tests—online, with a career coach, or in a book—your parents can be a great help in reviewing the answers. They are very familiar with your skills and talents, so their knowledge of you can help you understand results that may be confusing to you. For instance, they may remind you of activities you loved as a child that you may have forgotten about, but that show up as strong interests on an assessment test.

- **Rehearsing for interviews.** Just as our parents can be our biggest supporters, they can also be our biggest critics because they want us to be our very best. Many students ask their parents to help them practice for interviews, by running through questions, helping to choose an interview outfit, or videotaping a rehearsal. I recommend practicing with other people in your life as well (see Tip #82, "Mock Interview")—the more practice, the better.

- **Proofreading.** You can never have too many people checking your résumé, cover letters, and any other professional correspondence. If your parents have good grammar and spelling abilities, ask them to check some of your career-related writing.

- **Networking.** Your family members count as part of your network. Ask your parents if they'd be willing to sit with you to brainstorm any of their contacts who might be helpful. You'd be amazed at how many people come to mind when they really think about it. And I suspect that many parents don't even know exactly what kinds of connections their kids are looking for.

This was certainly the case in my family. As you know, in college I was considering becoming a lawyer and told my parents such. I ended up going to Australia for two and a half years, and by the time I came home I had switched my interests to writing. A few years later, when I got my first book coauthoring deal, I did what any good girl would do—I called my parents to share the news. When my dad picked up the receiver I said, "Dad, I have great news! I just got my first book deal!" He replied, "That's so great, honey! That will help you get into law school!"

I guess I hadn't exactly told him that my career dreams had shifted a bit. And as an English teacher, he may have had some contacts in the publishing industry for me, but I had never thought to ask.

Some people aren't comfortable asking their parents for help and connections. It's fine if you feel this way, and of course there are lots of other connections you can access. But if you are comfortable networking with your parents, then I'd make theirs the first contacts on your networking list.

Parents are also great for:

• **Accountability.** Ask one or both of your parents to check in on your job search progress. It can be easy to procrastinate if no one is keeping you accountable. Set goals on your calendar and ask your parents to check in with you by e-mail, text, or phone on specific accomplishments, such as the "Make This Work for You" activities in this book.

• **Bookending.** This is a lifesaving strategy I learned from my own mom. Whenever I am about to do something scary—make a cold call, negotiate a fee, have a difficult conversation with a colleague—I call my mom before the action to gear up and get confident. Then I make the difficult call. Afterward I call her to report on how it went. I've also heard this strategy referred to as "sandwiching"—picture the scary action stuffed between two warm, friendly pieces of bread. I urge you to try this when making a difficult call, going for an interview, attending a job fair, or pretty much any other time you need support.

When to red-light Mom and Dad's help:

In all of the above green-light situations, your parents' help is firmly in the background; it is invisible to any potential employers or recruiters. That is where mothers and fathers belong in the job search process. Otherwise, an employer will question your maturity, independence, professionalism, and work ethic. I've heard one too many stories from recruiters about parents' attending job fairs on behalf of their children because the student is "too busy studying" or "interviewing someplace else and couldn't make it." This is a huge red flag to an employer.

Parents should never be involved in a job search in the following ways:

- **Calling a recruiter or employer for any reason**—to pitch you as a good employee, ask why you didn't get a job, act as a reference, or for any other reason. This includes summer jobs, internships, study abroad programs—anything. Your parents should never talk to your potential employers about your career.
- **Attending a job interview or career fair.** If you need your mom by your side to get the job, then how will you function without her once the job begins? Don't even bring a parent into the waiting room for an interview—you should be completely independent.
- **Sending out a résumé.** Your résumé and any career-related correspondence should always come from your own e-mail address. Never have your parents send anything on your behalf. Again, it makes you look dependent and immature.

When in doubt about whether to involve a parent in any element of your job search, I'd err on the side of caution. Since you'll be out in the Real World on your own, now is a good time to start fending for yourself. Encourage your parents to support you, but not to do things for you.

Chapter 2

STOP BEING A STUDENT AND START BEING A PROFESSIONAL

In order to get a job in the Real World, you need to have the tools, habits, and professionalism expected in the Real World.

From the moment you send out your first résumé, show up for your first internship, or attend your first recruiting event, you are building your image in the professional marketplace. And today, that image, also known as your personal brand, extends from your in-person reputation to the image you set forth on the Internet. I'm sure you won't be surprised to know that your online image can matter as much as your live one when it comes to landing a job.

The good news is that your personal brand, both online and offline, is mostly in your control. There are many actions you can take to make sure you are putting your best face forward in the job market, and even small changes can make a big difference. Recruiters and employers are aware that you are, in fact, a college student, but they want to see that you'll be able to fit into the professional environment after graduation. The tips in this section will show you what they want to see.

11. UPGRADE TO GROWN-UP CONTACT METHODS

If you have a—ahem—less-than-appropriate voice mail greeting or ring back on a phone you plan to use for your job search
("Dude, leave a message" or a song with explicit lyrics as the only
information), record a new one. "Hi, this is Laura Roberts. Please
leave me a message, and I'll call you back as soon as possible."
That's pretty much all you need. Basically, potential employers
should feel as though they're calling another desk in their office,
because that's exactly where you want your phone to be someday.
This is a simple change to implement, and it can make a world of
difference.

The same goes for e-mail. LittleRoo (my sister's e-mail address
before I convinced her to change it), LakersManiac, and KegMan
don't exactly inspire confidence when listed on a résumé or posted
on a job search website. By all means keep your favorite address for
personal use, but for professional purposes, register a simple combination of your first name (or first initial) and last name at any of
the free web-based e-mail services, such as Gmail, Yahoo!, or Hot-
mail. If your college or university provides you with an address
that uses your name or initials, that's fine, too.

Another professional upgrade is to add a signature line, with
your full contact information, at the bottom of your outgoing
e-mail messages. Most e-mail programs allow you to set a template signature line that will appear at the bottom of all messages
you compose. They generally look like this:

Your Name
(505) 555-1212
Your.Name@gmail.com

Or, if you'd prefer, you can give a bit more detail:

Your Name
ABC University Class of 2012
(505) 555-1212
Your.Name@ABCUniversity.com

Every professional I know does this, so you should match their style. To keep your signature line most appropriate for job hunting, leave out fancy formatting, colorful fonts, and inspirational quotes from your favorite poet. Professionalism is the name of the game here.

By having your contact info at the bottom of every e-mail, if people want to respond right away by phone or mail, your information is at their fingertips. Even include your e-mail address in case your message is forwarded to several people, which is common when a company is sharing your résumé among different departments. Don't ever, ever, ever lose an opportunity because someone couldn't easily find your contact information.

Finally, when it comes to texting I advise against it in most professional situations as a job hunter. Many recruiters have told me that they regard texting as too casual for the recruiter–job candidate relationship. My professional rule of thumb is never to text anyone unless that person texts you first.

Make This Work for You

This one's easy. Just make each of these changes once and you're all set.

1. Record a professional outgoing voice mail message on any phone you plan to use for your networking

and job searching, or any phone you plan to list on a résumé.

☐ Done!

2. If you don't have one already, set up a professional e-mail account based on your name or initials, with absolutely zero cutesiness.

☐ Done!

3. Create a signature line for all outgoing e-mail messages, and set this as a template so the signature appears every time you compose a message.

☐ Done!

12. E-MAIL LIKE A PROFESSIONAL

Now that we've discussed what kind of e-mail address is appropriate for an aspiring young job seeker, let's talk about the contents of those e-mails. Since this is the primary way you'll communicate with networking contacts, potential employers, and pretty much everyone else during the career planning and job search process, make sure you know how to e-mail like the professional you want to become.

I find that most college students and recent grads have a ton of experience with e-mail, but they lack experience with *professional* e-mail. Remember that every interaction you have with a potential networking contact or employer, or his or her assistant, is contributing to your image and your chances of getting a job.

What are the rules a smart young professional should obey

when sending, replying, cc-ing, and attaching? Here are some dos and don'ts to make sure your important messages don't end up in someone else's trash folder:

- **DNUCAPE, or Do Not Use Cute Acronyms in Professional E-mails.** You never know whether people are familiar with the same abbreviations that you are. For instance, a few years ago a good friend used to use "LOL" in a lot of her e-mails to me. Because we're close, I assumed this meant "Lots of Love." Well, when a networking contact—a *male* networking contact—wrote an e-mail to me and inserted "LOL" after a funny comment, I was mortified. Had I misconstrued our professional relationship? Was he flirting with me? Luckily, my friend clued me in that "LOL" means "Laugh Out Loud." Oops. But keep in mind that the people you'll be e-mailing, especially the older ones, may be as clueless as I was.
- **Do use proper capitalization and punctuation.** my biggest pet peeve when it comes to some e-mails i receive from college students is that everything is in lowercase and there is very little punctuation if any at all trust me its not cute its really unprofessional so please dont do it thnx.
- **Do not use emoticons in professional e-mails.** Smiley faces are cute, but save them for your friends.
- **Do cool it on the exclamation points!** This is another big pet peeve among the older professionals I meet!! Young people e-mail them and use way too many exclamation points!!! They make you look really, really young and kind of annoying!!!! (A good rule of thumb is to limit yourself to no more than one exclamation point in a professional e-mail.)
- **Do not leave the subject line blank.** In today's overloaded inboxes and on the small screens of iPhones and Black-

Berrys, most people are likely to overlook or delete any message that looks like spam, so it's smart to include a helpful subject line. In professional situations, I'm a big fan of action-oriented subject lines, such as "Networking Request from a Young Alum" or "Internship Application Attached." If a professional receives an e-mail from someone she doesn't know and there is no subject line, she's likely to delete it.

- **Do not use "Hey" as your greeting.** While "Dear" is not necessary, greeting a professional contact with "Hey" is not appropriate and is a big pet peeve of many recruiters. Instead, use "Hi" or just the person's first name. If you are applying to a very formal organization, Mr., Ms., or Dr. may be appropriate.

- **Do not become the boy or girl who cried, "Urgent."** Use the red "High Importance" exclamation point sparingly. Sending in your résumé or asking for an informational interview is not particularly urgent to the person receiving such an e-mail.

- **Do a quick once-over of important messages, even after you've spell-checked.** Review the spelling of the recipient's name (you can double-check the spelling on the person's LinkedIn profile), the company's name, the accuracy of any important numbers you've mentioned, and the overall tone of the message (your dry sarcasm may come across as rudeness to a busy person reading your message).

- **Do make the e-mail address the *last* thing you type.** Just in case you accidentally hit send or realize at the last minute that you've addressed your message to the wrong person, leave the "To" line blank until you are ready to send your message. Then type in the recipient's e-mail address right before you click send. There is no worse feeling than sending an e-mail that you immediately want to recall.

- **Do not ever IM, BBM, or Gchat a professional contact.** I can't think of any reason why you would instant message anyone in a professional situation until you are regularly working with that person and they invite you to do it. I know a small-business owner who posted an internship opportunity on the web and received an IM from a college student who wanted the job. The business owner found this incredibly intrusive and wouldn't even consider hiring the student. There is no reason to use IM for any job search activity, ever.

The thing about e-mail is that it seems a lot more casual than it is. A professionally composed message can be as effective as a formal, typed business letter, and a casually dashed-off note can be as damaging as spray-painted graffiti on a potential employer's wall. When in doubt, have someone you trust proofread an important e-mail message. It's always better to be safe than spam-blocked.

13. GET CARDED

Whenever I recommend business cards to a student, I always get the same worried response: "But I don't work anywhere yet. What will be on my card?"

The answer is that you don't need a title or a company or a fax number or even a street address to have a business card. All you need is your name, a phone number (which can be a cell phone), and that professional e-mail address. Once you have a professional LinkedIn profile (see Tip #15), you can include that as well. If you're a student, it's nice to include your university and year of graduation, but it's not required. And that's it. But no matter what, you need a way to give people your contact information when you meet them. Writing your phone number on a cocktail napkin or ATM receipt is cute at a party, but it sends the wrong message when you're networking professionally. I am thoroughly impressed when I meet a student who has cards. It shows maturity, foresight, and an eagerness to have the appropriate tools for the working world.

Personally, I never go anywhere without my business cards—the gym, weddings, the beach, the bathroom. I keep cards in my wallet, all my bags, and my office. Why am I so obsessive about it? Because I never want to miss an opportunity to stay in touch with someone because neither of us happens to have a pen.

As for business card etiquette, you should request someone else's business card—"May I have your card?" is all you need to say—before offering your own. And when someone gives you his or her card, it's polite to read it before stowing it away in your pocket, purse, or card holder.

Your business cards should be the highest quality you can afford, but they don't have to be fancy. I recommend a nice, easy-to-read font (at least 10-point so people can read it) in a dark color on white or cream-colored card stock. You can go to an office supply store, your local FedEx Kinko's, or order from one of several websites (DesignYourOwnCard.com is my favorite source). I recommend ordering 250 to 500 cards in your first batch, which can cost anywhere from $25 for inexpensive paper stock to $150 for fancier thick stock. Another option is VistaPrint.com, which offers free cards in exchange for displaying the company's logo on the back. Or you can buy business card template pages to insert in your computer's printer and create cards that way. While these won't be as high quality as more professionally printed cards, it's better to have self-made cards than no cards at all.

And when you get your new job and you don't need your personal business cards any longer, you can always use the leftover cards as bookmarks, luggage tags, or scrap paper to make celebratory confetti.

Make This Work for You

Make or order business cards today. Be sure to have a trusted friend or family member review the card before you go to print to confirm that the cards look professional and contain no typos.

   If your name is difficult to pronounce, consider including a phonetic spelling in parentheses on your business card. Likewise, if your name is pretty common, consider including your middle initial to differentiate yourself: John K. Doe or Jane M. Smith.

☐ Done!

---

14. CLEAN UP YOUR INTERNET IMAGE

During the writing of this book I had dinner with an old college friend who is now a psychology professor at a very prestigious university. I was telling her about how much job research, networking, and reference checking is taking place online these days—very different from when we graduated college fifteen years ago.

   "Do I have a story for you!" she said.

   My friend told me about an experience she'd had the previous semester while interviewing undergraduates for paying jobs in her lab. About ten minutes before an interview with one young man, she decided to search for him on the Internet to learn more about him. She typed his name into Google and found much more than she'd bargained for. She clicked on the second or third link listed, and up popped a large photo of the student on another student's personal website. The caption of the photo listed his name, and then: "aka Fartchucker."

Fartchucker!

As you can imagine, my friend could barely keep a straight face during the interview. The student came dressed appropriately in a suit and gave all the right answers to her questions, but she couldn't stop thinking of him as Fartchucker. How could she hire Fartchucker? (Note that my friend is young and hip. Imagine the reaction of a stodgy corporate human resources executive.)

While sometimes you can't control what information appears about you on the web, often you can—such as asking a friend to remove an embarrassing photo caption from his website before you start interviewing for jobs.

You can also control what image you yourself send out into cyberspace. Make no mistake about it—employers are checking you out on the web. According to a recent Microsoft survey, 70 percent of employers have rejected a candidate because of information they found about that person online. Many recruiters I interviewed for this book admitted that they frequently Google job candidates to see what they might find on Facebook, Twitter, YouTube, or elsewhere.

It's fine to have social networking profiles while you're job hunting; just be smart about it. Here are some tips:

- **Make sure your security settings are airtight.** On many websites, the default setting is for everything you post to be public. Go in and change your visibility to private on any information or images you wouldn't want a recruiter to see.
- **Take down red flags.** Even with tight privacy settings, there is still some content you should remove entirely from the

web, such as photos of any illegal activity (including those "red plastic cup" party photos if you're underage), drugs, extreme profanity, and nudity. It's just not worth the risk of a potential employer coming across content that might hurt your chances of getting hired. In general, make sure any content you post has a PG rating.

- **Be careful with status updates.** More than a few recruiters have shared stories of students tweeting updates, such as "Going to another boring recruiting event." Even if you're kidding, the recruiter won't be amused.

- **Set up a Google alert (Google.com/alerts) on your name.** Once you set up an alert, you'll receive an e-mail any time your name is mentioned anywhere on the web, including social networks, video sites, news outlets, blogs, and more. Be sure to set up alerts for variations of the spelling of your name and include your middle name or initial as well. This is absolutely mandatory in today's day and age. If you see something incorrect or offensive, you can deal with it immediately.

I know some of these measures may seem extreme, but they really are necessary for job hunters today. The thing is, a recruiter will never tell you that your Facebook profile is the reason you didn't get the job. And it would break my heart if you lost an opportunity in this economy because you didn't clean up your Facebook page.

As a young man (who decided to tone down his blog) commented in a newspaper article I read recently, "I just knew I didn't want to jeopardize anything for my career. My real life is more important to me than my online life."

There are many aspects of a job search that are not entirely in your control; this one is. Having an embarrassing or inappropriate online presence is a completely avoidable mistake.

- - - - - - - -

Make This Work for You

Google yourself (aka ego-Google). Consider it a free background check. It takes two seconds to type your name into Google or another search engine (be sure to type in alternate spellings also if your name is easily misspelled), and the results you find may save you from embarrassment or, even worse, a lost opportunity. Remember to check Google Images as well. If you find anything potentially dicey, like an old posting on a bulletin board about an ex-boyfriend, remove the offensive content by changing it yourself or contacting the website's administrator. Media outlets won't change anything they've printed, but friends, student clubs, Greek organizations, and social networks should agree to do this.

☐ Done!

- - - - - - - -

15. SHINE ONLINE

Now that I've berated you with what not to do on the Internet, let's talk about what you *can* do to make sure that lots of good things appear about you on the web. Having an inappropriate web presence can kill your chances of getting a great job, but having no presence at all can be problematic as well.

Why? I've heard some people say that if you don't exist on Google, you don't exist at all.

Harsh, but these days, kind of true.

The good news is that you can improve your Google-ability

(or ability to show up on any search engine) so that people who search for information about you on the Internet will find you. And for our purposes of getting you your dream postcollege job, you can take steps to make sure that your image on the web is professional and impressive to networking contacts and potential employers. You're at an advantage over older professionals because you've grown up comfortable projecting an image on the Internet and forming connections through social networking sites. Best of all, this is one of those tips that you can do from the privacy of your bedroom, 24/7, with no phone calling or event attendance required.

Depending on what kind of career opportunities you're pursuing, you can develop an online presence by contributing to websites, reviewing online material, engaging in professional discussion boards, and commenting on blogs. Just as you become part of a campus community or a local town community, your goal here is to build your reputation in the vast online community. Here are some great ways to do this:

- If you belong to a student club or professional association, and particularly if you serve on a committee or hold a leadership position, offer to write a short online article on a topic related to your expertise, and then ask for this article to be posted on the organization's website. Most clubs, associations, and student groups are thrilled to have free content and happy to give you a byline.

- Review books on Amazon.com, BarnesandNoble.com, or send your review to a blog related to your industry. One student I know reads popular business books from the bestseller list and posts reviews on her own website and on the two major bookselling sites. She prints out her reviews and brings them to job interviews to share if any of the books come up in conversation. Note that for maximum exposure you should register to post any reviews with your real name and not a user name like MarketingMajor or IowaEconStud.

- Create a profile on LinkedIn. With more than 100 million members at the time of this writing, LinkedIn has become the clear leader in professional social networking around the world (full disclosure: I am a paid spokesperson for the site, a position I took because I am such a fan). The basic services of LinkedIn are free and provide essential tools for job hunters of all ages, including students and recent grads. Like other social networks, LinkedIn invites you to create a profile, but this one is 100 percent professional—essentially a longer, more detailed version of your résumé, including a professional summary, information about your (paid and unpaid) work experience, and even an area for you to post recommendations of your work. Then you connect with other professionals on the site and interact through group discussions, status updates, applications, job postings, and more. (See the Extra Credit sidebar, opposite, for more tips on making the most of LinkedIn.)

Once you've built up a professional online presence, make sure you don't get lost in cyberspace; you have to direct people to find you. Include a link to your favorite pieces of online content or the URL of your LinkedIn or other professional profile in the signature line at the bottom of your e-mail messages, and even on your résumé.

The last step to shining online is staying diligent about your online presence. If you haven't Googled yourself or set up that alert on your name yet, now is the time! This is particularly important before you venture out on an informational interview or formal job interview, when others are more likely to be checking you out online.

Extra Credit

As the largest and most vibrant professional social network, LinkedIn provides a wealth of opportunities. But LinkedIn doesn't work unless you work it. Here are some tips:

- **Write a professional summary statement.** Your LinkedIn summary statement should resemble the first few paragraphs of your best-written cover letter—concise and confident about your goals and qualifications. Remember to include all of your experience, including internships, volunteer work, and extracurriculars. You should also include key words and phrases that a recruiter or hiring manager might type into a search engine to find a person like you. The best place to find relevant key words is by researching the job listings that appeal to you and the LinkedIn profiles of people who currently hold the kinds of positions you want.

- **Display an appropriate photo.** Remember that LinkedIn is not Facebook. If you choose to post a photograph on your LinkedIn profile, opt for a professional, high-quality headshot of yourself alone. You don't necessarily have to wear a suit, but baseball caps, party photos, cartoon avatars, and glamour shots from last weekend's formal don't fit in the professional environment of LinkedIn.

- **Share your (career-related) news.** Like other popular social networks, LinkedIn provides the opportunity to share brief status updates with your connections. But again, remember to stick to the professional. I think of my LinkedIn status updates as brief conversations I would have at networking events: "I just read a really interesting article you might enjoy. Here is the link . . ." or "I'm attending our industry conference next week. Are you going too?" You never know what nugget might catch someone's attention and spark a conversation or opportunity.

- **Connect with friends and family.** Once you have a great profile, start building your LinkedIn network by uploading your online address book and connecting to friends, relatives, internship colleagues, and professionals you know in the Real World. The best networks begin with those you know and trust, and then grow based on personal referrals.

- **Customize your connection requests.** As you build your connections on LinkedIn beyond your friends and family, don't use the generic "I'd like to add you to my professional network on LinkedIn" note. Instead, always customize your connection requests with a friendly note and, if necessary, a reminder of where you met or what organization you have in common. You'll impress people with your personal touch.

- **Join groups.** To get even more out of LinkedIn, join groups related to your professional interests and communities. I recommend joining your university's LinkedIn group first, and then searching for industry groups related to the career or careers you want to pursue.

For more information about making the most of all of LinkedIn's features, check out learn.linkedin.com and the student video series (featuring the voice of yours truly) at learn.linkedin.com/students.

Make This Work for You

A great way to determine what kind of online professional image you'd like to have is to check out the online profiles of some people you admire—other students, alums of your school, family friends, or successful people in the fields you might want to work in. Run a search of such people and see where *they* show up online. Perhaps you can contribute to some of the same websites, join the same LinkedIn groups, or gather some tips on how to improve your online image overall.

☐ Done!

16. BECOME AN INDUSTRY EXPERT

As you know, one of my favorite career advancement recommendations is to read the news every day. This tip, my final recommendation for professionalizing yourself, is closely related. It is a daily habit that will serve you well through your postcollege job search, any future job searches, and for the rest of your career.

Be an expert about your industry. There is no reason why you can't read the same industry news, blogs, and tweets as someone already working in the field you want to enter.

Once you determine what profession to pursue (or even a few if you're not quite sure yet), begin to read anything and everything you can about that industry. Know which publications are essential reading, which companies are in the news, which executives are being profiled, where the conferences are held, who has the most Twitter followers, what buzzwords are popular, and of course what jobs are available. You can find this information through a variety of sources, including industry publications and trade magazines, Facebook fan pages, company and individual Twitter feeds, LinkedIn company pages, blogs written by industry leaders or expert analysts, and—my favorite source—e-newsletters.

Industry e-newsletters are generally free, and they require absolutely zero effort: once you sign up, they will magically appear in your inbox, just waiting to share their wealth of information with you. They are also time-savers. E-newsletters generally contain short articles or even synopses of articles. You can gather lots of information without spending lots of time. I subscribe to about two dozen e-newsletters and take only a few minutes to read each one. I usually spend the first twenty minutes or so at my desk in the morning reading through my e-newsletters so I'm in the know about my industry that day. Twenty minutes—that's it.

Why is it so important to be knowledgeable about the industry you want to enter? Because when you attend networking events, work in internships, write cover letters, and interview for jobs, you want to speak the same language and have the same reference points (company names, industry leaders, new product launches, future industry outlook, etc.) as the people you want to work with someday.

You also should pay attention to which e-newsletters you always delete or save for later or never seem to get to. This may be a sign that those industries, companies, or topics aren't as exciting to you as you may have thought. If there is a certain industry newsletter or company press release that you can't wait to open and read from top to bottom, that's a big sign that the industry would be a good fit for you.

Here is a list of some recommended websites that offer free e-newsletters or e-mail updates for particular industries:

Industry	Website Address
Advertising	www.adweek.com
Book publishing	www.publishersweekly.com
Business (general)	www.businessweek.com
	www.money.cnn.com
Finance	http://dealbook.nytimes.com
	www.institutionalinvestor.com
Media	www.mediabistro.com
Nonprofit	www.philanthropy.com
Science/health	www.sciencedaily.com
Technology	www.mashable.com
	www.techcrunch.com

If you don't see your interest area listed above, go to your favorite search engine, and type in the search terms "e-mail updates" or "e-newsletter" and the industry you want to access—such as real estate, human resources, fashion, beauty, environmental sciences, consulting, art, physical therapy, hotel management, etc. Remember, all of this is free, so sign up for as many as you'd like. Alternatively, ask professionals you admire what e-newsletters they receive, and sign up for those.

Another hot tip is to set up a news alert, using keywords related to the companies or industries that interest you. For example, you can set up an alert with the keyword "John Deere" or "Microsoft" to receive any news each day that mentions that company. Or you can do something industry-related, such as "fashion marketing" or "elementary education" to receive the day's articles on those topics. Google (www.google.com/alerts), Yahoo! (http://alerts.yahoo.com), and other websites allow you to set up such alerts for free. I have several alerts related to career issues for college students and young professionals, and I find these alerts to be invaluable in making sure I'm always in the know in my industry.

Make This Work for You

Subscribe to at least one free e-newsletter or keyword alert
from an industry or company that may be a career option
for you.

☐ Done!

Chapter 3

FIGURE OUT WHAT YOU WANT . . . AND WHAT YOU DON'T

One of the reasons that attaining your first job out of college can be so challenging is because it's the first divergence from the prescribed plan that you've been following for your whole life so far. Yes, you had choices of what classes to take or what college to attend, but the general concept was pretty clear: go to school. For eighteen years or so. Now you're facing an entire world of possibilities—more options than any generation in history. And everyone keeps asking you what sounds like an easy question but can be the hardest in your life to answer:

What do you really want to do?

(Please make special note that the above sentence does not read, "What do your parents want you to do?" or "What do you feel you *should* do?" or even, "What do most people with your college major go on to do?")

Most college students I've met find this to be the most difficult part of the career search process. It's not uncommon to feel paralyzed by fear and indecision. If you feel this way, I promise you are not alone.

So, what's my antidote to the indecision blues?

Action.

I don't believe that you can just sit in your dorm room or bedroom, think really, really hard, and figure out the best plan for your future. Thinking and self-reflection are definitely part of the equation, but you'll learn much more about yourself—and do it much more quickly—if you combine thinking with action. That's what this section is all about: taking actions that will help you learn what you want to do in the first few years of your career, and sometimes more important, what you don't want to do.

This section narrows in on specific activities that help you focus on what's right for you. Be patient with yourself, and be aware that very few people know exactly what career they want to pursue at a young age. Your goal should be to determine a few industries, jobs, or environments that match your interests and needs right now. That's all you have to do. You are by no means plotting your career path for the rest of your life right out of college. In fact, I'll let you in on a little secret: even if you do try to plot out your entire career right now, life is full of changes and surprises, so your ultimate path is bound to look quite different from whatever you imagine.

17. START A REALLY BIG LIST

I'm sure you already have a few ideas of companies you'd love to work for, internships to apply for, jobs that sound interesting, or people you've been meaning to talk to for advice or contacts. Now it's time to write it all down. Start an ongoing list in your career notebook, or on your computer or phone, of every career possibility that comes to mind. Try not to censor yourself at all; just write. Your Really Big List will come in handy in a variety of ways throughout this book and during your career planning and job search.

- **Your Really Big List will give you assignments.** Whenever you feel motivated to work on your career planning, it will serve as a to-do list of opportunities to research. Once you begin to gather information on any idea on your list, you should start a folder for what you find to keep track of it all.
- **Your Really Big List will help you network.** Glance through your Really Big List to prepare for any informational interview, networking event, or meeting with a career planning counselor on campus. Better yet, bring your list along. The people you meet are likely to know some of the companies or people on your list or how to reach them. Your list will turn a vague, "Can you help me find a job?" into a specific request for specific leads in specific organizations or industries.
- **Your Really Big List will help you assess yourself.** As your list grows, you'll begin to see patterns of what kinds of opportunities attract you. Perhaps you'll notice that many of the items on your list point you toward creative jobs, small companies, political work, African American organizations, living in Chicago, making a difference, going to graduate school, or something else. Or maybe you'll find a mishmash of stuff—which is okay, too. Don't see an all-over-the-place list as frustrating; instead, see it as reflecting the fact that a lot of different things will make you happy.

Make This Work for You

If you attempt no other tip in this book, please, please, please create your Really Big List. It will prove to be an invaluable resource as you get further and further down the path of career planning and job hunting. In fact, I bet that if you come back to this list in twenty years you'll be amazed at how many of the opportunities still interest you (or have related to your eventual career path) in some way.

I'll be referring back to your Really Big List at various points in the book, so be sure to keep it close by when you're reading.

☐ Done!

18. GET RID OF THE "SHOULDS"

As you begin to assess yourself and determine what you want in your career, an important step is getting rid of what other people tell you that you *should* want.

You may not even realize that you have some powerful predetermined ideas about how job searching works and what various career paths entail. In other words, much of what you think you know about the working world and your place in it may not actually be true. Why not? Because sitcoms, movies, magazines, and even friends, professors, and relatives don't always know what they're talking about—or they give advice based on their own personal knowledge or experience, or on current economic conditions, and not necessarily what's best for you. Add to this that career trends change over time, and it's pretty clear that some people's impressions may not be entirely accurate.

It may be that you're interested in some jobs or career fields simply because you know people or have heard about people who are in those fields. While it's great to follow in the footsteps of those you admire, you may not want to limit your options to the careers of people in your immediate frame of reference—or to jobs that you currently understand how to perform. I guarantee there are thousands upon thousands of careers, companies, and job titles that you've never even heard of. One of those may just be the winning ticket for you.

Here are some common "should" myths that you may need to bust before you can move on and seriously consider what kind of job you want:

MYTH: You should get a job that's directly related to your college major.

FACT: English majors get job offers from investment banks. Premeds change their minds and go to law school. Philosophy majors are marketable outside of academia. While some industries may require that you take a few extra classes to prove you can do the work required, your major should not hold you back from pursuing a career that feels right to you.

MYTH: You should try to get the highest-paying job you can.

FACT: Well, sure. You should try to get the highest-paying job you can … as long as it's something you really want to do. Taking a high-paying job that doesn't interest you is a big—and common—mistake. Now is the time to start at the bottom and build a career in something you enjoy. Believe me; it will be much harder to give up a big salary in ten years to switch careers into something you love rather than doing it now. There is no shame in taking a lower-paying job now to build a career path in an industry you like. Don't worry about keeping up with your friends in more lucrative industries (see Tip #21 for more about money matters).

MYTH: You shouldn't even try to get a job in a glamorous industry unless your last name is Spielberg or Chanel.

FACT: It's harder to get a job in a glamorous industry—such as film, fashion, magazines, television, or professional sports—than in, say, telemarketing, but it's not impossible at all. Most of these industries don't have formal college recruiting programs, so you'll have to do more work on your own. The major fact about glamour industries is that virtually everyone starts at the bottom, so in these fields it's all about getting your foot in the door—any door you can. You may have trouble convincing your parents that your college degree is well used while you bartend and direct short films, but they'll understand in a few years when your full-length feature wins a prize at Sundance.

MYTH: If you're good at something it should be your career.

FACT: It's a great idea to pursue your natural talents, but remember this: just because you *can* do something doesn't necessarily mean you *should* do it. The reality is that most college students are good at a lot of things; that's how you got into college in the first place. You *can* write well. You *can* analyze a math equation. You *can* plan a fund-raiser. But just because you can do all of these things doesn't mean they would make you happy as a career choice. Choosing a career path is a combination of your abilities and your interests. It's perfectly okay to be good at something but not do it for a living.

Make This Work for You

What is your biggest "should" about getting your first job after college? What message is playing over and over again in your head? Whatever you're telling yourself, there is one thing you must do right now: Find out if the "shoulds" are true. Test your assumptions. Take your top three "shoulds" about your particular situation and write them below.

Examples:

- I'll never get a job in a big city because I go to college in a small town in Maine.

- I shouldn't even try to find a job in corporate America because my parents didn't go to college and they don't have any connections.

- I should be a teacher because that's what English majors do.

- I shouldn't try to be a professional singer because most people fail.

Your "shoulds":

1.

2.

3.

Now go out and gather information to see if you need to wipe these beliefs from your mind. Ask your professors. Ask your college career services office. Ask alumni of your school. Post these questions on an online bulletin board devoted to career advice. Bring these questions to your next informational interview. If you find out that any of your worries are unfounded, then erase them from your mind. My hunch is that you'll learn that no path is impossible, though some are harder than others. But once you know what you're really facing, you'll be able to make a more informed decision about your future.

☐ Done!

19. DON'T BE CAUGHT "HITCHHIKING": ASSESS YOURSELF

Reality Check

"I wish I had known myself better. You learn a lot of technical skills in school but spend very little time learning about yourself: your own preferences, values, passions, and interests. I think self-awareness is the single most important ingredient for building a happy and successful career and life."

Celeste Blackman, global consultant and cofounder, Green Zone Culture Group

While there are few shortcuts in the figuring-out-what-to-do-with-your-life process, there is definitely a way to put yourself a few steps ahead of the pack: you can take a thorough career assessment test (don't worry—this is a test that everyone passes). Completing an assessment is the ideal way to narrow down the entire universe of potential careers into a few manageable categories that fit with your skill set and interests. Assessment is a good idea for anyone, but it's absolutely essential if you have a wide variety of talents and passions or you're completely unsure of what you want to do.

For expertise on this topic, I turned to Peggy Bier and Jerry Sturman, president and CEO, respectively, of the Career Development Team, creators of CareerPortrait®, a comprehensive career assessment process. Their company has been helping people figure out their ideal careers for over thirty years.

Here is how Jerry explains the importance of assessment testing:

"Finding and managing a career that's right for you is like a game. Games have rules. You wouldn't want to play poker for money without being absolutely clear about the rules. In the same way, you wouldn't want to manage your career without knowing the rules. Well, the first rule is, 'Do a thorough assessment.'

"Career mastery, at any level, from entry to CEO, is a function of doing what you do best and what you like most, and then developing yourself to get as good at it as possible. Starting the process in college or postgraduation with assessment will get you moving in the right direction."

According to Jerry, there are four important things you need to understand about yourself in relation to your work life. And these are what a career assessment will help you determine:

- Your style: how you do what you do
- Your motivation: why you do what you do
- Your skills: what you use to do what you do
- Your internal barriers: what blocks you from doing what you do as well as possible

A thorough assessment test analyzes all four of these areas, which will help you make clearer decisions about your career choices now and throughout your life.

"Everyone knows people who have 'hitchhiked' into their

careers," says Jerry. "They come out of school, stick their thumbs out, and take the first job that looks halfway decent. With rare exceptions, these people are dissatisfied, if not downright unhappy, in their work. The job may not provide what it is that motivates them in their work lives. Or they're not using the skills they're best at, or most interested in using. Or the environment is wrong. Or they don't fit well with the kinds of people with whom they have to work. Or they're incompatible with their managers.

"Learning about yourself in relation to the work world will help you find and keep a job and create a career that will be fulfilling and satisfying for you."

Make This Work for You

Ready to take your own assessment test and ensure a career free of "hitchhiking"? There are many different kinds of tests available through university career services offices, licensed career coaches, and various books on the market. While a complete career assessment provides information about your style, motivation, skills, and internal barriers, the single most important piece of information is your true motivation. The Career Development Team has graciously offered to provide their Career Drivers™ motivational assessment without charge to readers of this book. To access the assessment go to: www.careerdriversassessment.com/CtoC.

☐ Done!

20. EXPLORE A PASSION

A young woman—we'll call her Cheryl—came rushing up to me after a workshop I gave at her university. She was spunky, dressed in a bright tank top and jeans, and had a friendly, open face. "I need your help!" she shouted out as I turned to say hello.

Before I could get a word in, Cheryl launched into her career dilemma. "I'm a sophomore and I love film. I've always loved movies—I've seen everything—and I would so love to work in Hollywood. It's been my dream since I was little. But I know it's a really hard industry to break into, so I'm planning to major in accounting so I can get a job at a big firm that recruits on campus. What do you think?"

"I think you should get any job you can in film," I said.

"But it's so hard! And I don't live in California! And it doesn't pay well when you're just starting out!"

"It's clearly what you want to do."

"Yeah, but . . ."

"It's clearly what you want to do."

I'm not a psychic or anything, but I swore I had two future visions of Cheryl: one was of her in a designer gown accepting her Academy Award in fifteen years, and the other was her sitting in an office surrounded by spreadsheets in fifteen years, calling up a career counselor to schedule an appointment to talk about the hard task of making a midlife career change from accounting to entertainment.

Reality Check

"It's impossible to be truly successful without passion, so loving what you do is the key to future happiness."

Soraya Darabi,
cofounder, Foodspotting
.com, and digital strategist,
ABC News

Unfortunately, I've met dozens of people who are similar to the latter version of the future Cheryl. Over the years I've worked and volunteered for several organizations with the mission of helping people achieve their career dreams, and I wish I had a dollar for every person who had pursued a "safe" career choice when they were young and now wanted to pursue a lifelong passion. The problem is, by their thirties and forties, people had kids, mortgages, and lots of experience doing something they didn't want to do anymore. And the prospect of starting all over again as an entry-level employee was not very enticing.

Don't let that be you.

If you have a clear passion, why not avoid this midlife fate and pursue your passion right now? This is the time in your life to experiment, follow your dreams, and, if necessary, work for lower pay in order to do something that you love. This may require moving back in with your parents for a while or taking on a second job to help make your student loan payments. It's worth it.

Pursuing a passion now—before you have dependents, a mortgage, and years of experience behind you—should really be considered a *career strategy*. I am very serious about this. I have met with dozens of people at all stages of their careers and eventually everyone comes around to the same conclusion: to be ultimately happy in your career—which is a big chunk of your life—you have to work at something you enjoy. If you pursue something you don't really enjoy, it's highly likely you'll eventually try to change careers to something you're passionate about.

At the very least, add a passion to the list of careers you're pursuing. This is what Cheryl finally agreed to do: to look for opportunities in both accounting and film, and see which worked out.

My fingers are crossed for the film job.

Make This Work for You

What passion could you pursue as a career, and how would you go about getting paid to do it? Here are some steps to propel you toward a career pursuing a passion:

1. **Define your passion (or passions).** There's a very simple question you can ask yourself: What would you do for a living if money were not an issue? Would you ski all day? Be a fashion designer? Write code? Travel the world? Write screenplays? Paint? Invent toys? Read?

2. **Make it real.** Research every job that relates to the passion or passions you've just defined. Since money *is* an issue, find all the real ways you can make money doing what you love to do. Here are some examples:

   • **If your passion is skiing:** Consider opportunities as a ski instructor; work in marketing for a ski resort; write for a skiing website; work for a company that designs or produces ski equipment or clothing; work for a company that makes skiing videos.

   • **If your passion is travel:** Consider opportunities working for a travel magazine or travel-related cable show; work for a travel agency or travel website; work for an airline, hotel chain, resort company, cruise line, or tour organization; work for an advertising agency that specializes in travel industry clients; work for the tourism bureau of your town, state, or favorite country.

   • **If your passion is painting:** Consider selling your paintings online or at local arts and crafts fairs as

62   Lindsey Pollak

your full-time job or in addition to any other work
that brings you close to paintings, such as: working
for an art gallery, museum, or art school; teaching
painting in public school, private school, art school,
community centers, hospitals, or retirement communities; working for a government arts council; being a
tour guide at a museum with your favorite paintings;
learning about opportunities to "paint" with computers and working for a graphic design firm or for a
textile design company; working for the arts division
of a corporation that sponsors painting exhibits;
working for a publishing company that specializes in
art books; working for any division of an art or design
magazine.

3. **Hang out with passionate people.** The first lesson I always
share with aspiring writers is to start hanging out with
other people who are writing—or doing anything creative—for a living. If all of your friends are working in
corporate cubicles and you want to be an actress, you're
more likely to feel frustrated than if you're spending
time with other actors. If you're still in college, make
sure you develop a network of students hoping to pursue a passion professionally—this will be great for job
ideas, moral support, and mentoring.

☐ Done!

21. PUT MONEY INTO PERSPECTIVE

There is no doubt about it: jobs and money are intricately related. While people work to be productive, to express themselves, to leave a legacy, etc., everyone also works for a paycheck. The recent global recession has made this fact clearer than ever.

Every student's and recent grad's situation is different when it comes to money: you may have massive student loans that you want to start paying off right away, you may have experienced a parent's unemployment, you may possess a lifelong dream to be a multimillionaire by age thirty, or you may not care about money at all. Whatever your situation, it's important to include your feelings and goals about money as a factor in your career decisions.

Notice I said that money should be *a* factor. I did not say that money should be *the* factor. One of the most striking results of my survey of professionals was the number of people who commented on the fact that the best-paying job is not always the right job. Take it from people who've learned from experience:

"Go into a career that you can see yourself doing every day of your life. Making money is great, but hating what you do every day isn't worth it."

Anonymous, purchasing manager

"Don't worry about the money. Take a job in an industry that you are naturally attracted to. It will lead to a happier 'first job' experience in that you'll be working in an area that you already love. The money will come later as you successfully progress."

Stephen Mätt, marketing executive

"All that glitters is not gold. I took the highest-paying job
I could find coming out of undergrad. I learned quickly
I had *zero* passion for the industry and became dis-
illusioned. 'How could I have gone down such a wrong
path so quickly?' I asked myself. After two years I quit
that first job out of school to follow a dream. It's been a
smoother ride ever since."

Brian Kurth, founder, VocationVacations

"But wait," some of you may be thinking. "I have serious student loans to pay off. Money *is* the most important factor in my
decision-making process right now."

Okay, then. If this is the case for you, by all means your number one criterion for your first job should be earning as high a
salary as possible. But I urge you to remember that your first job
is not your last. If you feel that you are sacrificing some of your
passion or happiness in order to make a higher salary in a job that
pays well but is not ideal, there are still things you can do to keep
money in perspective and not give up on any nonfinancial interests
or dreams you may have. You can join professional associations
related to the fields that interest you (even if you're not working
in that field right now), subscribe to blogs or e-newsletters related
to industries that represent future career dreams, volunteer your
time to organizations you care about, or take online classes that
keep you stimulated and connected to your interests. All of these
are opportunities to get experience, skills, and networking contacts that will come in handy if and when you decide to pursue
your passion in the future.

22. DECLARE A TAKE YOURSELF TO WORK DAY: JOB SHADOW

While most experts advise people to step out of the shadows, my advice is to step right into them—job shadows, that is. By this point I hope you have some idea of what career fields might interest you, so don't wait another minute to start learning more about any job, company, or industry that's on your Really Big List. Job shadowing is a great way to do this. The concept of job shadowing is simple: you sign up with a working person to follow him or her around for a day (or more) to learn about that person's daily reality. The goal of job shadowing is to learn what a person's job and company are really like, to scope out whether you'd like to be in the same shoes someday.

You can shadow anyone at any career stage, but I particularly like the idea of shadowing an entry-level person in the kind of job you might apply for. Your college alumni network is a good place to look for such people. Another option is to shadow the kind of person who hires or manages entry-level people. Then you can observe the workplace from the perspective of a potential future boss—the person who can show you what the company needs from its young workers and what a future career path for you might look like.

Job shadowing can be formal—coordinated by your school's career services office or a professional association—or it can be informal, involving simply asking someone, "Can I follow you around for a day to learn about your job?" Either way, you can make the most of a job shadow experience by following these guidelines:

- **Be very clear about what you want to learn from the job shadow.** When you request to shadow someone, tell the person what exactly you want to observe and what interests you about his or her organization. You might want to observe internal meetings, technical work, client interactions, research trials, on-site customer visits, rehearsals, or something else, depending on the kind of job and organization. The clearer you are on what you want, the better the professional can choose a day where you'll get the most relevant information.

- **Offer something.** Since this person is doing something for you, it's a nice idea to invite the person to start the day with breakfast, or offer to take the person to lunch or a coffee after work (your treat, of course). You'll be showing your maturity and professionalism, and you'll also guarantee some alone time with the person to ask any specific questions that aren't answered the rest of the day. Plus you'll have the chance to connect on a personal level so you can share a bit more about yourself and your goals.

- **Do your homework.** Before your shadow day, research as much as you can about the person you'll be shadowing, his or her specific department, and the company itself (LinkedIn and Twitter are great for this). When you're adequately prepared, less of the day will be spent teaching you what the company's products or services are, and more of the day will be spent experiencing the culture and learning what really goes on.

- **Dress appropriately.** Remember that a day of job shadowing is also an opportunity to show anyone you meet that day that you are a serious young person who wants to have a successful career. Don't show up looking like a scrappy student; look like someone who could be an employee at the company. Call ahead and ask the person you're shadowing what is appropriate attire.

- **Listen.** As my grandfather used to say, there's a reason why you have two ears and one mouth: you should listen twice as much as you talk. On a job shadow day, you'll want to turn off your cell phone and take in every bit of information you can, from the general atmosphere of the organization to business challenges they're facing to casual conversation in the lounge. Keep a notebook with you to jot down questions as you have them; then ask your questions when you are one-on-one with the person you're job shadowing.

- **Use your peripheral vision.** Being inside a company on a typical day offers a wealth of information that no one could ever tell you and you could never read about on the company's website. Pay attention to everything: How old are most of the employees? Do people go out for lunch or eat at their desks? Is the office particularly quiet or loud? How new are the computers on people's desks? Do people have photos of their kids and friends, or are the walls all bare? What is the pace—fast or slow? What are people wearing? What time do people arrive and leave? Do employees seem happy?

- **Get specific.** Come prepared with a list of questions about opportunities for entry-level employees or internships, or about the company in general. The person you're shadowing will know that the reason for the shadow is that you want to work in a similar company or job, so usually he or she will be happy to answer questions. However, if the day becomes very busy and the person appears stressed, it's better to request another time to meet when he or she has more time.

- **Keep the connection.** The person you shadow is now a member of your network and a good contact for you. Keep in touch with this person on social networks and especially report back if you end up in an internship or job that was inspired by your shadowing experience. People love to know that they've made a difference in someone else's career. Note, too, that if you end up getting a job at the company where you shadow or even in the same industry, this person can become a good mentor or adviser for your future career.

23. TWEET

If you think Twitter is frivolous or just for celebrities, it's time to change your mind. While Twitter certainly has plenty of 140-character tweets about people's cats and what Ashton Kutcher (@aplusk) ate for lunch today, it also contains some of the best career information available on a minute-by-minute basis. From here on in, start thinking about Twitter not just as a social network, but as an essential career tool.

Whom to follow:

All of the following types of people use their Twitter feeds to share career advice articles, job search tips, real job and internship opportunities, event announcements, and much more. If you're not on Twitter, you're missing out on a tremendous amount of free and valuable information.

- Influential people in the industry you want to join (check out www.wefollow.com for a directory of top tweeters by topic area)
- Recruiters for the companies you want to work for (examples: @GECareers, @googlejobs, @PwC_US_Careers)
- Your university's career center (visit my comprehensive list of career centers with Twitter feeds at twitter.com/lindseypollak/college-career-centers)

- Me! (@lindseypollak)
- Other career experts who tweet advice, links, and resources (check out my frequently updated list at twitter.com/lindseypollak/career-workplace)

Just as you read the news headlines every day, when you log in to Twitter you can see the daily updates of people who are very important to your job search. And remember that unlike other social media sites, you can follow people on Twitter without those people following you, so don't be shy.

How Twitter can help you land a job:

Besides the fact that following the above-mentioned people on Twitter can alert you to real job listings in real time, here are some additional ways Twitter can help your job or internship search:

- **Twitter enhances your online professional brand.** As long as you tweet appropriately, Twitter provides yet another way to enhance your online reputation and increase your professional Google-ability with recruiters. Be sure to represent yourself with a professional-looking headshot, a professional user name (ideally some version of your real name) and a career-driven profile summary statement, such as, "Ohio State senior looking to enter the start-up world."

- **Twitter can get you noticed for your knowledge.** Because Twitter is such an open, public networking and sharing forum, you can make your mark by helping others, sharing valuable resources (such as links to interesting articles in your industry or about a topic you care about), and helping other people share information by retweeting their comments. I definitely keep track of people who retweet my blog posts or comment on questions I tweet. Sometimes it takes awhile to get noticed, but if you are consistent in your tweeting (even just once or twice a day) and you focus as much on listening and sharing as on self-promoting, you never know who might pick up on something you say and offer you an opportunity.

- **Twitter augments your experience of live events.** Since many conference planners, speakers, and campus recruiters are on Twitter, you can stand out from the crowd at a live event by tweeting before and afterward. For instance, you might tweet something like, "Looking forward to attending the @GenMillsCareers event in the Student Center tonight!" and then, when you introduce yourself to the General Mills recruiter, you can say that you were the one who tweeted the message. Likewise, after an event, you can stand out by tweeting a thank you, such as, "Thank you to @zappos for an inspiring speech. Will be applying to work at Zappos this week!" if a presentation by Zappos.com CEO Tony Hsieh inspires you. You never know who might take notice of such a communication.

- **Twitter offers real opportunities.** Several websites, such as www.tweetmyjobs.com, and a number of Twitter feeds, such as @craigslistjobs, exist to tweet out internship and job postings all day, every day. Many local and industry-related Twitter feeds do the same, so be sure to research the options that apply to your job search. Some employers even use Twitter as a job application in itself. A 2011 *New York Times* article reported that Minneapolis-based advertising agency Campbell Mithun conducted a search on Twitter for six paid internships (in four areas: account management, creative, media, and technology). Applicants were asked to submit 13 comments on Twitter in 13 days and tag their comments with the hash tag #L13. According to the article, 425 people registered as applicants and more than 300 submitted comments to Twitter. Not a bad way to land a job, huh? Since many organizations are seeking employees with social-media knowledge, I would expect to see a lot more unconventional hiring practices like this in the near future.

Make This Work for You

If you haven't taken the Twitter plunge, now is the time to go for it!

- Set up a free profile with a professional user name, a good head shot of yourself alone (no cartoon avatars, sports logos, or group photos), and a brief professional bio so people know who you are.

- Before you tweet a word, start following about 20 professionals from the aforementioned list—such as industry VIPs, career experts, your career center, etc. (By all means follow @ladygaga if you want to, but she doesn't count for this exercise!) Just "listen" for a while and get a feel for what people tweet about and where you might contribute.

- Tweet! Following others' lead, tweet out a link to an interesting article, talk about an event you're attending, or comment on a tweet by somebody else. Just remember that, even though Twitter moves fast, everything you tweet is becoming part of your ongoing online reputation.

☐ Done!

24. CONSIDER A COACH

If you needed extra help in a class or for a grad school entrance exam, you'd hire a tutor. If you wanted to learn to play an instrument, you'd hire a teacher. If you wanted to get into serious shape, you'd hire a personal trainer. Why not use the same strategy for your career planning?

Career coaching has become increasingly popular for entrepreneurs and executives, and it's recently spread to the world of college students and recent graduates. Although private coaching can be costly, some students find it invaluable to have an experienced professional adviser completely dedicated to helping them reach their career goals. And almost all college career services offices offer free one-on-one career coaching to students and young alums. If you choose to work with a private coach, Randi Bussin, founder of the career coaching company Aspire! recommends that you work with someone who specializes in your life stage. "Choose a coach who has worked with college students so they understand how to relate to and how to coach your age group," she advises.

What exactly can a coach do for you? According to the International Coach Federation, the industry's professional membership association, "Coaches are trained to listen, to observe, and to customize their approach to individual client needs. They seek to elicit solutions and strategies from the client; they believe the client is naturally creative and resourceful. The coach's job is to provide support to enhance the skills, resources, and creativity that the client already has." And these days, many coaches will work virtually, conducting sessions by phone or Skype. To be more specific:

- A coach will help you assess your skills and talents to help you determine which career path(s) to pursue. Many coaches are trained to thoroughly evaluate the results of assessment tests.

- A coach will help you prioritize. A coach will assist you in determining what steps to take to determine your career and job search strategy, and which steps to take in what order.

- According to Randi Bussin of Aspire!, a coach specializing in college students will help keep you on track with many of the topics covered in this book: clarifying career goals, résumé writing, networking, interview preparation, and follow-up. Having a coach means having an accountability partner making sure you do what you know you need to do.

- A coach will challenge you to think big. Maggie Mistal, a career coach I have worked with who hosts *Making a Living with Maggie* on Martha Stewart Living Radio, likes to ask her clients, "What would you do if you knew you couldn't fail?" Then she works with her clients to achieve their seemingly impossible dreams. According to Maggie, "People don't often give themselves permission to pursue their dreams." Coaches encourage you to give yourself that permission. Maggie believes this is particularly important for young people. She coaches her youngest clients to take risks. "When you do scary things, you want to do the next scary thing," she says. "Get used to it now. And if you fail when you're young and pretty inexperienced, you won't have very far to fall!"

Make This Work for You

If you're interested in finding a coach to help guide you through your job search and career planning, here are three suggestions:

- Visit your school's career services office and ask about one-on-one coaching. Remember that coaching is often still available for recent grads.

- Check out an online coach referral service such as the International Coach Federation at www.coachfederation .org or Coach Inc.'s www.findacoach.com.

- Ask for a referral. You can ask around at networking events or post a query to your social media connections. Personal recommendations from people you know are generally the best source of referrals.

☐ Done!

25. HERO WORSHIP

Another great way to figure out what you want in life is to think about the people you most admire and want to learn from. The people you look up to are people who have what you want, and when you know what you want, you can set a path to get it.

You can use this exercise for any aspect of your life, but for our purposes you should focus on people whose careers you admire. Try this simple three-step process for turning your hero worship into an actionable career strategy in college and beyond.

Step one: Identify your heroes

Write a list of the people whose careers you admire in some way— your heroes. Your list can include parents, family, friends, celebrities, people you've read about in the news, professors, alumni of your school, politicians, CEOs, historical figures—anyone. I recommend selecting at least three people, but feel free to list as many as you'd like. Even include people who intrigue you in some way, even if you're not totally sure what attracts you to that person's career or if only one aspect of that person's career inspires you. Next to each person's name, write down what you admire about this hero. Here is a simple chart to help you get started:

Hero	The Reasons I Admire This Person

Step two: Follow in their footsteps

Now that you've identified some people whose careers you admire (and, therefore, identified some potential career paths for yourself), do some further research on Google and LinkedIn: What degrees did they receive? Where did they have their first jobs? What awards have they won? Who do/did they hang out with? Who were their mentors? What networks and professional organizations do/did they belong to? What companies employed them? What do they tweet about? Learn as much as you can, and then use this information to brainstorm a list of opportunities, internships, companies, and people you might consider looking into for your first job after college (add these ideas to your Really Big List, of course).

Also look for patterns that might give you a hint to what you might want to do: Do the majority of your heroes have MBAs? Did your heroes work for the government at some point? Did they all start at the bottom of an organization and work their way up? Did they each work for social justice in some way? Your heroes will likely provide clues to your own ideal career path and the choices you might want to make along the way.

Step three: Contact them

What? Am I kidding? Wasn't this supposed to be a fun little self-assessment exercise and not a *real thing*? Actually, it's both. Thinking about and researching your heroes is a great assessment exercise, and it's also a real career planning and job search tactic—if you take the final step of contacting your heroes directly. You have to be a bit gutsy to try this, but I promise that getting in touch with your heroes can pay big dividends.

Just ask Bobby Lopez, who won a Tony Award in his twenties for cowriting the music and lyrics to the Broadway musical *Avenue Q* and went on to collaborate with *South Park* creators Trey Parker and Matt Stone on *The Book of Mormon*. As a high school student and aspiring musician, Bobby wrote a letter to one of his idols, Stephen Sondheim. Because Bobby attended school in New York City and was active in the theater community, he found a contact who knew Sondheim and helped make the connection.

"I'm shy," Bobby says. "I didn't just write a letter. I met someone who knew Sondheim and got that person to give it to him. What I've learned is that people do answer unsolicited letters. Everyone you respect and admire got where they got with help from people they admire. Everyone is willing to 'pay it forward.' People understand how much a word from them means. It took Sondheim five minutes to write back, but to me it was like a word from God."

Now that Bobby has made a name for himself in the musical theater world, he's the one getting letters: "I write back to everyone who writes me. I enjoy getting letters," he says. "I would definitely encourage everyone from college to write to their idols. Don't write a distant-sounding letter or a cold, formal letter, but something that reflects your real passion for the field and the person's work. Write something genuine that expresses your admiration. Ask for advice, or ask a question, or just say that you'd love to take that person to lunch someday."

According to Bobby, John Tartaglia, the original star of *Avenue Q*, wrote a letter to Muppets creator Jim Henson when John was fifteen or sixteen years old, saying that he dreamed of being a Muppeteer someday. Sadly, Jim Henson died soon after that, but Kevin Clash, the principal Muppeteer of the character Elmo, found the letter and invited Tartaglia to come audition. By the time Tartaglia was eighteen, he had a job at *Sesame Street*.

Don't worry that this tactic only works for creative types. I once typed up a letter to one of my idols, *Cosmopolitan* editor in chief Kate White, after she wrote a book I loved, *Why Good Girls Don't Get Ahead but Gutsy Girls Do*. I told her that I aspired to be a writer and work on career issues, and asked for her advice about breaking into the publishing world. A few weeks later I received my letter back, with White's handwritten notes in the margins of my letter, offering her answers to my questions. We didn't become best friends, but I got real advice from a real star in the field I work in today.

Proof It's Possible

Here is an excerpt from the hero list of Tammy Tibbetts, a recent grad of The College of New Jersey:

Hero	Reason
Katharine Graham, publisher, *The Washington Post*	Journalist and editor who reconciled her modesty with assertive leadership. Graham, who died in 2001, transformed expectations for the female sex.
Dana Canedy, Pulitzer Prize–winning journalist	I met Dana Canedy at New York Women in Communications, Inc.'s student career conference. I admire her in-depth reporting and writing style, particularly when addressing a hot-button issue.
Anna Quindlen, author, journalist, columnist	We both graduated from South Brunswick High School and were coeditors of the student newspaper, the *Viking Vibe*. The fact that she's won a Pulitzer Prize and has written for the *New York Times* makes me hope that the parallels in our lives won't stop there.

Hero	Reason
Oprah Winfrey, talk show host, magazine founder	Though not a journalist, Oprah Winfrey earns my respect for her impressive interviewing skills and successful magazine *O*, which is credited as being the most successful magazine launch in recent history.

Tammy was very clear on the career path she wanted to follow—magazine journalism—but it's a hard field to break into, so her hero list was most helpful in setting her sights high and keeping her focused on her dreams. She even took the project a step further: she not only made a list of her role models, but also posted the list, photos and all, on a page on her personal website. Here's where the story gets a little magical.

One day, after posting her role models on her website, Tammy received an e-mail from—believe it or not—one of the women listed! Here is a copy of the e-mail:

Subject: I'm honored
From: Dana Canedy
To: Tammy Tibbetts

Hi Tammy,
My sister, who I guess gets bored from time to time, occasionally checks me out on Google to see the latest information that is listed about me. She came across your website and your listing of me as one of your role models. I cannot tell you how incredibly touched I am. Please do

call or write any time if I can help you as you embark on your journalism career. It would be my honor. Thanks for making my day.

Best,

Dana

It doesn't get any better than that—your hero contacting you and offering to support your career dreams! Of course Tammy accepted Dana Canedy's kind offer, and Canedy has become a mentor to Tammy as well as a role model. I'm sure it won't surprise you to know that Tammy had internships at *Jane* magazine and *Ladies' Home Journal* and landed a job at the Hearst Corporation working in digital media when she graduated.

"I'd say 50 percent of what I do comes from my own inner drive, and 50 percent comes from the inspiration/support of my role models, mentors, professors, parents (who drove me to the bus station every day I interned)," says Tammy. "So that's why my biggest piece of advice to my peers would be to get out there and meet people you can emulate."

No doubt Tammy Tibbetts will be someone's hero someday.

26. SEEK A MENTOR

How can you turn a hero into a real career adviser? Cultivate a mentor.

A mentor is a professional adviser who agrees to provide expertise to mentees, or protégés, in order to help them build and succeed in their career, develop their skill set and experience, and build their networks. Mentors are an asset to any career, and most successful people over the course of history, in every field, cite one or several mentors as important factors in their achievements. Socrates mentored Plato. Haydn mentored Beethoven. Johnny Carson mentored Jay Leno. Whitney Houston mentored Brandy. Usher mentored Justin Bieber.

But don't worry that mentoring is only for highly accomplished people who want to be superstars. According to Peer Resources, a nonprofit Canadian educational corporation, "It is a myth that mentoring is a rare experience and only occurs for a few great people. Informal mentoring is probably the most frequent method of transmitting knowledge and wisdom in society; virtually everyone has experienced it." By creating a more formalized mentor-protégé relationship, you'll have a more regular forum for increasing your knowledge and wisdom.

In some ways, a mentoring relationship is like a long-term informational interview. It's also a kind of friendship. This means that you and your mentor have to have a natural affinity for each other and genuinely enjoy talking and watching each other's success. So, how do you find this person? First and foremost, you have to be proactive; a mentor usually won't come seeking you. As Andrea Jung, CEO of Avon Products, has said, "Some people just wait for someone to take them under their wings, but they should just find someone's wings to grab on to." Gaining a mentor is up to you.

Here are some tips for finding and making the most of a mentor, based on what's worked for me and many of the successful professionals I know:

- **Seek a mentor in your existing network.** If you're new to this concept, seek mentoring from someone you know already. You might approach a former boss, professor, friend of the family, or local community leader whose career you admire. Professional associations, even if you've only attended one meeting, are a great place to find a mentor—many organizations will even set you up with a mentor as part of their services. Alumni of your college or university are great to look to as well. Some schools have formal programs, and others encourage students to find mentors in their alumni databases—check with your career services office for the proper protocol. And, as you saw in Tip #25, sometimes a mentoring relationship can be developed with someone you greatly admire simply by contacting that person.

- **Investigate professional organizations with mentorship programs.** The Asian American Professional Association (www.aapamentoring.com) and the American Society of Journalists and Authors (www.asja.org), just to name a couple, help connect young people to excellent mentors in their chosen fields. Note that some associations do charge a fee for this service.

- **Start small.** "Never ask, 'Will you be my mentor?'" advise Eric Henderson and Heike Currie, formerly of Management Leadership for Tomorrow (www.ML4T.org), a nonprofit organization that runs programs to increase the presence of minorities in fast-track, entry-level jobs and major graduate business schools. "This unfocused request puts the person you ask in an awkward position. Although he or she is not likely to give you a flat no, it is very likely that you will have closed off a potentially meaningful conversation by positioning yourself as someone who simply wants a favor. Instead, ask an experienced person a focused and informed question about something you need to learn about your career. This will begin a dialogue that can grow into a mentoring relationship." Mentoring can start with a simple chat over coffee, where you discuss just one issue or ask for general advice. You don't have to set up weekly or monthly meetings right from the start; ease into your relationship.

- **Be specific about the kind of help you need.** When someone agrees to be your mentor, tell that person exactly where
  you need help—determining what career path to pursue
  after college, learning how to be a professional, becoming
  a more confident negotiator, whatever. The more specific
  you are about your needs, the more specific a mentor can
  be with his or her advice.

- **"Meet" any way you can.** In today's superbusy world, it
  may be hard to have regular, face-to-face meetings with a
  mentor. Or you may want to develop a mentoring relationship with someone who lives far away. This is absolutely
  fine. You can have a productive mentoring relationship
  over the phone or with e-mail interactions. You can even
  talk for free through Skype or Google Chat.

- **Ask your mentor to make you accountable.** It's a great idea
  to find a mentor who is willing to follow up with you about
  your goals. When my mentors give me ideas or networking
  connections, we set a deadline for me to report back on my
  results. This also means that you should always be prepared
  when you meet with your mentor: have specific questions
  or situations ready to review—it's totally appropriate to
  bring a list of items you'd like to discuss.

Proof It's Possible

Having a mentor can be particularly helpful if you are a
member of a minority group or if you plan to enter a nontraditional field. For instance, I recently met a young woman
who wants to work in fire safety, a field that is heavily male-
dominated. My advice to her was to find a woman in her
field and ask that person to mentor her up the ranks.

According to Gaby Rodriguez, a Hispanic woman and graduate of Northwestern University, mentors can be particularly helpful for minority students. Her mentor, Marilyn Skony Stamm (also mentioned in Tip #33), helped her transition from teaching into a career in business. Gaby says, "Many minority students, particularly first generation American-born, don't have people in their families they can ask for career advice, or they don't know people in their fields of interest. They might not even know what's possible. For example, unlike in Mexico or Latin America, in the United States you can switch professions. I didn't know I could switch from being a math teacher to multicultural marketing at a bank where I am now.

"Marilyn played a crucial role for me, giving me insight I didn't have. She helped me to see my advantages in the marketplace, such as being bilingual and learning very quickly, and to understand my challenges, such as not understanding the corporate environment, having a different understanding of body language, and having feelings of uncertainty or not fitting in. She became my confidante about very personal things—salary negotiation, difficulties with managers, seizing the moment, and getting up the ladder."

Gaby advises every student to network with alumni of your college and other professionals who have similar interests or have overcome similar challenges to any that you face. You don't have to walk into a vast and scary maze; find someone who has a map to guide you.

Extra Credit

A relatively new concept in career management is called
"co-mentoring," in which two people, often of different
generations, advise and support each other. The traditional
model of mentoring, of an older person bestowing wisdom
on a younger person, can be very beneficial and maintains
an important place in your career, but the concept of co-
mentoring is gaining popularity.

According to Janet Hanson—founder of 85 Broads
(www.85broads.com), a network of current and former
female employees of the Wall Street firm Goldman Sachs
and young women from the world's leading colleges and
universities—co-mentoring "describes the connection
between women in our multigenerational network, which
we believe is and should be viewed as a relationship of
equals—in essence a collaboration built on respect for the
contribution made by both younger and older generations of
women." (The same concept works for men, of course.)

Why is mutually beneficial co-mentoring possible?
According to Janet, it's partly because of the technology gap
between generations. "There is BT—before technology—
and AT—after technology. Young people have cognitive
function that is different from mine. They have a technical
language proficiency that I don't." The idea of co-mentoring
also guards against what Janet fears could become "a
huge, Grand Canyon–like divide between generations." Co-
mentoring keeps everyone connected.

In a co-mentoring relationship, what the younger
person—that's you—can offer is an understanding of new
technology, new trends, and new media outlets—all of
which are important for older workers, even just five or ten

years your senior, to know about. According to Hanson, what you also have is "enthusiasm and energy and talent," which many older workers will find refreshing and encouraging.

What does your mentor have to offer in return? Experience, experience, experience.

I love a situation where everyone wins.

━━━━ ━━━━ ━━━━

27. RELAX—A JOB IS NOT A SOUL MATE

There is one more myth I'd like to bust before we move on. It applies to everyone, but particularly to those of you who have read up to this point and still feel overwhelmed by career options and unsure what path to pursue. I invite you to relax and sink into the comfort of this tip.

When romantic girls and guys dream about falling in love and getting married, they often fantasize about meeting "The One"—that perfect soul mate, Prince or Princess Charming, who is the sole person in the world one is meant to be with for eternity.

While I'm not entirely sure that there really is only one person on earth for each of us, I can absolutely guarantee that this is *not* the case when it comes to jobs. I've met so many college students and recent grads who are looking for the one "perfect" first job. This is

━━ ━━ ━━ ━━ ━━

Reality Check

"Your first job isn't the end-all, be-all. You should try some things out, and don't be afraid to admit that something might not be right for you."

Danielle Calnon Martin, vice president, integrated marketing, major television network not just false, but a great way to stress yourself out, particularly in tough economic times.

While I do think there are a lot of jobs that could make you actively *unhappy* (such as working alone as a computer program- mer when you love interacting with people, or working in sales if you are painfully shy), I'm confident that there are many, many, many jobs that would be a great way to start your career.

There will be many more pointers in this book to narrow down your choices, but first I'd like to offer my philosophy of making a good first job decision. If you're feeling totally paralyzed about what to do after college, I recommend opting for one of these three relatively fail-safe options:

1. **Take a job where you will have a great boss.** Don't underesti- mate the importance of a good manager early in your career. Your first "real" boss is the person who will show you the ropes, develop your skills, and may even mentor you for the rest of your career. If you come across someone you'd love to work for and learn from, you've found a good opportunity.

2. **Work for a company with a strong brand name.** If you sus- pect you may make a few stops on your way to career bliss, consider the benefits of having a brand name on your résumé: a major corporation (any Fortune 500 company), a well- known nonprofit (such as the American Cancer Society or the Special Olympics), or another prestigious institution (such as an Ivy League university, a respected news outlet, a prestigious professional services firm, or a boutique luxury goods brand). This applies to undergraduate internships as well. According to Lauren E. Smith, partner in a major executive search firm, "If you're with a big company early on, it will stay with you for the rest of your career no matter what you decide to do. Espe- cially if you want to build a corporate career, the best brand

and biggest-name companies are always more impressive to potential employers than no-name companies." Working for a major company is certainly not for everyone, but it does help open more doors in the future. Note that if you live in a small town or city, working for the biggest companies in your particular geographic area will be most impressive.

3. **Do something you totally love doing.** Even if a job is not very prestigious and doesn't have the best boss in the world, I think you'll still be happy if you absolutely love the work you're doing every day or you're working for a cause you believe in deeply. There is no substitute for spending eight hours or more a day working on something fun, exciting, or fascinating.

If you take a job that contains one or more of these elements, I think you'll have a positive first job experience that gives you lots of room for advancement, happiness, and future success. Of course, if you can find a job that offers all three of these characteristics, take it immediately!

Chapter 4

TALK. LISTEN. REPEAT. (I.E., NETWORK)

Who you know, aka networking, is one of the most important attributes of career success. About 70 to 80 percent of jobs are found through networking, so you should spend 70 to 80 percent of your job search and career planning energy on networking. This is, bar none, the single most important activity you can undertake to find real job opportunities and get hired.

I encourage you to drop any negative connotations you associate with networking—images of schmoozy guys shaking dozens of hands and giving out their business cards like free samples at a supermarket. In my definition, networking is about building and maintaining mutually beneficial relationships. These can be personal, professional, online, offline, international, one-on-one, in communities, or anything else that works for you. And most important, networking is not just about who you know; it's about *who knows you*. You've got to get out there, introduce yourself, and become known and respected.

Like your fingerprints, your personal network is entirely unique to you and stays with you forever. Connections to people, places, associations, industries, information, and ideas will help you now and every step of the way as your career grows and changes. Your network is no less than your professional lifeline. And even better, networking is also really fun.

28. TALK. LISTEN. REPEAT.

The most important tool you need to network is your mouth. Just begin by having conversations with people everywhere you go. My instructions to beginners are simple: Talk. Listen. Repeat.

Whether you're sure or unsure of your career direction, whether you're happy or stressed, whether you're flying high or in a seemingly endless rut—basically whenever and forever—there is one action you can take to make sure your career is always moving forward: *keep building your contacts.*

Why? Ultimately, it will be a *person* who hires you, a *person* who promotes you, a *person* who signs your paychecks. The sooner you get comfortable with meeting and talking with new people, the more successful you're bound to be. No one has ever built a career all alone.

The rest of the tips in this section will advise you on the ins and outs and ups and downs of networking, but at its essence, networking boils down to two main rules of thumb:

DON'T wait until you need a network to make connections with people. Networking is

Reality Check

"Network! Let everyone know you're looking for a job and tell them what they can do to help."

Jill Perlberg, senior manager, workforce solutions company

not something to do when you need a new job or promotion or new client. It is not something you can buy, beg, borrow, or steal when you need it. It must be part of your life and activities as an ambitious, success-oriented young person. You can't build strong relationships overnight.

DO make sure all networking relationships are mutually beneficial. While you may feel you have nothing to offer older, more experienced contacts, you never know what you might be able to do for them. Simply ask any networking contact, "Is there anything I can do to help you?" and you may be able to lend a hand, from touring that person's daughter around your college campus to suggesting some cool music downloads for your contact's new iPod. And in a few years when you're flying high in your career, you'll be amazed at how quickly you'll become the person people are calling for connections. The best way to combat the discomfort of asking people for help is by knowing that you're always willing to return the favor.

Make This Work for You

Have one conversation today (and every day, if possible) with someone you don't know—a friend of a friend, the barista at Starbucks, a teaching assistant, your mail carrier, anyone. Get into the habit of talking to people everywhere you go.

☐ Done!

29. BE ABLE TO INTRODUCE YOURSELF

"So, tell me about yourself."

This may be the most intimidating phrase you'll hear during your networking and job search activities, from informal chats to formal job interviews. Be prepared, because you're going to hear it all the time.

Why is this question so hard? Because "tell me about yourself" sounds like a book-length essay question, but people expect a response that's only a few sentences long. And at this stage in your life, "So, tell me about yourself" is Real-World-speak for, "So, tell me why I might be helping you get a job someday."

By taking the time to learn the key elements of introducing yourself, you'll be able to impress anyone you meet in a professional situation, from a networking event to an internship coordinator to a hiring manager at the company of your dreams. Luckily, you've already read about many ways to narrow down your interests and position yourself as a mature professional, so what you need to do now is put all of those elements together.

For help with this task, I turned to Laura Allen, cofounder of 15SecondPitch, a company that trains people how to sell themselves more effectively. According to Laura, the best answers to "So, tell me about

Reality Check

"Understand and promote your personal brand. Your personal brand tells a prospective employer what you can offer them that is unique and valuable. Be able to articulate what makes you distinctive professionally and personally in thirty seconds."

Holly Paul, U.S. recruiting leader, PwC

yourself" demonstrate confidence and leave the other person wanting to know more about you. And a successful answer combines preparation and presentation—it's not just about what you say, but how you say it.

According to Laura, "Whatever you do, don't wing it!" There's nothing worse than meeting an important contact or job interviewer and completely blanking when asked to introduce yourself. Take some time *before* you start meeting with people to think about what you're going to say.

To get started crafting your answer, Laura recommends that you ask yourself the following questions and write down your answers in your career planning notebook:

- Which of your previous jobs, even if they were part-time or volunteer positions, provided you with experience relevant to what you hope to do now? If none, what about internships or academic experiences? What about courses you may have taken that gave you an understanding of the industry you're pursuing?
- What are your strongest skills?
- What can you say about yourself that will set you apart from other young people or entry-level job candidates? In other words, what makes you memorable and special?
- In what ways do your answers to these questions align with your online personal brand? It's important to be consistent.

Now let's look at Laura's step-by-step advice on how to craft your own personalized response, using some of the information you determined above.

Step one: Tell them who you are

Remember that your primary goal is simply to introduce yourself. What's the most memorable thing you can say about yourself and your accomplishments? What can you say that will immediately make the other person want to know more about you? Begin with that.

Some examples:

- "I am a student [or recent graduate] from ABC University and . . ."
- "I'm a chemistry major and recently received a research grant."
- "I graduated magna cum laude with a B.A. in art history."
- "I am a jazz saxophonist. I've been managing a band to put myself through college."
- "I am an extreme sports enthusiast. I love to skydive, and I just got my pilot's license."
- "I am a volunteer EMT and president of my fraternity."

Step two: Tell them what you're good at

Next, you can leverage the skills you listed earlier and frame them in a way that is meaningful to an important networking contact who could lead you to, or be, a potential employer. This may not be necessary or appropriate in a casual networking environment, such as the bleachers of a hockey game, but it's a smart strategy when talking to a recruiter. Remember to keep your tone positive and confident but also humble. Here are some examples:

- "I'm a really great organizer. In my internship as a production assistant I received three promotions in one summer."

- "I would say that my biggest strength is project management. In my internship as an editorial assistant I read two scripts a day while juggling administrative tasks for an office of ten people."
- "I'm a quick learner. In my year abroad, I achieved fluency in Japanese."
- "I love working with people. As a volunteer for the Red Cross I consistently won high praise for my ability to put first-time blood donors at ease."
- "I have design experience with a number of social media platforms, including Facebook, Twitter, and Tumblr."

Step three: Provide a call to action

The call to action is how you let someone know what you're looking for. It's critical to convey that you are keenly interested in networking with this person or getting a job from him or her. People, especially hiring managers, want to recommend or hire someone who is passionate about a particular position or industry, not someone who is wishy-washy or will decide to leave a job after six months. You can put yourself on anyone's short list of young people to recommend or hire by making it clear that you really know what you want and will do a great job. If you can work in some information you've learned about your listener's organization, even better.

Examples:

- "My principal career goal right now is to attain an internship at a talent agency, and I would love to hear more about what it takes to succeed in your agency's summer program that I read about on your website."
- "I believe very strongly in your company's mission to serve

children and families living in poverty. I'd love to explore with you how I might make a contribution to that mission, especially your new project in Guatemala."

Step four: Practice your presentation

Last but not least, it's time to think about how you'll deliver your answer and practice, practice, practice. Laura recommends that you think of your presentation in terms of the three Cs: be clear, creative, and concise.

Also be sure to tailor your delivery to the interpersonal circumstances of the moment: the goal is to maintain a conversational tone and not sound rehearsed. Think of the above elements—who you are, what you're good at, and your call to action—as sound bites that you can inject into the flow of the conversation. You don't necessarily have to pitch yourself in one continuous monologue. And be sure to maintain eye contact and appropriate body language. These nonverbal cues say a lot about who you are and how ready you are to take on responsibility.

While most other college students and recent grads are likely to stammer and ramble, you'll be delivering a confident and polished introduction of yourself. You'll be ahead of the pack from the first few minutes you meet anyone.

━━ ━━ ━━ ━━ ━━ ━━ ━━ ━━ ━━ ━━

Make This Work for You

You can study all the tips in the world about preparing an answer to the question "So, tell me about yourself," but the only way to know if you've got a great answer is to test it out for yourself. Here are four tricks to try:

1. **Tape yourself.** I cringe every time I hear the sound of my voice on tape, but this reality check can be incredibly

helpful. Speak your introduction into a recorder and ask yourself: Do I sound confident? Am I clear, creative, and concise? Is it apparent what I want? Am I being polite? Do I have any weird speech tics, such as using lots of "ums" or "likes" or speaking too quickly?

2. **Study other people's pitches.** Learning by example is a great way to improve your skills. Check out www.15secondpitch.com, www.videobio.com, and www.shatterbox.com for lots of pitching inspiration.

3. **Test your introduction with a friendly audience.** Once you're happy with the way your intro sounds to your own ears, try it with friends, family members, advisers, or career services counselors. Remember that every time you test your introduction and get feedback, you're also getting more and more comfortable talking about yourself.

4. **Create a cheat sheet.** Write your intro on an index card or on the back of one of your business cards and keep this in your wallet or handbag at all times. (Laura Allen even creates business cards with fifteen-second pitches on the front for her clients.) Refer to your card before you walk into any situation where you might use your introduction—a networking event, informational interview, job interview, or anyplace else. Take a quick peek for extra confidence and clarity.

☐ Done!

30. NETWORK WITH YOUR NEIGHBORS

Remember the very first tip in this book, "Start Wherever You Are"? The same principle applies when it comes to networking and connecting to people who can help you figure out and achieve your career ambitions: start with whomever you know.

Everyone has a network. Your friends, family friends, classmates, employers, graduate teaching assistants, hairdresser, dean, librarian, professors, and, yes, neighbors, are all in your network and can help you expand your contacts. No one starts from scratch and you never know where any connection may lead.

How do you start to engage your existing network in your career planning and job search? First, and especially if you're actively looking for a job right now, make sure your closest friends and family know what you want, so they can help connect you to any relevant people in *their* networks. Sit down with your Really Big List of all the things that interest you and your database, LinkedIn connections, or address book (or whatever you're using to keep track of your contacts). Then go through your current database person by person, and note each name next to any item on your list where you think he or she might be able to help you or introduce you to someone in a field related to your interests. (You can do this on the same pages as your Really Big List, or you can create a new page in your notebook.)

Then ask your existing contacts—your nearest and dearest— for help. Don't be shy about doing this. It's really much easier to start with people you know, who already have an interest in you and your future.

The best strategy is to ask your closest contacts to introduce you to anyone they know with direct experience working for the companies or in the industries that interest you.

There is absolutely, positively no better strategy to figure out what career or careers you might want to pursue, and then break into that field, than talking to people who have done it themselves.

Think about it: When police and lawyers want to prove a case, they talk to eyewitnesses. When journalists want to report a story accurately, they talk to sources "in the room" with the people they're covering. We read first-person memoirs to understand what it's like to experience drug addiction, celebrity, or political power.

The same principle applies in a career search. You can check out as many websites as you'd like or read as many job search manuals as you can handle (and those strategies have a part in any comprehensive career plan), but nothing beats talking to a person who knows firsthand the day-to-day experience of the careers you're considering. The formal name for this strategy is informational interviewing, and I believe it's the most effective form of networking for college students and recent grads.

Recommending informational interviewing is the advice I give most often to job seekers. Here is a common scenario: Someone comes up to me after a talk and says, "I'm looking for a job in advertising. What do you recommend?" I'll say, "Talk to as many people as you can who work in advertising and get their advice. It's those people who can tell you where to look for jobs, those people who can best critique your résumé, and those people who can tell you what associations to join. All of this will help you decide if that career choice is right for you and will direct you to great job leads."

Take a look at the list you developed of all the people in your existing network and ask them if they'd be willing to introduce you to any eyewitnesses they know so you can request an informational interview. Note that informational interviewing in the fields you want to enter does not require that you meet senior-level hotshots. In fact, senior executives are not always the best contacts for entry-level networkers, because they can be quite disconnected from what happens at the entry level of their companies. By all means contact the CEO if it's your best friend's dad's college roommate, but don't worry if you don't have VIP connections.

Here is a sample e-mail message, which you can adapt to your own style, or use as a basic phone script, to ask a close personal contact for help:

Sample E-mail Message to Close Contact

Subject: Would you help with my career planning / job search?

Dear Aunt Meredith,

Hi—I'm writing to ask you a favor. As you know, I'm starting to think about my postcollege career plans, and I'm working on finding a great first job. At the moment, I'm most interested in careers in these areas: [Insert career fields here, e.g., pharmaceutical sales, public relations, human resources—you can either send all of your interests to everyone on your list, or you can target particular fields to people who are more likely to have contacts in that area].

Since you are a successful and connected person, I'm wondering if you might be willing to chat with me about your career or connect me to anyone you know in one of these fields who would be willing to talk to me and provide some career advice. I would be extremely grateful.

Thank you so much for your help!

Most people who know you already will be happy to help and downright flattered that you think they are successful, connected people. (Don't tell them the secret that *everyone* is connected!) As you begin to receive names and contact information from people, keep track of the referrals in your notebook. And graciously thank anyone who helps you.

You'll want to act on any referrals as quickly as possible. In the next tip, we'll look at how to do that.

- - - - - - - - - - - - - - -

Make This Work for You

Call or e-mail one person in your immediate network at least once a week to ask for their career advice or their help introducing you to people in their networks who might be willing to speak with you.

☐ Done!

- - - - - - - - - - - - - - -

31. SET UP INFORMATIONAL INTERVIEWS

Now let's talk about how to act on the referrals you receive.

Here is a simple step-by-step strategy for requesting and setting up informational interviews:

1. **Do your research.** Before contacting anyone, you have two assignments:
   - First, chat with the person who made the referral, and ask for as much information as your contact is willing to give: Where does your potential informational interviewee work? Does he or she prefer to be contacted by phone or e-mail? Do you know if this is a particularly busy time? Has your contact mentioned that you might be in touch?

- Second, type this person's name into an online search engine or LinkedIn to find out as much as you can on your own: approximate age, alma mater, family, previous jobs, association memberships, etc. If they have a blog or Twitter account, follow them and read through some posts as well. You want to feel as if this person is familiar to you and not a total stranger. Familiarity will make you less nervous and will prepare you for topics that are likely to arise when you begin to communicate. You may also find a point of connection that will help you build rapport—such as hailing from the same hometown, sharing a love for dogs, or being in the same fraternity or sorority.

2. **Make the request.** I recommend e-mail as the best form for requesting an informational interview. It's less intrusive than calling someone on the phone, and it allows you to write out exactly what you want to say and how you want to say it. The only exception is a situation in which the person referring you has suggested that you call by phone. In this case, you can use the e-mail template below as a guide for a phone script.

Anatomy of a great informational interview e-mail request:

1. **The subject line.** These days, people are so bombarded by e-mails and often check their messages by phone, so a clear and compelling subject line is crucial. Avoid generic or misleading subject lines. Opt for one that is descriptive and recognizable, and include a name or reference point if possible.

Wrong: "Request," "Getting together!" "Let's meet!" "Interview"

Better: "Request for an informational interview," "Request for career advice"
Best: "John Doe suggested I contact you"

Reality Check

"Informational interviews will get you further than online applications. Talk to anyone who will give you even five minutes of their time."
Anna Schilawski, coordinator, communications and events, Victoria's Secret

2. **The opening.** Although e-mail is less formal than a letter, in this case you want to be as formal and polite as possible. I'd go with "Dear Mr. Jones" or "Mr. Jones" followed by a comma. If your referrer says to call the person by his or her first name, it's okay to do so, but err on the side of formality if you're uncertain.

3. **The body of the e-mail.** I recommend a three-part e-mail: a) **Introduction** (who you are and your connection to this person); b) **Explanation** (why you are writing to this person in particular—show that you've done your homework!); and c) **Specific request** (what you want). Here is an example:

Dear Ms. Goodman,

(a) "Hello. I am a student at ABC College considering a career in magazine editing, and my journalism professor, Joe Nicholas, said you might be willing to offer some advice. (b) I'm particularly interested in hearing about your work writing celebrity profiles for your magazine and how you got started in that area. (c) May I take you out for coffee near your office, or perhaps call you to chat for twenty minutes or so?

I like this format because it provides ample information and alternatives. You are giving your contact enough information to make a decision about meeting with you, and you are making it easy for the contact to say yes by indicating that you will not take up too much of the person's time. You want to avoid having too many back-and-forth e-mail exchanges. In some cases, your contact may be too busy, so he or she may forward your e-mail to a colleague. This is a great outcome, and by providing details about what you're looking for, you've made it easy for an alternate person to be determined.

Note: Do *not* attach a résumé to a request for an informational interview. It is too presumptuous. Also, attaching a résumé implies that you want this person to give you a job, which puts the person on the defensive. All you are requesting at this point is information and advice. Do not send a résumé unless the other person asks for it.

4. The closing. Here is where lots of people mess up big-time. Do not assume that the person will say yes, and do not ask the person to call you—this puts an inappropriate burden on the person. "Please call me at your convenience" is a burden. "Please let me know a good time to call you" is polite. In the closing, the burden is on *you* as the asker to be grateful and follow up to make a plan.

> **Wrong:** Please call me at your convenience as I look forward to meeting you.
> **Right:** I hope that we will have the chance to meet or chat. Thank you for your time and your consideration of my request.

Then sign off with a polite, formal closing: "Sincerely," "Best regards," or "Thank you" are all fine.

5. **The signature line.** Never forget to include your full name and contact information (phone, e-mail, and LinkedIn URL) at the bottom of any e-mail request. Then the person you're writing to can decide if he or she would like to call you directly; if your e-mail is forwarded or printed out, all of your contact information, including your e-mail address, will be intact.

In general, remember always to be:

- **Specific:** explain exactly how you got this person's name and exactly what you'd like advice about
- **Gracious:** be polite, humble, and respectful of the person's time and expertise
- **Generous:** offer to treat the person to coffee, to show that you want the meeting to be enjoyable for him or her.

My prediction is that most people will be kind in return and flattered to be asked to share their wisdom. Some may be busy and not able to meet for a while, some may prefer the phone, and some may just ask to respond to a few questions by e-mail, but very few people will turn you down entirely.

32. MAKE THE MOST OF INFORMATIONAL INTERVIEWS

Once you've contacted your eyewitnesses and they've agreed to meet you for informational interviews, be sure you make the most of each opportunity. I am a humongous advocate of informational interviewing, so over the years I've developed a template to guarantee that the meetings are a positive experience for both the interviewer and the interviewee. I believe you can never go on too many informational interviews, and this strategy can benefit you over the course of your career—especially if you decide to change industries, start your own business, or go back to school someday. It's always a smart idea to learn from people with more experience in a situation than you have.

Step one: Confirm twenty-four hours in advance

I mostly learned this tactic from being on the other side of the equation. It's irritating when a young person asks to meet with me and I agree, and then I never hear from the person again and can't help wondering if I'm going to arrive at an empty coffee shop. In the Real World, people always confirm meetings, since everyone is busy and cancellations are common. Don't make your interviewee question whether or not you're still on. Confirm with a short e-mail, like this one:

Subject: Confirming coffee meeting tomorrow

Ms. Goodman,

Thank you again for agreeing to meet with me tomorrow at 10 a.m. at the coffee shop in your office building. I look forward to seeing you then. By the way, I have red hair and I'll be wearing a beige coat. If you have any problems and need to reach me, my cell phone number is 310–555–1573.

Best regards,

Emily Corcoran

Step two: Get ready

Preparation for an informational interview is similar to that for a real job interview. Dress for the job you want (see Tip #80 for help), bring a list of questions, know exactly how to get to the meeting location, and make sure your résumé is up to date. I recommend bringing a copy of your résumé, but not offering it until it comes up in conversation or the interviewee agrees to see it (we'll address this issue in step five). Remember, this is an informational meeting, so you don't want to put your interviewee on the defensive by acting like you are desperate for a job. You've asked for information and that's what you should plan to receive.

Step three: Arrive early

Be sure to arrive at your designated meeting spot about ten minutes early. This will allow you to choose a quiet table where your interviewee can easily spot you and you can chat uninterrupted (i.e., avoid sitting near the bathroom or the cappuccino maker). Take a few minutes to relax, breathe, set your phone to vibrate, and get settled with a notebook and pen. Don't order anything, though. Wait for your guest to arrive.

Step four: Start strong

When your guest arrives, show your confidence and eagerness by standing and reaching out to shake hands. A big smile is really important, too. This person is giving up his or her valuable time to meet you, so show that you are grateful and that you'll be pleasant to spend time with. As soon as your guest is settled, offer to get the person a coffee, tea, or cold drink. If you have a waiter serving you at the table, it's polite to invite your guest to order first. If you're at a place with counter service, take your guest's order and go get the drinks yourself. If there's a superlong line, you might decide to chat first and then go get the drinks when there will be less of a wait. Don't waste time on your informational interview by standing in line while your guest is sitting and waiting.

Step five: Conduct the interview

Now it's time for the good stuff, the moment you've been waiting for. Here in front of you is a real, live person who can give you insight and advice about the career you might want to enter. Do not let this opportunity go to waste; it is incredibly precious. Most important, do not spend the meeting talking about yourself! Spend the time listening to what the other person has to say. This will build the relationship and make sure you get the information you're seeking.

1. First things first, express your gratitude for your guest's time and willingness to share advice with you.

2. Next, briefly remind the person about your situation and the kind of advice you're looking for. For example, "As you probably remember, Professor Joe Nicholas recommended that I meet with you because I'm graduating next year and I'm interested in pursuing a career in magazine journalism. Right now I'm studying communications and I'm working on the weekends at a local newspaper. I'm really interested in hearing about your career path and specific advice you have for getting the right experience early in my career. I'm hoping to stay here in the Los Angeles area."

3. I advise bringing a list of questions in case you feel nervous or the other person isn't very talkative. However, if your guest is engaged and open and talking freely, you'll probably deviate from the questions on your list. This is great, but it's absolutely fine to refer back to some of your questions if your interviewee goes off on a tangent. You can gently say, "That's very helpful, thanks. If you don't mind, may I ask you another

question?" Here are some great informational interview questions to consider asking, depending on where you are in your career planning process, and what field(s) you're hoping to enter. Obviously, these are only a guide and you won't ask them all, but I wanted to give you a lot to choose from (special thanks to Tina Adolfsson for offering her favorite questions to add to this list):

- How did you find and get hired for your current position (or your first job)?
- Please tell me about your job. (What is a typical day like? What are your primary responsibilities? With whom do you interact? What hours do you work?) Try to get a balanced perspective by asking for pros and cons.
- Tell me about how you made the decisions in your career path—why you chose this field, why you took positions and left positions. If you could do things all over again, would you choose the same path for yourself? If not, what would you change?
- What does your company look for in the people they hire? (Note: it puts people on the defensive to ask if their company is hiring right now. Instead, keep your questions more general.)
- What part(s) of your college experience best prepared you for your career?
- What is the best decision you made as an undergraduate with respect to your professional life? What actions should I take now to set myself up for getting a great job?
- Who were your mentors when you first graduated and began your career? How about now?
- How do you build a relationship with someone you want to be your mentor?
- What skills and experience are most impressive in your field? How would you recommend I get that experience?

- What are the typical entry-level job titles and functions? What entry-level jobs do you feel are best for learning as much as possible?
- How is the work-life balance for most people in your company or industry?
- What media sources, blogs, Twitter feeds, etc. should I be reading to be in the loop in the industry?
- What organizations do you recommend I belong to, and what events should I attend?
- What people do you admire in the industry? How can I learn more about them?
- What do you think is the outlook for your industry?
- Do you have any specific advice for me, based on my background and experience?
- Would you be willing to review my résumé and offer your opinion and advice for improving it?

Notice that many of the questions involve asking your interviewee to recommend actions you can take—experience to go and attain, media sources to read, people to research, résumé improvements to make. This is critical. When a new contact recommends actions, you not only get some great ideas to pursue, but you also get a reason to follow up with this person in the future.

For instance, you can apply for an internship an interviewee recommends and send an e-mail thanking him and asking him to put in a good word with the internship coordinator at his company. And you can revise your résumé according to the person's suggestions and then send an e-mail thanking him for the great suggestions and asking if he might be willing to pass that revised résumé along to his company's HR department. By following through on the advice recommended by your new contact, you show that you are a responsible, trustworthy, action-oriented young person who is truly appreciative of the help you receive.

4. Last, all informational interviews should conclude with one essential question—perhaps the most important of all:

   Would you be willing to connect me with anyone else you know who might be able to offer some advice? If you've formed a nice connection with your interviewee and he or she seems to want to help you, one of the best outcomes of your meeting is to find another person to interview. This will limit the number of cold calls you have to make by helping you get "warm" leads—many of which lead to real jobs. If your interviewee agrees to make an introduction, it's a good idea to get the other person's name and contact info on the spot. You can either ask your current interviewee to make an e-mail introduction for you, or ask if it's okay to use your interviewee's name when contacting the person on your own.

Step six: Close

As the interview is wrapping up, it's time to show your thanks again and to close the deal. To make sure this person remains in your network, ask for his or her business card and ask if it would be all right to keep in touch. If you haven't offered your résumé yet, now is another good time to ask if it would be okay to provide it, or to send it by e-mail for the interviewee to take a look and offer some advice.

Step seven: Say thank you

As with a job interview, it is essential to send a thank-you note or e-mail within 24 hours after your informational interview. It's a good idea to customize the note by referring to some of the most helpful advice you received. For instance:

> Ms. Goodman,
>
> Thank you very much for taking the time to meet with me yesterday and providing such helpful advice about my career. I especially enjoyed hearing about your first job and your tips for attending the magazine association trade show next month. Thank you also for the referral to your colleague Mr. Baird. I will contact him this week.
>   Thank you again for your time, and I look forward to keeping in touch.
>
> Best regards,
> Emily

It is also important to send an additional e-mail to your original contact who made this introduction, to let him or her know that you had your meeting and you are grateful for the referral. As time passes, remember to keep both your original contact and your interviewee in the loop about your job search, particularly if your interviewee has introduced you to other people. Send a note when you set up the meeting with that next referral, and keep your original contact posted on how the next meeting goes, and about your job hunting in general. Be sure to add any informational interviewees to your database, and to LinkedIn if the person accepts your connection request. Then circle back with each person when you eventually get a job. This takes a lot of time, but it is how a genuine professional network grows.

One final note about informational interviewing: just like eyewitness accounts, an interviewee's story represents only one person's viewpoint of a company or industry. People offer advice based on their personal experiences—which may be good or bad, representative or out of the ordinary. While every informational interview is helpful, do not take anyone's word as gospel. This is another reason I recommend interviewing as many people as possible—you will start to hear themes and similarities that will help you get a balanced, comprehensive view of a job or industry and make an informed decision from there.

- - - - - - - - - -

Make This Work for You

This week, contact at least one person who works in a field that interests you and invite that person out for coffee.

Bring a notebook and write down all the advice you receive.

If this whole process sounds a bit daunting, practice an informational interview with a career services staff person, family member, or friend.

☐ **Done!**

- - - - - - - - - -

33. BECOME AN ACTIVE ALUM . . . EVEN BEFORE YOU GRADUATE

After the people you know and the people they know, the next easiest group to approach for networking is the alumni of your college or university. If you want an express ticket to networking nirvana, get involved with the alumni activities of your college or university. Whether you went to Princeton, Penn State, or Podunk U., college alumni connections are among the most valuable you possess. This is because one of the keys to networking is having an affinity with the people you want to network with. Sharing the same alma mater is one of the best affinities you can find. And alumni are easy to contact, thanks to LinkedIn alumni groups and online databases at virtually every college and university. These resources are gold mines for eager networkers! You can ask alumni for informational interviews using the same strategies in the previous tips, except that this time your connection is your school instead of an individual person.

Your school's alumni really do want to meet you. According to Catherine Stembridge, executive director of the Northwestern University Alumni Association, "What undergrads do not understand is how interested alumni are in their lives and how willing they are to help. *Anyplace* that I go and talk to alumni, what they want to know is what's going on with the students. If undergrads understood that, a lot more of them would be making connections with alumni. Alumni are a tremendous resource to undergrads and recent grads. They just need to take advantage."

If you are currently a student, there are several ways you can get involved with your school's alumni network, and you can do all of this even before you get your diploma.

Join your university's alumni group on LinkedIn. There are tens of thousands of college and university alumni groups on LinkedIn, and many of these groups accept, and often encourage, current undergraduates as members (send a quick message to your group's manager if you're not sure of the policies for joining). While you want to make sure you are professional and appropriate at all times, it is completely acceptable to post a discussion asking alumni for advice or guidance in your job search.

In fact, I recently heard a great story from a career services director at a liberal arts college in North Carolina. He directed a student to their university's LinkedIn alumni group because this student really wanted to move to Southern California after graduation. There weren't a lot of LA-based companies recruiting on campus, and he didn't know a soul on the West Coast.

After following the career director's advice and joining the group, this student posted a polite discussion about his interest in moving to the Los Angeles area after graduation. Within a few days, several alums based in that area responded to his discussion post, welcoming him with open arms—"Surf's up! So glad you're moving to Cali!"—and offered their assistance and support to the student. The student was thrilled with the response and set up several informational interviews to help him get started in California.

If you're not yet comfortable posting publicly in an alumni group, another strategy is to search for group members who are working in the geographic location or industry you want to join and reach out to these people privately on LinkedIn to ask for an informational interview. By mentioning that you are a member of the LinkedIn group they belong to, you are likely (but not guaranteed, of course) to receive a positive response.

Speak on panels. Many schools invite current students to speak on admissions panels for prospective students (and their parents, who are potential networking contacts) and to alumni visiting campus. This is a nice opportunity to talk about your experience as a student, and your postcollege goals, and to improve your public speaking skills in a relatively safe and low-pressure environment.

If you've already graduated, here are some alumni networking strategies you can implement:

Attend reunions. While most formal reunions aren't held until you're five years out of school, informal reunions take place all the time. If you're in a major metropolitan area, be sure to sign up for any e-mail lists, Facebook fan pages, or regional LinkedIn groups for alumni in your area. If nothing exists or you're in a smaller town, host your own reunion by planning a small get-together for anyone you know from your school—and ask everyone to bring friends. And as soon as your school starts planning your fifth reunion, volunteer to serve on the committee. This is a great leadership position to include on your résumé, and it will ensure that you get a chance to meet, or at least know about, all of your classmates and what they're up to. Remember, peer-to-peer networking is among the most effective.

Send in your news. I love reading the notes about members of my class and members of other classes when I get my alumni magazine in the mail. Many schools have such magazines, newsletters, or websites, where alumni can post their news and updates. What a great opportunity to promote what you're doing, where you're living (to find fellow alums in your area), and to scout out any graduates who report that they're working in an industry or for a company that interests you. If you find such a connection, search LinkedIn or your alumni database for that person's contact information and send a quick e-mail: "I saw your news in the alumni magazine, and I'd be very interested in hearing more about your new position. Would you be willing to spend a little time talking to a fellow alum?"

The additional benefit of doing any networking related to your school is that you stay connected to your life as a college student—which for most people holds lots of great memories. Rather than lamenting the good old days of college life, stay connected by becoming an active alum.

Proof It's Possible

Some universities offer specific programs to help alumni
connect with current students and recent graduates. One
such program is Northwestern's Council of One Hundred, a
program started by Catherine Stembridge with the mission
of offering women alumnae the chance to come back to
campus to mentor undergraduate women.

One alumnae networking and mentoring relationship
that grew from the program was between mentor Marilyn
Skony Stamm and mentee Shanna Wendt. Shanna, a 2000
graduate of Northwestern, says, "I had heard of the Council
of One Hundred, and on a whim I went to an event. Marilyn
gave a presentation at that event, and something about it
connected, and I thought, 'I need to introduce myself to this
woman and ask her advice.' It was mid- to late autumn of
my final year, so I was at that soul-searching point.

"Marilyn listened to me and what I was interested in,
and she started to provide really practical counseling and
guidance. She shared her experiences and people she knew.
What she did that I think is so important is that Marilyn
opened up a world of contacts that I didn't have.

"It's true that the opportunities that came out of the
discussions with Marilyn were much more time intensive—
making calls, time on the phone, making trips to the East
Coast, etc. But all of that time was an investment in my
future, and it paid off in real job opportunities.

"Marilyn once told me something so true: that people
want to help you, to give back. They've all been in your
shoes. They know what it's like. Don't shy away from
approaching people."

34. ASSOCIATE

How can you meet even more people? No matter what your career interests, I can almost guarantee there is a professional association to support you and introduce you to new people, from the United States Bowling Congress to the Direct Marketing Association to the American Translators Association to the National Association of Social Workers. Thousands of associations exist, some as small as ten or twenty people, others as large as major corporations. To explore a wide variety of professional associations, check out the American Society of Association Executives at ASAEcenter.org.

I've worked for several professional associations as an employee or consultant, and here is the secret: they want new members. Their business is membership. And they particularly want *young* members to sustain their organizations into the future. I strongly advise you to explore this world, which is entirely designed to facilitate networking, networking, and more networking.

So, what do associations offer that can help your career at this point? Here are a few opportunities:

- **Social networking access.** Because sites like Facebook and LinkedIn have grown so large, it's helpful to find smaller communities, such as professional associations, within these networks. The vast majority of associations have LinkedIn groups, Facebook fan pages, Google Groups, and/or Yahoo Groups, and some of these are open to non-members as well as members (shh—don't tell anyone—but this means you can enjoy some of the benefits of membership without paying any dues). Associations use these online networks to post networking event listings, share job opportunities, encourage member-to-member communication, and promote industry best practices.

- **Young professionals groups.** If an association is particularly large, it may include a student or young professionals group that offers you the chance to network with other people in your peer group. Young professionals groups often host social outings and workshops targeted to young people and their needs. Often young professionals groups will have their own web presence and their own separate meetings. The nice benefit of young professionals groups within major associations is that any educational content or programming will cater to your life stage (i.e., you won't have to sit through a lecture on retirement options before you can network with other members). For a list of many young professionals chapters of major national associations, see the resource guide at the end of this book.

- **Jobs.** Many smaller employers often recruit through their industry association publications, websites, and LinkedIn groups rather than through major national recruiting sites like CareerBuilder.com or Monster.com. Check out an association's online job postings to see if any listed positions appeal to you.

- **Mentoring programs.** If you're interested in finding a professional mentor, but you're not sure how to ask for one, consider finding a mentor through an association. As you learned in Tip #26, many organizations have formal programs, or you can call an association you belong to and ask for a referral to a potential mentor. By belonging to the same organization, you already have something in common with this more experienced person.

- **Membership benefits.** Benefits to association members typically include free subscriptions to industry publications, discounts on event attendance, online learning programs, and discounts on professional products or services, such as office supplies or insurance. Some memberships even include access to proprietary information that can be very helpful to job seekers, such as industry salary surveys. Often the value of such benefits more than justifies the annual membership dues.

Make This Work for You

Spend fifteen minutes on the website or social networking group of one professional association that you might be interested in joining—ideally, one that represents an industry you're pursuing.

☐ Done!

---

35. CONNECT WITH DIVERSITY

Did you know that one in three members of your generation is a person of color? That means the Millennial generation is the most diverse generation in American history. If you live in a major city or an ethnically diverse community, you're probably aware of this fact. If not, it's time to start understanding the way multiculturalism will impact the future of our country and the working world you're about to enter. And if you're a member of a minority group, there are many organizations and programs that exist to meet your specific needs.

If you identify as a minority, or if you'd like to learn more about professionals of other backgrounds to diversify your network, there are several actions you can take. One idea is to subscribe to publications for professionals of diverse identities, follow them on Twitter and LinkedIn, and fan their Facebook pages. Just like subscribing to magazines or e-newsletters for an industry that interests you, this is a way to learn about a particular community—the issues, the major players, the companies that are friendly to the group, and, of course, job opportunities. There are many national organizations as well as local networking and professional development groups that provide in-person networking opportunities as well. Check with your career services office for recommendations to suit your unique needs.

One resource for minority students is Management Leadership for Tomorrow (www.ML4T.org), an organization with the mission of "increasing the presence of minorities in fast-track, entry-level jobs and major graduate business schools as preparation for leadership positions in corporations, nonprofit organizations, and entrepreneurial ventures." MLT's career preparation (CP) program offers a comprehensive curriculum designed to identify career opportunities; develop the skills, competencies, and attributes that hiring organizations require; and prepare high-achieving minority students for the job search and interviewing process. The no-cost program is open to students who identify as being African American/black, Latino/Hispanic, or Native American and who are college juniors and seniors. Although the program is business focused, it's open to students from all disciplines and interests. Application information is available at ML4T.org.

Why is it important for minority students to seek organizations and resources specifically catering to their needs? According to Eric Henderson, a former director of marketing and communications for MLT, "If we consider minority achievement gaps in historical and cultural terms, we can see that those gaps have infinitely less to do with aptitude than they do with simple access and exposure. Minority-focused organizations strive to level the playing field in this regard, allowing the student to focus on what's really important—working hard to learn and grow, not just to get in the door."

And what do organizations like MLT offer that minority students can't find elsewhere? Henderson says, "There is no other place where minority students will find so many successful people specifically committed to helping them achieve great things. At MLT, for example, staff members come from high-impact careers with Fortune 100 companies, business schools, and entrepreneurial ventures, making MLT a one-stop shop for the essentials that minorities have traditionally lacked: the coaching, experiences, relationships, and skill development they need to realize their full potential."

36. WORK SOME NEW ROOMS

My college friends often laughed at me when I left campus to attend luncheons or spent summer days inside over-air-conditioned hotels attending professional conferences. Well, no one was laughing when I scored an internship at the conference I attended during spring break of my junior year. Professional conferences in particular are the mecca of career development and networking opportunities. And you will put yourself at a huge advantage in the postcollege job market if you have the experience of attending them, especially when so many members of your generation are much more comfortable hiding behind a computer screen.

Here is an easy-to-follow process for learning about, attending, and making the most of professional conferences. Note that this tip is called "Work Some New Rooms," not just "Walk into Some New Rooms and Hang Out." Attending a conference or networking event isn't going to get you as far as actively engaging. You have to work it!

1. **Be in the know.** To attend a professional conference or networking event (such as a breakfast, after-work reception, or workshop), you first have to know that it exists. Conferences and events take place for virtually every industry and in cities and towns across the country. If you live or go to school near a major city, you're likely to have more event opportunities, but college campuses are common conference and workshop hosts, so don't worry if you're based in a smaller town.

   Other places to look for event opportunities include:

   - **Your school's career services office.** I know that they offer many workshops and receptions, because I often speak at them. If you haven't already, be sure to sign up for event announcements or the Twitter feed from your school's office.
   - **Your professors.** Ask about what conferences and events they attend or receive information about. You might request an invitation to tag along.
   - **Craigslist.org.** Craigslist features postings in dozens of cities, ranging from Albuquerque to Richmond to South Bend. Click on the "Events" link in your area to find information about conferences that might interest you.
   - **Professional associations.** As mentioned in the previous two tips, associations exist to provide networking opportunities, so they frequently host a wide variety of get-togethers, both formal and informal, live and virtual.
   - **LinkedIn and Facebook.** Most event organizers now regularly post their events to these social networks. When you find an event on these sites, you also get the additional perk of being able to check out who has RSVPed to attend.
   - **Religious organizations.** Local churches, synagogues, and religious community groups often host discussions, socials, and other events. Sign up for e-mails from any organization that appeals to you.

- **Bookstores.** Local booksellers, from your nearest Barnes & Noble to small, indie shops, often host readings by authors who have recently published. While such events are not officially business or networking functions, they are a great way to be in a room full of interesting, interested people. Even more so if you attend a reading about a book related to your career interests. Pick up a schedule at your nearest bookstore, or check the store's website or Twitter feed for listings. You can also check the speaking schedules of your favorite authors on their websites to see if they'll be visiting your area.

2. **Register without going bankrupt.** The major drawback of conferences is that they can be über-expensive—sometimes in the thousands of dollars. Most attendees are able to have their companies pay the registration fees, so conferences can get away with the high prices. Occasionally conferences offer student rates, but I think there's a better way to get in without paying an arm and a leg: ask for a discount or free admission. You have nothing to lose by asking: all it takes is an e-mail or phone call to the conference organizer. In my experience planning various conferences, event organizers are usually happy to help a genuinely interested young person. Here is a simple script for making the request:

   "Hello, my name is Olivia and I'm a student [or recent graduate] from UVM. I'm very interested in attending your upcoming conference, but as a student [or recent graduate], I'm unable to pay the full registration fee. Do you have any student or young professional scholarships available?"

   If the answer is no, ask if you might volunteer to work at a portion of the conference in exchange for attendance at some of the sessions. Again, my experience has been that most conferences could use some extra help from a smart young person—handling registration, ushering people to seats, handing out materials, etc.

If you absolutely, positively cannot get a conference organizer to budge on the registration fee, it's worth asking your university if it has funds to sponsor students who want to attend an event. The department of your major is a good place to look, or the budget of any clubs to which you belong.

3. **Research.** A few days (or, better yet, weeks) before you are scheduled to attend a conference, study up on what topics will be covered, which experts will be speaking, and what companies will be represented as sponsors or attendees. Decide based on your research if there are specific people or organizations you'd like to meet at the event. (Many conferences provide this information on their websites or, if the event is posted on Facebook or LinkedIn, you can scope out the attendee list there.) Decide which breakout workshops would be most beneficial to you at this point. If you're not sure, make your decision based on the people you want to meet rather than the topic of the session. For instance, if you're interested in learning more about careers in finance, attend a session discussing the financial industry rather than the topic of personal finance. This will maximize your chances of sitting next to a financial professional who might share some advice with you or might even have an internship or job available.

If you see information about a sponsoring company, professional association, or nonprofit organization associated with the event, visit the website and social media profiles of that organization to learn more before you attend the event. Likewise, read the bios of every person speaking at the event. Check out the LinkedIn profiles of the speakers and sponsoring organizations, and follow them on Twitter as well. See if you have anything in common with them (same university, same hometown, similar hobbies) to find a point of connection if and when you meet them.

The overall goal of all of this pre-event research is to avoid spending valuable time learning the basics about any organization or person you'll meet at the event and be able to cut to the chase of networking with them. In other words, if you find that your dream role model is speaking at the event, rather than introducing yourself and asking about how she got her current amazing job, you can say, "Hello. I've read about your work in this industry, and I noticed that you started your career in management consulting. May I ask how you made the transition to what you are doing today?" The person will be impressed that you've done your homework and know that you're seriously interested in making a connection.

4. **Dress the part.** If you're attending a professional conference, make sure you look the part of a professional —which usually means wearing a suit. Additionally, you'll want to bring your business cards and career notebook or a laptop or tablet to take notes.

37. MAKE EVERY NETWORKING EVENT A SUCCESS

It's great to sign up for lots of networking events, but most people show up and say, "Well, here I am. I hope something really great happens!" and they expect to make a dozen connections. You have to be more strategic . . . and more realistic. I recommend setting a goal before every event you attend.

Here are some goals to consider:

- **Gain general industry knowledge.** Use the conference to attend sessions and make contacts that will tell you more about what jobs exist in a particular industry, what companies might be good to work for, what common career paths exist, and what the outlook is for the future of that field.
- **Make a great one-on-one connection.** You may decide to look for a person to ask for an informational interview, a potential mentor, or even a potential future employer, perhaps one of the people you researched in the previous tip.

  Once you do meet someone, be sure to close the deal and set a time to follow up with this person after the conference. Simply say, "I've really enjoyed meeting you, and I'd like to follow up with you if you're willing. What is the best way to get in touch?" This way you'll find out if the person prefers to be reached by e-mail, by phone, on LinkedIn, or through his or her assistant. You'll also learn if the person is about to go on vacation or is particularly busy at the moment. Request the person's business card, and jot down the contact instructions you receive on the back of the card. Then follow up exactly as you've been told!
- **Become a better networker.** A great goal for attending an event is to sharpen your networking skills; remember, even if you are shy, networking skills can be learned. You don't have to be born with the schmooze gene. One way to improve your networking is to study other conference attendees who appear to be strong networkers and borrow their tactics. You don't have to reinvent the wheel—learn from people you admire. How do you observe people without looking like a stalker? Try this: when people line up to talk to the speakers after a conference panel or workshop, stand nearby and watch each interaction—see how people introduce themselves, what they ask, and how they offer to follow up.

Networking events really are meant to be fun and beneficial, even if you consider yourself to be shy or just a little antisocial. If you do feel a bit awkward, try these strategies to become a more comfortable event networker. If you start to apply these ideas, I have no doubt you'll be an expert connector in no time.

Bring a friend. Some networking experts frown on the idea of bringing a wingman to an event, since some people use this as an opportunity to stand together in the corner and avoid all other human contact. I trust that you won't do this, so if you feel more comfortable and confident attending an event with a friend, then go for it. In fact, in many cases a friend can spur you to be more gutsy and talk to more people. If you do choose to bring a friend, I dare you to bring your most outgoing pal, who will kick you in the butt and push you to talk to people about your job search.

Call ahead. Make yourself known—call or e-mail ahead and introduce yourself to the person listed as the RSVP contact, or just call the host organization's new-member director. Explain that you are a student or a recent grad and new to the organization, and that you'll be attending their upcoming event. Then when you arrive you will have someone to look for. This person will surely take you under his or her wing and introduce you around. And everyone will want to talk to the special guest who is walking around with the host!

Plan your conversation starter. Having a conversation is simple; starting a conversation is challenging. If you feel paralyzed by the idea of walking up to a stranger and talking, then it's a good idea actually to memorize exactly what you're going to say in such a situation. And I have the perfect opening line for you. It's easy and it works every time: "Hi, my name is _____. What brings you to this event?"

If for some reason that doesn't lead to some decent chitchat, then here are a few other good conversation starters and fillers:

- Have you been to any other good events lately?
- Which speakers have you enjoyed/are you looking forward to hearing today?
- Hi, may I join you/join your conversation? I don't know anyone here/I'm new to this networking thing, and you seem friendly.

Finally, I will share with you my favorite event networking trick of all time. It works for shy and outgoing people alike, and it never fails: hang out by the food. This will always give you something to talk about ("How about that spinach dip!"), and if no one pays attention to you, just nibble until someone comes by. I admit it's not the most glamorous strategy, but it totally works.

38. NIX THESE NETWORKING EVENT NO-NOS

Now that you have lots of ways to network effectively at live events, there is one last step: avoiding some common mistakes that can sabotage your best-intended efforts. Here are some networking missteps to avoid:

- **Don't be needy.** The golden rule of networking is to give more than you receive. Nothing irks me more than meeting people who immediately launch into telling me all about what *they* need and how *I* can help *them*. This is a huge turnoff. It is always best to make a genuine, friendly personal connection first, and then broach the subject of your career needs and how you and the other person might help each other. A good rule of thumb is to listen more than you talk.

- **Don't be negative.** Avoid focusing on negatives, particularly with new acquaintances. It's easy to make conversation at a networking function by criticizing the speaker, the venue, the length of time between bathroom breaks, or even the weather, but this can leave people remembering you as a complainer. Make an impression as a positive young person. This includes being positive about yourself—don't put yourself down when you meet new people!
- **Don't be cliquey.** While I definitely advise bringing that wingman if you want to, don't bring an entire flock. I've attended lots of events where all of the college students or young professionals arrive together, stand in a corner together, and leave together. By all means spend some time with your friends, but make an extra effort to introduce yourself to unfamiliar faces.

The biggest mistake of all is not showing up. If you sign up to attend an event, go to that event. You never know which event may be the one where you make the connection that leads to your dream opportunity. Vow that you will stay for only fifteen minutes, if that makes you feel more comfortable. But go. Show up. Always.

39. BE THE FIRST TO FOLLOW UP

A very shy friend of mine recently told me that he fell in love at first sight with a woman behind him in line at Starbucks. He even got up his nerve and asked for her phone number.

"That's so great!" I said. "Did you call her?"

"No."

And that was the end of the story.

This sad tale reminded me of the crucial importance of follow-up. Now that the last few tips hopefully have inspired you to be a bit gutsier, let's put that confidence to use immediately.

Woody Allen once said, and I agree, that 70 percent of success in life is showing up. I propose that the remaining 30 percent of success comes from following up. Yes, it's very important to go out and make valuable face-to-face connections, but the real prize—whether it be a date or a job or most anything else—comes from persistence.

It is not always easy to contact a person you may have met only once, especially if you are shy like my friend. But you must maintain momentum if you meet someone at a networking event with whom you would like to develop a relationship. Make the first move . . . quickly. (Unless you were advised otherwise.)

The best time to follow up is directly after meeting someone, while you're still fresh in his or her mind. This is the case if you've met someone anywhere, such as a networking event, during a volunteer project, at a neighbor's barbecue, or on an airplane. Send a brief "It was so nice to meet you" e-mail (phone calls can sometimes be intrusive and Facebook friend requests can be too personal), and suggest a specific next step. Remember, it is easier for someone to say yes to a specific request rather than a generic "We should get together!" You might invite the person for coffee, lunch, or a scheduled phone call for an informational interview, or share an invitation to an upcoming event where you might connect again. If you're not interested in meeting with or speaking to this person in the near future, you can still send a short message saying that you enjoyed meeting and would like to keep in touch, and ask the person if it's okay to drop a note once in a while or to connect on LinkedIn. The important thing is to express your interest in keeping a connection. You can go out and meet dozens of people, but what's the point if you never keep in touch with them?

I know this sounds like a lot of effort, but I urge you not to sit around and wait for people to follow up with you. Never forget that at this stage of your life, you are the one who is seeking information and contacts. Most people will be happy to offer you guidance and information when you ask for it, but it's doubtful they'll contact you to offer unsolicited advice.

As a general rule, in the Real World lots of things will happen only if you make the first move.

40. KEEP IN TOUCH

Remember the beginning of this section when I defined networking as building and maintaining mutually beneficial relationships? Now we've reached the maintaining part.

Just like any relationship, networking connections need regular attention. You also want to demonstrate to people that you are not someone who only reaches out when you need something. You may be surprised to learn, however, that regular attention in this situation means contacting someone just two or three times a year—once a quarter at most. When it comes to a networking acquaintance you don't see on a regular basis (or LinkedIn connections you might not see at all), this is plenty of interaction to stay on a person's radar screen.

There are a few different methods of keep-in-touch communications that you can use to maintain and nurture your networking connections:

"I saw this article and thought of you" e-mails. Here is another reason why it's so beneficial to read the news and industry e-newsletters every day. Whenever you see an article or item that reminds you of somebody you know, forward that article with a brief note. This is a great way to show that you have this person in mind and want to provide him or her with information, support, a lead to a professional opportunity, or just a laugh or smile. Often I'm the lucky recipient of such notes and clippings. For instance, my website mentions that I like to bake and decorate cupcakes, so contacts will often e-mail me articles about new cupcake shops and even the occasional recipe with a note saying, "Lindsey—I know you'll love this!" And of course I do. (Note: Do not, however, send those mass joke forwards. Most people just delete them.)

Your news. Another great time to send notes and e-mails to contacts is when you start a new position, or have any personal or professional update to share. This is especially important when you start a summer internship or a full-time job; be sure to alert everyone who helped you along the way.

Holiday cards. If you're looking for a reason to get in touch with someone, you have a terrific opportunity during the December holidays. I send about two hundred cards every year, with personal notes on each. (I know that sounds like a lot, but I read that the President of the United States sends over a million a year!) Holiday e-cards are fine, but I believe real cards that people can hold in their hands and display on their mantles have more of an impact.

Social media status updates. While you probably have more than enough experience updating your various social networks with personal updates, now is the time to increase your professional-related updating, especially on LinkedIn. Status updates are a way of staying on people's radar screens in a nonintrusive way. Status updates keep you on people's minds, and you never know what nugget might catch someone's attention and spark a conversation or opportunity.

I recommend updating your status with a professionally related message at least once or twice a week. Think of your status updates as brief conversation starters you might use at a networking event. Here are some examples:

- "Just read a really interesting article [share the link]. What do others think?"
- "Registered for this Thursday's Career Services Job Fair [include link]. Who else is attending?"
- "On my way to volunteer at a local elementary school for Earth Day. Looking forward to it!"
- "Finished reading [name of book]. Highly recommend."

I once updated my LinkedIn status to let my network know that I was on my way out to Los Angeles from New York. By the time my flight landed, I had a message on my voice mail from a news producer in LA who had seen my update and asked if I could be a guest on his show the next day. Of course I said yes (and updated my status to invite my network to watch the segment!).

And last but absolutely not least, **thank-you notes**. Thank-you notes never fail to impress, and I am shocked at how few people send them to professional connections. In my opinion, expressing gratitude when appropriate is one of the most important elements of professional etiquette. Never let a good, helpful deed go unthanked. This is particularly important for young professionals, who are usually on the receiving end of advice.

There are times when thank-you notes are absolutely essential, and there are many, many, many other times when sending a thank-you note is an excellent form of networking and will guarantee that you stand out from your peers. Here is a primer:

Thank-you notes are absolutely essential in these situations:

- Immediately following a job interview or informational interview
- When someone refers you to another person for networking or a job lead
- When someone provides a professional reference for you

Thank-you notes are smart networking when sent to:

- The host of an event you found particularly valuable (note that this category moves up to "essential thank-you" status if someone lets you into an event for free or gives you a discount)
- The author of a book or article you enjoyed
- A mentor or other person who offers particularly good advice
- Anyone else who assists you in your career or job search, in any way, for the rest of your life

In most cases e-mail thank-yous are acceptable because business moves fast and many people—especially recruiters—are rarely at their desks to receive snail mail. However, in some industries and situations (such as interviewing with a small business owner or thanking a family friend for providing advice, perhaps), a handwritten thank-you is a good strategy. When in doubt, there's nothing wrong with sending both a brief e-mail thank-you and a follow-up card in the mail.

If you do choose the handwritten option, I also encourage you to think about what kind of notes to use. This small choice can be an extra way to make a memorable impression and keep you top-of-mind with the people in your growing network. For instance, you may choose to send thank-you notes to alumni of your school using stationery with the school's logo or mascot. If you are networking with people in the film industry, you may choose stationery with old film posters pictured. When I thank colleagues in the publishing industry, I like to send thank-you notes that have a picture of a typewriter on the front. (And of course I have a huge supply of cupcake stationery.) All of these choices show that you have an attention to detail and you are willing to go the extra mile to make a positive impression.

The thing about follow-up and thank-yous of any kind is that they make recipients feel acknowledged—and make those people want to help you again in the future.

Chapter 5

GAIN REAL WORLD EXPERIENCE

"Are you experienced?"
—Jimi Hendrix

Who knew that Jimi Hendrix had a second calling as a hiring manager? "Are you experienced?" is the most important fact most employers will want to know when you express an interest in working for their companies. Along with building your network, getting experience in the Real World of work is crucial for getting a head start in the career game. It is never too early to start building your experience, and you can still make strides even if you're starting late.

This, of course, leads to the classic college-student conundrum: How do you get experience without a job, and get a job without experience? Rest assured that it's possible, because if it weren't, then nobody on earth would be employed.

The tips in this section offer an overview of some of the most common and well-established ways for college students and recent graduates to gain the kinds of experience that most impress entry-level employers.

Remember that experience is something that no one can teach you, give you, or buy for you. You have to put in the work and the time completely on your own. This also means that no one can ever take away the experience you have. It's yours forever. And experience counts. Big-time.

41. BE A LEADER

When I asked recruiters and hiring managers what kinds of activities, extracurriculars, and work experience they most admire in entry-level job candidates, they all gave different responses. The truth is that the importance of different kinds of experience varies widely depending on the kind of job and industry you're seeking. For instance, an accounting internship is way more impressive if you want to be an accountant than if you want to be an engineer. But in my interviews with recruiters and human resources experts, one preference rang out loud and clear: employers want to hire leaders.

Gaining leadership experience and demonstrating leadership success can be accomplished at any age or stage of life (think of the Girl Scouts and the Boy Scouts, which are most people's earliest experience with leadership training).

> ### Reality Check
>
> "The same skill set that made me successful in running organizations in college has helped in the business world."
> Anne Mercogliano,
> manager of business
> strategy, Arnold
> Worldwide

I'm confident that you've already shown some leadership in your life so far, because this is a strong factor in college admissions. Colleges like to admit sports team captains, student government officers, club presidents, and first chair violinists. I'm sure it doesn't surprise you to learn that employers like these types, too. Let's look at the topic of leadership in greater depth to see how it can play a role in your job search and career planning.

What's so important about being a leader, anyway?

"Leaders are what make things happen. Period," says Alice Korngold, nonprofit leadership expert and author of *Leveraging Good Will.* "Every organization, from business to nonprofit to politics to coffee shops, needs people who will say, 'This is where we need to go' and will make sure you get there."

Why is leadership important to entry-level job searching and career planning?

Looking at the leadership experience you've had in your life so far is another good way to see where your skills, talents, and interests lie. My guess is that you wouldn't be president or founder of an organization or event you didn't like. So leadership positions give clues to the kinds of jobs that might make you happy and fulfilled.

Being a leader in any capacity also builds real skills that employers will find valuable in entry-level candidates. The trick is to take any leadership experience you have, from leading a tennis team to being the manager-on-duty at Banana Republic, and translate that experience into words, phrases, and stories that will impress potential employers.

Here are some examples of skills that you build through leadership experience:

- Thinking on your feet
- Dealing well under stress
- Being responsible for other people
- Developing interpersonal skills
- Earning the respect and trust of your peers/bosses/people you manage
- Getting diverse people to work well as a team
- Seeing projects through from beginning to end
- Being a self-starter
- Paying close attention to quality

Consider applying these phrases to the stories you tell about yourself in job interviews, the phrases you use on your résumé to describe your accomplishments, and the essays you might write to apply for internship programs, scholarships, or special honors.

What if I don't have any leadership roles to put on my résumé?

Everyone can't be captain of the debate team. But I firmly believe that everyone can develop some leadership skills, and probably everyone has. Think of the military; one of the main ideas of military training is to empower every single soldier to have personal leadership skills and the self-confidence to act in the face of danger. The same can be said, to a different degree of course, about many types of activities. You can show leadership skills and development without being in charge. According to leadership expert Karlin Sloan, there are many ways to learn leadership skills as a member of a group or team. Here are some phrases Karlin recommends using in cover letters or while telling stories about your experience if you haven't held any clear leadership positions:

"I learned leadership skills by . . .

- "communicating with the diverse people on my team/in my club/at my place of work."
- "managing/being responsible for a certain part of a project (e.g., coordinating our math team's fund-raiser or handling promotional displays for the pharmacy where I worked)."
- "being in a competitive environment (e.g., on a sports team, working in a retail store with competition down the street) and contributing to my team/company's success."
- "developing my own competence to contribute to the success of my team."

Every single type of experience you get as a college student or recent grad provides opportunities to learn, demonstrate, and excel at leadership. I can't overemphasize how important leadership is in the minds of the people who want to hire you.

42. BE A JOINER

On the Saturday afternoon of my college orientation week, every club, society, organization, and activity on campus set up a booth on the main quad and tried to enroll eager freshmen in their ranks. When I think back on that event now, I see that every single booth held an opportunity. While the last tip addressed the importance of developing general leadership skills, this tip drills down to more detailed ways to use your undergraduate activities to help your career planning and job searching.

By all means participate in extracurricular activities that interest you and are fun, but you can be strategic and turn them into marketable Real World experience as well. Here are some pointers:

- **Build a career-related skill.** No matter what extracurricular activity interests you, you can enjoy the fun of it while gaining marketable experience at the same time. For instance, if you love to sing and you think you're interested in a career in public relations, volunteer to be the student in charge of promoting your choir's events. If you're in the honor society and want to pursue a career in finance, volunteer to be the society's treasurer.

- **Participate in an organization related to your career interests.** If you want to work in politics, then participate in student government. If you want to work overseas at some point in your career, join the French club. If you want to be a teacher, volunteer to run a tutoring program at a local school. If you want to be an engineer, join the engineering society. This advice may seem obvious, but many students don't take advantage of the career-building opportunities that are right on their campuses.

- **Test the waters.** If you have no idea what you want to do careerwise, trying a variety of extracurricular activities is a great way to get a feel for what a particular career might be like. For instance, if you're considering jobs in the business world, join the economics club or a prebusiness club. See if you like the people, the activities, the topics of discussion. This will give you insight into what your future colleagues and professional culture might look like.

- **Start a new organization.** If you can't find an extracurricular activity that fulfills your needs, then take the initiative and start your own—an entrepreneurial club, a current events discussion group, a sculpting club, an environmental awareness crusade, a Korean students association, a web design collective, anything. This is another great way to show initiative and leadership combined with expressing your deepest interests.

- **Engage your faculty adviser.** If your extracurricular activities have a faculty member involved, develop a relationship with that person. He or she will likely have input on the skills and talents you've shown through the activity and can provide an opinion on good career paths or specific job opportunities you might want to pursue. Your adviser would be a good person to ask for a professional recommendation on LinkedIn, as well.

- **Show results.** If you take the time to be part of an extracurricular activity, it's worth making an effort to accomplish something in the process. Instead of simply participating in events, consider hosting a fund-raiser for the group, coordinating an alumni reunion for former members, building the group's membership, balancing the organization's budget. Make a tangible, measurable contribution to any student organization or extracurricular activity you belong to, just as you would if you took a paying job with an organization. These accomplishments will be strong bullet points on your résumé and will provide you with specific, results-oriented stories to share in future job interviews.

One last point about extracurriculars: don't spread yourself too thin. Employers are more impressed by someone who is strongly committed to a few activities rather than someone who dabbles in a bit of everything. Go deep, not wide.

Make This Work for You

If you're still in college, join or focus on at least one extracurricular activity that can help your career planning and job search. Join a career-related club, take on a responsibility that will develop the skills you'd like to apply in your future career, head up a volunteer project that will produce tangible results, or start your own club or a subgroup of an existing club.

If you've already graduated, look at the extracurricular activities you participated in during your college years and analyze them from a strategic career perspective: note down your responsibilities, skills you learned, interests you pursued, or accomplishments you achieved. Then be sure to include these on your résumé and your LinkedIn profile.

☐ **Done!**

---

43. INTERN . . . EARLY AND OFTEN

"It used to be that students spent summers as a lifeguard or cutting grass," says Rick Klotz, director, human resources, Tyco Fire Protection Services–SimplexGrinnell. "Internships were the exception. But now they're the rule. Most student applicants come to us with relevant work experience." This trend is supported by survey findings as well. According to the National Association of Colleges and Employers, in 2008, 50 percent of graduating college students had held internships. While there has been some controversy in recent years over the issue of unpaid internships and whether they flout labor laws (and I encourage you to carefully consider whether an unpaid internship is a realistic financial option for you), the reality is that most employers expect to see at least one internship on your résumé and paid internships are not always easy to find.

Some organizations—mostly large corporations—have formal programs that require students to apply for a limited number of spots, while other firms may have more of an informal program. Some internships are summer programs, while others take place year-round. Some pay, some don't. Some offer course credit. No matter what type you choose, I highly, strongly, totally recommend internships to students, young professionals, and even to more experienced people who are looking to change careers. Nothing beats real, honest-to-goodness experience in the industry—or even the company—you want to work in someday.

Here are some additional benefits of internships:

Internships build your résumé. Internship experience can and should appear on your résumé and LinkedIn profile. The better the brand name of the company, the more impressive this experience will be to prospective employers. An internship of virtually any kind allows you to get real professional experience under your belt. Besides having a job to list on your résumé, you will also have completed projects to discuss during job interviews, which allows you to show results you've achieved in a professional setting.

Internships build your professionalism. Internships are also a great chance to learn some of the basics of business interaction: how to write a concise e-mail; how to leave professional voice mail messages; how to interact in a meeting; and how to interact with the mailroom, the IT help desk, and other professional support services that are crucial to get-

> ### Reality Check
>
> "If you get an internship, recognize that it is absolutely your best shot to establish yourself as indispensable and unforgettable. It's relatively rare to see interns who recognize that they are responsible for their growth and advancement and go after it hard every day. I'm not looking for careerists or suck-ups, but the people who fail to lean forward and grasp the opportunity simply don't make it."
>
> Jay Porter, general manager, San Francisco, Edelman

ting things done. It's better to learn these things (and make beginner mistakes) in an internship rather than when you're working in a real, paying job, where your superiors may be far less forgiving.

Internships build your contacts. Every person you work with during your internships is a contact to add to your growing network. If you succeed in your internship and impress people, you may be able to call on them in the future for reference letters, job leads, or even employment opportunities.

Internships build your industry knowledge. Before an internship at a magazine, you might not know what "TK" means. (It's editor-speak for content that is "to come.") Before an internship at a law firm, you might not understand the concept of billable hours. Internships are a great place to learn the lingo for an industry. If you want to work in an industry that doesn't generally offer internships, such as equity research, then the best advice is to get as close to that field as you can. In the case of equity research, that would mean securing an internship in another area of finance.

Finally, a great advantage of internships is that they can help you decide what industry you might not want to work in, and what jobs you might not ever want to pursue. This information can be just as valuable for you to learn about yourself.

━━ ━━ ━━ ━━ ━━ ━━ ━━

Extra Credit

A relatively recent development is the advent of virtual internships, which are—just as the name implies—internships that don't require working from an organization's office. While these opportunities are still relatively rare, they are increasing in popularity thanks to the massive growth of technology and social media. For more perspective on the world of virtual interning, I turned to Cari Sommer, cofounder of Urban Interns, an online marketplace where small businesses source part-time workers and interns, including virtual ones.

LP: What is a virtual internship and what are the advantages of this type of experience?

CS: A virtual internship is like any other internship except the majority, if not all of the work, is done remotely. Virtual interns will sometimes work in the same city or geographic location as an employer, which provides opportunities for occasional face-to-face meetings. In other instances, interns and their employers are many miles apart and communication is solely online or by phone.

Since they don't have official office hours, virtual interns can work on their own schedule, provided that their work is done and they are meeting deadlines. Virtual internships also provide access to opportunities beyond where a student or young professional lives.

LP: How can a student or recent grad go about finding a virtual internship?

CS: There are consistently a number of opportunities listed on UrbanInterns.com. Internships.com is also a great resource.

LP: What are some examples of responsibilities a virtual intern might have?

CS: Virtual interns may be asked to do anything, including blogging, maintaining social-media profiles, helping to execute an SEO (search engine optimization) strategy, and even some administrative work. There often is a wide range of tasks.

LP: What are some tips for succeeding in a virtual internship?

CS: Being organized is key. Whether a virtual intern is work-ing from home or a coffee shop, it's imperative to impose some structure and organization to make sure work is being done on time and effectively. It's also important to commu-nicate regularly with your boss. You want to make sure that out of sight does not equal out of mind.

Make This Work for You

What is the best way to find an internship that meets your individual interests and job aspirations? Here are some sug-gestions:

- **Online listings.** There are several websites you can search for internships across the country. Try Internships .com, UrbanInterns.com, OneDayOneInternship.com, InternJobs.com, InternWeb.com, and AfterCollege.com. Smaller companies may list internship opportunities on industry association websites (best found through a general Google search on the industry name and the word "internships"), LinkedIn groups, Facebook, Twitter, or Craigslist.org. Many companies post their internship information on their own websites as well.

- **Your school.** If you're a current student or recent gradu-ate, contact your college or university career services office for information about available internships. Do this as early as possible, as more opportunities will be available and some formal internship programs have early deadlines, particularly for summer internships. Look for internships offered by alumni of your school: if

they are specifically seeking an intern from your college
or university, you'll have a better chance of winning the
position.

- **Your professors.** Don't forget to ask your professors as
  well. Many professors are connected to companies and
  other organizations tied to their field of study, so they
  often hear of opportunities for student interns or part-
  time workers. Tell your professors that you're looking for
  internship opportunities so you're top-of-mind if they
  hear about anything. I found an internship in graduate
  school from a flyer posted in my academic department—
  it turned out I was the only one who responded!

- **Professional associations.** Just as alumni of your school
  are more likely to hire students affiliated with their alma
  mater, members of professional associations are eager to
  hire young people connected to their professional membership associations. Research associations in the fields
  that interest you and scan their websites, newsletters,
  social media pages, and member magazines for internship opportunities. If you're not able to view any of these
  resources (some are limited to association members
  only), call up the association and express your interest.
  I received such phone calls at one of the professional
  associations where I worked, the National Association for
  Female Executives, and we sometimes offered internships to the students who called.

- **Your network.** If you know what kind of internship opportunity you're seeking, spread the word to your network of
  friends and family. A simple e-mail message like this one
  may result in some leads for an internship crafted to your
  needs:

Subject: Seeking contacts for an internship

Dear Friends and Family:

As many of you know, I'm very interested in entering the hospitality industry when I graduate from college in two years. This coming summer I would like to build my experience in the field by working in an internship position at a hotel or bed-and-breakfast in the Kansas City area. If you know of anyone who may be looking for an enthusiastic, hardworking summer intern, please let me know. I would really appreciate your help. Thank you very much!

☐ Done!

----

44. PRACTICE THE EIGHT ESSENTIALS OF INTERNSHIP ACHIEVEMENT

I'm pretty sure I know what you're thinking right now. I'm, like, the millionth person who's told you to get an internship so you'll have some tangible experience to include on your résumé. So you get an internship, or you've already had one or many. But during the long hours of the internship, you often wonder how filing, answering phones, or just sitting around (which are all pretty inevitable, even in the most challenging, productive internships) really gives you skills that will make you stand out among all the other students who did internships, too.

I wondered the same thing, so I set about asking a variety of internship coordinators what really makes an intern get noticed and even get hired for a full-time job once the internship ends. No matter what organization, what work they give you, or what

industry you think you might want to work in, here are some tips
to make sure your internship works for you:

1. **Learn how work is different from school.** Of course the most
   exciting difference between college and the Real World is that
   you get a paycheck instead of grades. However, there are a few
   other changes an internship can help you adjust to. For instance,
   missing a deadline has major consequences. According to
   Tammy Tibbetts, the recent journalism grad whose story you
   read in Tip #25, "Hero Worship," "If editors need something,
   they need it. If you are late handing in an assignment in school,
   your grade is docked. If you're late at a magazine, you can slow
   down the production process." As an intern, you're supporting
   full-time employees whose jobs are their livelihoods—there's
   no room for messing around with projects they're relying on.
   Furthermore, your work as an intern could directly impact the
   bottom line of the organization you're working for, particularly if you're dealing directly with clients or customers. Your
   professionalism is not requested; it's required.

2. **Step outside your comfort zone.** Tammy, who had several
   impressive internships, credits her success to "learning how
   to step outside my comfort zone . . . that's the thing I sense
   is most difficult for my peers. As an intern, I was asked to do
   things that seemed nearly impossible at first—find homeless
   women who live in their cars, find women who've quit their
   jobs to start cool businesses, find a place to rent video projec-
   tion equipment for a party in LA happening in two days . . .
   and try to get it for free. Those were all tasks that challenged
   me to think outside the box. And I learned that if you can't
   find an answer using plan A, you need to come up with a plan
   B, C, D, etc. I always felt I could go to an editor for help, but
   I know they largely expected me to figure things out myself."

Internships are a great time to take risks, face your fears, and challenge yourself to try some big new things.

3. **Be proactive.** Chris Salvatore, formerly a senior book publicist for a major media company who oversaw college interns every summer, advises interns not to wait around for work to be assigned. She admits that there can be a lot of downtime, especially when employees are busy with other projects, but that's no reason to start texting your friends. Chris suggests that interns ask their managers this smart question: "What is a good thing for me to work on when you're busy and I have nothing specific to do?" This question shows that you are a go-getter who wants to contribute and learn as much as possible. And you may get assigned a cool project that no one else was smart enough to ask for—something that you can highlight on your résumé and promote in future job interviews. Remember, raising an internship from the "busywork/no experience" level to the "real experience" level is in your hands.

4. **Read what you file (with permission!).** This is another great suggestion from Chris. "One thing you often have as an intern is the luxury of time," she says. "So, as long as your boss tells you it's okay, take time to read through the documents you're filing, and you'll learn a lot." Be sure to heed her warning—you don't want to snoop through confidential contracts or legal records—but if you get approval, this is a shrewd strategy. Chris herself remembers reading through hundreds of book reviews in the early years of her career, which helped her later on when she was the publicist promoting books to those same reviewers.

5. **Set up informational interviews.** While you're at an organization in the role of intern, you have a rare opportunity for face time with people you otherwise might not be able to

meet. Check with your internship coordinator to make sure it's appropriate, then pinpoint a few people in the organization whose jobs interest you and ask them to meet with you. Don't miss this opportunity to shoot fish in a barrel—during an internship you are literally surrounded by informational interview prospects! As appropriate, connect with them on LinkedIn as well. If you can, you should also set up a meeting with someone in the human resources department to talk about future full-time job opportunities—this is a golden lead for your first postcollege job. One internship coordinator in the entertainment industry shared with me that he is shocked at the lack of interest he sees in some of his organization's interns. "I work with interns now, and they're all on Facebook all day," he says. "I can't believe they're not taking advantage of the people around them!"

6. **Network with your fellow interns.** Chris Salvatore also reminds interns to network with your peers, not just your higher-ups. In addition to chatting during work hours, try to attend as many after-work events and informal get-togethers as possible, and connect with your fellow interns on social media so you can keep in touch after the internship ends. These people are great contacts; you never know where your fellow interns are going to end up someday—or who else they know right now. Since you landed at the same internship, your fellow interns must share some common interests with you. So ask them what other careers, companies, internships, or opportunities they're considering or have pursued already. This can be a great source of ideas and contacts for you. And if you're intimidated by the general idea of networking, it's often easier to practice this skill with your peers than with more senior people.

7. **Collect references.** Don't assume future employers will take

your word for the fact that you gained valuable experience and skills during your internship—get proof! Ask your internship supervisor and any other professionals with whom you work to write written references or recommendations on your LinkedIn profile to help with your future career pursuits. You can also ask people to write on company letterhead addressed "To Whom It May Concern" so you can use the letters for various purposes. When you ask for any type of recommendation, remind your internship supervisor what you've achieved over the course of your internship—projects completed, results achieved, departments you interacted with, events you attended, and any other significant experiences or contributions. Putting together such a reminder list will also serve to help you when you add this internship to your professional résumé. Make a copy of your note and any reference letters you're able to collect, and put them in a folder in your filing system. It's a good idea to keep reference letters in a plastic folder or sleeve so they stay in good condition.

8. **Keep in touch.** Supervisors, employees, fellow interns, and everyone else you meet through your internship are now relationships and should be added to your contact database, your LinkedIn connections, and the people you follow on Twitter. (Facebook is generally not appropriate unless you're connecting with a peer.) Here's my recommended way of adding people you meet during an internship to your network: ask them! Simply say toward the end of your stint, "I've really enjoyed meeting you and working with you during my internship. May I keep in touch with you in the future and check in with you once in a while?" Most likely people will say yes, and they'll appreciate the respectfulness of your asking. Then send each person a hello note, LinkedIn connection request, or e-mail within a month of ending your internship (just to say hello and prove you really

do want to keep in contact), and send an e-mail or note about twice a year—perhaps once during the December holidays and once in the spring when classes end.

Additionally, you can keep in touch by offering yourself as an active alum of an organization's internship program. If it's a large corporation, you can offer to speak to potential future interns and help them prepare for the internship. For any organization, you can help recruit future interns from your college or group of friends. Let your internship supervisors know that you'd like to be as helpful to their organizations as they've been to your career. This will keep you top-of-mind when full-time opportunities become available.

45. TEMP

Particularly in tough economic times, you may not be able to secure an internship or even a paid part-time job. Another option to consider is temp work, which may not be your ideal scenario but which offers some benefits you may not have considered.

What's intriguing about temping is that it's similar to being an intern—you are able to gain on-the-job, in-the-office experience—but the length of commitment is up to you.

What's very different, of course, is that in an internship the employer knows that you are there partly to learn. In a temp job, you should not expect any coaching or mentoring. However, I believe that you can turn any situation into a career opportunity, so here are some tips for being a tactically minded temp:

Get a temp job that will help your career prospects.

• Temp in an industry that interests you. Do your research

to find temp agencies that specialize in the industries you might want to work in full-time. (The American Staffing Association website [www.americanstaffing.net] can help you locate temp agencies in your desired location and industry.) Then you'll gain experience in that industry through your temp job, and you'll be in a better position to raise your hand if a job opportunity arises while you're temping.

- **Temp in a major corporation.** If you're unsure of what industry you'd like to work in, do your best to get a temp job in a major corporation. The good news is that corporations are more likely to hire large numbers of temps. Why is it helpful to temp at a corporation? Employers are always impressed by brand-name corporate experience because of the level of professionalism found in large, respected companies. Even if you're just sitting at the reception desk of such a company or unpacking boxes in a back room, you'll still be exposed to how such companies run and what the environments are like. That's experience you can use to determine if corporate life is for you, and even mention in a corporate job interview if you choose to pursue that route.

Make the most of a temp job once you have it.

- **Think like an intern—or, better yet, an employee.** Just like an internship, any work opportunity, even a temp experience, is a chance to show your skills, meet people, and learn about the Real World. You never know who's around the corner watching . . . or hiring. Always raise your hand for additional assignments and get to know any colleagues or fellow temps who seem open to networking. You can even request a meeting with someone in HR to discuss your interest in any full-time positions that might become available.
- **Be positive.** In full-time job interviews or any time you talk about your temp work, be positive about the experience.

You can probably guess that saying, "I graduated without a job and would have taken anything at that point!" is not the best strategy. Instead, talk about the best experience and skills you gained from temping—exposure to the corporate environment, learning about different functional roles at the company, etc.

Proof It's Possible

This story begins with a simple networking connection. Erin Berkery, a graduate of Binghamton University, took Laura Allen's 15SecondPitch workshop (see Tip #29, "Be Able to Introduce Yourself") and met a young woman who was temping at the time. The young woman gave Erin a reference to her temp agency in New York City, and Erin received her first assignment as a receptionist at the publishing company Rodale Inc. Here's how Erin turned temping into a full-time job where she quickly moved up the entry-level ladder:

"Apparently all of the receptionists they had before me were complete idiots, because when I started, the phones weren't even turned on. This meant my job was to sign for package deliveries—that was it! I worked temporarily for three months, when I was hired on full-time to work as the assistant to the office manager and the director of Human Resources.

"When I was working in Human Resources my boss said to me, 'You're too smart to be working this job, so if you want to do anything else in the company, just tell me and I'll get you the job.' I told her that I was interested in writing, so when an editorial assistant position opened up, I applied and got the job.

"I got the job because I did *everything* as a receptionist. At one point, neither of the doors into the office would
open without a security tag, which meant I had to walk all
visitors over to the doors, which were about ten feet away.
I did this *every* time someone came in, and also when
employees forgot their security tags.

"I also kept asking for work. I felt guilty sitting there,
with no phone, reading the paper cover to cover every day.
I couldn't believe that they paid me to do this. I kept saying to the office manager, 'If you need me to do more, just
let me know, because I'm willing to do the work.' And she
eventually took me out of reception and put me in a cube
next to her to help organize her work.

"I also think it helped that I didn't complain. When I
went full-time, there was nowhere for me to sit, so I had to
move back to the reception desk, where I acted as a receptionist in addition to doing all of the duties that Human
Resources and Facilities needed. I wouldn't get ruffled
when people would get angry because the 'receptionist' was
away making sure a new employee had all of her paperwork
in order. I think it was this resolve that my bosses appreciated, and that's what led them to give me the second job."

46. VOLUNTEER

The great thing about volunteer jobs is that you can always get one.
No previous experience necessary. You can volunteer on your college campus, in your community, in a foreign country, or even from
the comfort of your home. There are opportunities everywhere.

In addition to the great feeling you'll get from supporting a good cause, volunteering your time also offers extensive learning, networking, and experience-building opportunities. Some good websites to look at for volunteer opportunities include VolunteerMatch .org, Idealist.org, Serve.gov, and DoSomething.org.

Here are some career-enhancing volunteer opportunities to explore:

Volunteer to pursue a passion. If you love animals, volunteer to work at a nature center, zoo, or animal rescue center. If you love science, donate your time to a hospital, science museum, or laboratory. While you are helping support a cause that's important to you, you can also test what it's like to work in various environments. You may think you like working with children until you spend an entire summer volunteering at a nursery school and realize it's just not for you. You may decide that a legal environment feels too controversial for your shy nature. Or you may decide that you really do want to pursue a career working in your dream field, and volunteering will get you even more excited— and experienced.

Volunteer to build your skills and experience. If you're looking to develop or refine specific skills in anticipation of a job search, consider volunteering for tasks that will help build your experience in your professional discipline. If you're a techie, offer your services in programming or database management. If you want to be a PR professional, help write press releases and build media contacts for your favorite cause. Most volunteer-based organizations are more than happy to accept assistance in any area, particularly if you can contribute specific professional skills. And once you've been volunteering for a while, be sure to request LinkedIn recommendations or reference letters detailing the professional services you've provided. These will come in handy during your job search.

Volunteer to build your leadership skills. In addition to taking on more specific tasks, consider taking leadership of an entire project, serving on a nonprofit committee, or even chairing a junior committee event for an organization. Don't wait to be asked. Raise your hand for additional responsibilities, committees, strategic planning sessions, and other opportunities to be more visible, and show your talents and willingness to learn. As you've already read, having this type of leadership listed on your résumé, even at a volunteer job, can really help you stand out from the crowd.

Volunteer to build your network. Think of all the people you interact with through volunteer work—other volunteers, nonprofit staff, fund-raising prospects, sponsors, nonprofit agency clients, donors—who may be potential sources of job leads, career advice, and mentorship. Most of these contacts would be happy to help a dedicated volunteer or at least have a chat. So politely spread the word about your career goals, and explain exactly what sort of opportunities you are seeking. And, of course, always offer to help others in return.

Volunteer to build your résumé. Many people don't realize you can—and should—include volunteer work on your résumé and online profiles. Employers often prefer to hire employees who are active volunteers because this demonstrates a commitment to one's community and the organizational skills to manage both work and outside activities. When including volunteer experience on your résumé or discussing it in a job interview, emphasize the skills you've developed in your nonprofit work that are transferable to the professional world. Use terms such as "leadership," "fund-raising," "public relations," "people management," and "budgeting" to describe your activities.

Volunteer in order to get a job with a volunteer organization. Sometimes the best jobs are right under your nose. If you love your volunteer work, consider career opportunities with the organizations to which you donate your time and skills. Many nonprofits recruit paid staff members from their own volunteer ranks. Ask the organizations where you volunteer for available opportunities in their organization or in related ones. Working in the nonprofit sector has become an increasingly popular choice since the 2008 financial crisis. According to an analysis by the *New York Times*, in 2009 alone, 11 percent more young college grads worked for nonprofit groups than the previous year. With approximately 1.5 million nonprofit organizations in the United States, this trend is sure to continue.

Make This Work for You

Volunteering is a great thing to do, but it's also time consuming. Sometimes it can be hard to donate your time for free when you really need to study or earn money to pay your rent and make a dent in those student loans. Or you get excited to volunteer for a while, but then your interest fades. If this has happened to you or you suspect it might, try these strategies before giving up on the idea of volunteering:

- **Commit to a specific and manageable time frame.** Volunteering can become a big burden if your regular hours and the length of your commitment are not clearly defined. When you sign up to be a volunteer, set up a game plan with the volunteer organizer to keep both of your expectations in check. For example, "I'd like to be a Big Brother to an inner city boy one Saturday a month for six months," or "I'll answer phones at the youth crisis hotline from 7:00 p.m. to 10:00 p.m. every other Thursday until the end of the school year." Then mark the commitment on your calendar for its duration.

- **Consider volunteer efforts that can be accomplished virtually.** If you want to contribute but time is tight, donate your efforts from home. This will still allow you to get many of the career benefits of volunteering (such as experience, connections, and knowledge) as well as the "feel-good" benefits, while fitting in the work when it's convenient for you. You can volunteer to do off-site computer or database programming, write articles for a newsletter, make fund-raising phone calls, or help with Web design. Most nonprofit organizations have small offices anyway, so they'll be happy to sign you up as a virtual volunteer. VolunteerMatch.org is a good resource for finding virtual volunteer opportunities.

- **Volunteer with a friend.** Lots of people have gym and yoga buddies who make sure they get to their work-outs, so why not enlist a volunteer buddy? Commit with a friend or a group of friends to a volunteer activity you can do together, such as landscaping an urban playground, cooking in a soup kitchen, or handing out flyers for a carnival. To make sure you get the maximum career experience from your volunteer efforts, partner with a friend or classmate who has similar professional goals.

☐ Done!

━━ ━━ ━━ ━━ ━━ ━━ ━━ ━━

47. SKIP SOUTH BEACH

I first learned about the concept of alternative spring breaks from a special on MTV. I was hugely impressed by the students featured in this program. Rather than partying or sleeping their way through spring break (which, of course, there's nothing wrong with doing if you need a break!), these college students were doing community service.

One of the most marked characteristics of Generation Y is your commitment to community service, and this has been reflected in a huge growth in the alternative spring break movement. To learn about such opportunities, check out the Corporation for National and Community Service (NationalService .gov), which includes programs such as AmeriCorps, organizes thousands of students each year to build houses for low-income families, care for AIDS patients, and tutor inner-city children. If you'd like to volunteer overseas, check out Projects Abroad (www .projects-abroad.org).

Over one hundred college campuses around the country have chapters of Break Away (www.alternativebreaks.org), which offers an even more comprehensive approach to alternative spring breaks: Break Away teams spend months preparing for their experience by educating themselves about the social issues and the community in which they will be serving, while also team building, fund-raising, and planning logistics. Students perform short-term projects for community agencies and learn about issues such as literacy, poverty, racism, hunger, homelessness, and the environment.

Consider an alternative spring break service-learning trip at some point in your college career, or even after you've graduated. These trips and projects are often available during winter and summer breaks as well. In any industry or area of the country, you'll stand out from your peers who spent their vacations lying on the beach—and, who knows, you may just end up on MTV.

48. BE SUPERSTRATEGIC ABOUT PART-TIME WORK

As a college student or recent grad living in uncertain economic times, you will likely want or need a part-time job to make money. Many young people don't consider that a part-time job can help their career plans, but it absolutely can. You just need to be strategic.

Many people take whatever job they can get, particularly if it's part of a work-study program, but at many schools you can request the kind of job you'd like. What a great opportunity to explore some career options that interest you. For instance, if you're interested in landscape design, work at the physical plant. If you love fashion, work at a clothing store. If you want to be a lawyer, be a receptionist at a law firm. If you want a medical career, work in a hospital or medical clinic. Even the lowest-level job can expose you to the skills, language, habits, and people that can help you land a full-time job in the future. Or a part-time job can help you to discover that a particular field or working environment is not at all what you expected.

Any job also offers a chance to build your skills, many of which will be transferable to a full-time job. Here are some examples of skills you might learn at a part-time job, which can turn into stories to tell in a job interview or phrases to use when describing a part-time job on your résumé or on your LinkedIn profile:

- Customer/client service
- Communication skills
- Managing a budget
- Meeting deadlines
- Managing people
- Programming

- Social media management
- Patience
- Leadership/responsibility
- Teamwork
- Problem solving
- Time management
- Multitasking
- Prioritizing

Part-time jobs, for a student or recent grad, can also meet other needs. Besides making extra money and building skills and networks, many part-time jobs these days offer health benefits and quick advancement opportunities. Some companies, such as Starbucks, UPS, Wegmans grocery stores, REI, and the Container Store, even promote themselves as good places for recent grads to start out as part-timers and work their way up. A 2006 article in *Kiplinger's*, a personal finance magazine, referred to such opportunities as "stepping stone" jobs.

Beyond working part-time in a good environment with excellent benefits, these companies are all big employers of full-time, corporate employees as well. Starting out behind the counter will give you an

Reality Check

"Working as a waitress provided me with ample opportunities to get to know people and understand the true value of connecting with customers and building good working relationships. Getting along with the cook turned out to be one of the most important factors in providing good service and getting good tips! I also learned the value of hard work and how to balance work, life, and school."

Celeste Blackman, global consultant and cofounder, Green Zone Culture Group entrée into the corner office if you impress your managers and show an interest in moving up the ladder. But you can't be shy—ask your manager to connect you with the HR department to find out about opportunities to apply for full-time positions.

If a part-time job is part of your career path, even if it's just a stopgap on the way to your "real" future, always have a good attitude and do your best. You absolutely never know who might walk through the door and notice your hard work, drive, and discipline. Every job, no matter how short-term, low-level, or monotonous, is a chance to shine. And everyone has to start somewhere. Even Madonna once worked behind the counter at Dunkin' Donuts.

49. PUT OUT YOUR OWN SHINGLE

I once attended a business planning workshop where the instructor told us, "All you need to start a sole proprietorship is a pulse." So, congratulations! You are totally qualified to start your own business no matter how old you are, where you live, or what skills you have. These days, everyone is the CEO of his or her own career, so it's a great move to start and run a venture in college or in your early twenties. Perhaps you've already considered this. According to a 2011 study by Buzz Marketing Group and The Young Entrepreneur Council (of which I am a member), 79 percent of Gen Ys are interested in entrepreneurship and 27 percent are already self-employed in some way.

Additionally, the concept of "sidepreneurship" is increasing in popularity. According to the same Buzz Marketing/YEC study, more than 35 percent of Gen Y respondents who have jobs have started a business on the side in order to supplement their incomes. Even if you have no desire to run your own business, there is a strong likelihood that at some point in your career you'll work for an entrepreneur. You might be surprised to learn that 99 percent of all independent enterprises in the United States employ fewer than five hundred people. In other words, most Americans *don't* work for big corporations. (For tips on how to find opportunities with small businesses, see Tip #70, "Start Small.")

Starting and running a venture, full-time or part-time, can give you phenomenal experience and skills, whether you aspire to be a lifelong entrepreneur, a corporate employee, a doctor, a teacher, a government worker, or a trapeze artist. Entrepreneurship can develop your financial acumen, networking skills, sales ability, confidence, maturity, creativity, and much more. And you might just hit on a business idea that launches your career into the stratosphere. And these days, because of the ease of access to technology, starting a business might be easier than ever. Just look at how many recent ventures have started in college dorm rooms.

I asked some entrepreneurs across a wide variety of industries, ranging from high-tech to social entrepreneurship, to share their best advice to students and recent grads considering this path. Here are their words of wisdom:

> "There's no better experience, no better learning opportunity, than entrepreneurship. The best thing about starting a company is that you're a better person and a better employee because of the experience, even if you fail. And failure is okay. In fact, success is just another failure away."
>
> *Mike Hudack, cofounder/CEO, blip.tv*

> "People who are good entrepreneurs have probably been doing some version of it all their life, maybe without realizing it. If you're like that, great. If you're not like that, make sure you know what you're getting into. Being an

entrepreneur is hard. It works if you create something that you can learn and grow from, and if you have a good sense that you can actually support yourself and/or raise money from your idea."

Katie Orenstein, founder and director,
The OpEd Project

"Students should consider entrepreneurship if they have a bright idea, have a network to help them execute on that idea, and are committed to success. I don't believe that entrepreneurs should just 'wing it.' Instead, you could start a business while having a full-time or part-time job, like I did for a few years. You may have loans and living expenses, so don't risk your life on something that might harm you."

Dan Schawbel, founder of Millennial
Branding and author of Me 2.0

"If you're feeling *on fire* about an idea or passion and you can see a way to monetize it, there's no better time than when you're young to take some big risks. Trust your gut."

Jenny Blake, blogger/speaker/life coach,
author of Life After College

■ ■ ■ ■ ■ ■ ■ ■ ■ ■ ■ ■

Make This Work for You

If you're thinking about becoming an entrepreneur or side-preneur, here are some tips for taking the first crucial steps toward business ownership, even while you're still a student or hoping to work full-time first:

- **Find real and virtual mentors.** I guarantee you are not the first person to start a business in your industry. Use the web, your personal network, and professional organizations to make connections with people who have started similar businesses (though not direct competitors—that makes some people cranky). Ask people how they got started and what advice they have. You can also use the web to research successful entrepreneurs. What do their websites look like? What experience is listed in their bios? What professional credentials do they maintain? Take notes!

- **Increase your entrepreneurial education.** In recent years, more colleges and universities have added entrepreneurial courses to their offerings. If you're still in school, enroll in one of these classes, where you'll not only gain skills, but also connect with other students who are launching new ventures. If you want to study on your own, some of the most popular books on entrepreneurship include *The E-Myth Revisited* by Michael Gerber, *The Art of the Start* by Guy Kawasaki, and *The Four-Hour Workweek* by Timothy Ferriss.

- **Understand the essentials.** It's not the most exciting part of starting a business, but it's crucial to research the licenses, taxes, and insurance you'll need to deal with before going solo. Start a list to keep track of everything, and don't be afraid to ask experts for help. You can call on freelancers unions, entrepreneurial networking groups, and the Small Business Administration (www.sba.gov) for free or low-cost help in determining what official steps are required.

- **Build your independent brand.** In order to attract customers, clients, or investors, you will need a professional reputation beyond your résumé. Beef up your LinkedIn

profile, attend entrepreneurial networking events, sign
up for entrepreneurship listservs, join committees of
industry organizations to make yourself visible to members (who may be future clients of your new business), or
volunteer at a nonprofit organization related to the business you'd like to start.

Each of these activities will increase your leadership experience, expand your network and, perhaps most important,
build your confidence that there is a world outside of full-
time employment. The plunge into entrepreneurship could
even take place sooner than you thought possible. Or, if you
find yourself resisting these actions, it may be a sign that
you're not quite ready to leave the regular paycheck pool.
Either way, it can't hurt to get started.

☐ Done!

50. GOTV

Office politics exist in virtually every workplace, so what better
training for any future career than to spend some time working
on a political campaign? Whether you consider yourself Democrat,
Republican, Libertarian, Green, independent, or any other political
persuasion, there is sure to be a candidate for you. Even in years
when there is no national presidential election, you can find dozens
of local, state, and congressional races that are thrilled to have young
volunteers. To find volunteer opportunities, check out the websites
of the Democrats (www.democrats.org), Republicans (www.gop
.org), or a nonpartisan organization such as RocktheVote.org.

GOTV, or "Get Out the Vote," is one of the jobs to which a young volunteer will likely be assigned. Calling registered voters and reminding them to go to the polls on Election Day and knocking door-to-door require little experience but lots of enthusiasm. Candidates and their staff members will love your youthful energy and your connection to other young voters. If you yourself are considering a career in politics or public service, this is experience that you absolutely must have.

In addition to getting out the vote, campaign volunteers may have the opportunity to help fund-raise (a crucial skill for a future job in sales, the nonprofit sector, or an entrepreneurial venture), design marketing materials, coordinate and attend rallies and speeches, research policy initiatives, answer queries from constituents, or help to design a website or social media initiative. Political campaigns will give you as much responsibility as you are willing to handle. They always need free help.

What can you do if you end up stuffing envelopes day and night and you don't seem to be contributing much to the campaign or to your own career development? According to Alice Korngold, author of *Leveraging Good Will*, you have to take initiative to work your way up the volunteer ladder, just as you would in a job. Alice says the best way to do this is to really observe what's happening on the campaign. "Once you know what's going on, you can see where you can help," she says. For instance, if you notice that a particular staffer is overworked, you can volunteer to be his or her assistant. If an event seems to be highly disorganized, you can volunteer your type A organization skills to create a more organized RSVP system. Come up with a plan and bring it to the campaign coordinator. Everyone loves a problem solver.

Working on a political campaign will also familiarize you with the important issues in your city and state. You're sure to impress potential employers if you can talk intelligently about the strength of the economy, public safety challenges, procurement opportunities, taxes, real estate assessments, or funding for education and the arts.

This is also a phenomenal networking opportunity. As a political volunteer, you can meet and interact with civically minded people as well as key players in your area. Observing politicians is a great way to see how networking happens. Politicians are masters of communication, mutual opportunity, compromise, and—let's be honest—schmoozing. You may not like the style of every politician, but you can use the opportunity of working on a political campaign to observe how deals get done and how candidates get people to vote for the people and issues they support.

"Politics is all about relationships," says Rafael Mandelman, a former member of the San Francisco Democratic County Central Committee. And as Rafael is quick to point out, not all relationships in politics are exactly friendly—which makes working on a political campaign a great chance to learn negotiation and conflict resolution skills as well. "If you can deal with political conflict, you can deal with any conflict," he says. "And even a summer intern will see some of this."

Rafael, who is an active member of the gay community, also points out that politics offers lots of career opportunities for members of minority groups. "If you are not a white man and you have an interest in politics, you should absolutely do it, because this is not a white male country. Ultimately, we will need nonwhite males to run it! If you are Latino and interested, absolutely do it. There's such a need for you. [Hispanics are the nation's largest and fastest-growing minority group.] The political culture is looking for people who are not white."

The same goes for women, who represent over 50 percent of the U.S. population, but only about 15 percent of our elected congresspeople. If you're a young woman interested in running for office, check out the White House Project's Vote, Run, Lead campaign at www.voterunlead.org. The organization offers lots of resources and training programs to equip young women with the skills to run for office and win.

Even if politics is not a career choice you're actively considering, I'd still recommend attending a workshop or even just a volunteer training session on how to run a campaign. You never know what opportunities could emerge.

──────────────────────

Proof It's Possible

Sarah Stewart Holland is a graduate of Transylvania University and American University's Washington College of Law, and she participated in political internships as an undergraduate and as a law student.

"I got both of my internships through friends who had previously interned at each place," she explains. "I think a lot of students think your network needs to be a CEO or one of your parents' friends, but your own classmates are your best resource. At both internships I put the friend's name in the first sentence of the cover letter saying that person had recommended the internship to me. I think it really helped having someone to vouch for me."

How did Sarah get started in politics in the first place?

"I had always wanted to work in politics, but it was the 2004 election that really pushed me to take the next step in pursuing my goals," Sarah explains. "In college I interned at NOW PAC [the National Organization for Women Political Action Committee], where I gained valuable fund-raising experience and overall knowledge of elections from a PAC [lobbying] point of view."

In law school, Sarah served as a congressional intern for a lawmaker from her home state of Kentucky. "It was an excellent networking opportunity," she says. "This internship in particular was what you made of it. So I stayed late and volunteered for all types of jobs. I learned quickly how to write constituent letters, which made me valuable to the overworked legislative assistants. By the end, I wrote one of the congressman's monthly columns."

As you can see, Sarah is a hard worker and willing to go the extra mile. In fact, that's her best advice to college students interested in political internships: "They say that luck is what happens when preparation meets opportunity, and I think nowhere is this more true than in politics. The best way to get a job is to network, network, network, so when that opportunity arises, people think of you first. The other part of preparation is not only networking, but also making yourself indispensable. It is very easy in political internships to coast through without making an impact. You have to go out of your way to prove you are the person they want to keep around."

Rafael Mandelman agrees with Sarah's advice: "Hard work really gets noticed. If you're there volunteering, making the phone calls, being responsible and diligent and doing a good job, you will get noticed."

---

51. GO GLOBAL

"Globalization" is a major buzzword today—so what does this mean for you? In a world where more companies are doing business with foreign countries from China to Germany to Peru, international experience is growing more and more important for career success. Dr. Kerry J. Sulkowicz made this prediction in *Fast Company* magazine, with which I wholeheartedly agree:

"I'm convinced that in the future, the most successful among us will be those who understand that they are citizens of the world. Keeping up with the effects of globalization takes both openness and work—openness to learning, reading, and seeing the world, and work to adapt to the competitive, intellectual, and cultural shifts before they bite you in the rear."

You can put yourself ahead of your peers (and avoid that rear-biting scenario) by chalking up international experience before you venture out into the workforce. If you have the opportunity to study abroad, do it. According to the Institute for International Education, about 262,000 American students studied abroad in the 2008–2009 academic year. That sounds like a lot, but it actually represents less than 1 percent of undergraduates in the country. Think how much you can stand out from the crowd in an increasingly global world by having international experience.

In 2005, Goucher College in Maryland took the unique step of making study abroad a mandatory requirement for graduation. How did this come about? According to Dr. Eric Singer, associate dean of International Studies, Goucher has always had a strong commitment to "experiential education," such as an internship requirement for graduation. In 2001, when the faculty engaged in a strategic planning process, "we looked at what a twenty-first-century liberal arts education would constitute. We began to recognize that the notion of global citizenship ought to be taken seriously,

> ### Reality Check
>
> "The study-abroad experience done right—not just travel and partying—can really open up a new way of thinking and new possibilities that will impact your working life."
>
> Trudy Steinfeld, assistant vice president and executive director of the Wasserman Center for Career Development, New York University

and we talked about the means by which we could promote this and make it an integral element to one's academic and experiential training."

Is Goucher's mandatory study abroad program the way of the future? That's yet to be seen, but I think it's a sign of the growing need for Americans to be experienced in dealing with other countries and cultures.

In addition to study abroad programs offered by colleges and universities, there are a variety of scholarship programs that send undergrads, graduate students, and young professionals all over the world—and sometimes for free. Rotary International, which provided me with a scholarship to earn my master's degree in Australia, is the world's largest privately funded international scholarship program, awarding more than one thousand scholarships each year. A great searchable database of other study abroad scholarships can be found at www.InternationalScholarships.com. If you've already graduated and want to go overseas, check out programs such as the Japan Exchange and Teaching Programme (www.jetprogramme.org), AIESEC (www.aiesec.org), and the Fulbright U.S. Student Program (www.cies.org).

I was struck when interviewing people for this book how many said that studying abroad had been a fantastic "life experience" and they had learned a lot about themselves while overseas, but that it had not impacted their job search or career plans. I think this is wonderful, but it is a missed career development opportunity. If you go into a study abroad situation with your career in the back of your mind, you can use the experience to your advantage in many ways. But be aware that recruiters often tell me that the fact that you've studied abroad isn't impressive by itself—it's what you *do* with that experience that catches the eye of a potential employer.

If you've already studied abroad:

If your international experience is already over, there are several ways you can maximize that experience to impress potential employers.

Offer to mentor students planning to study in the same country where you traveled. Contact the coordinator of your study abroad program and volunteer yourself to help students involved with their upcoming programs—answering questions, reading applications, serving on question-and-answer panels, or helping to manage the program's Facebook fan page. Employers will be impressed with your desire to take your knowledge and share it with less experienced people. This is an especially great skill for a future teacher, corporate manager, or business owner.

Finish your fluency. Many people spend a semester or year abroad and begin to learn another language, but never become fully fluent. If you've made it far enough in your language skills to get around a country, why not go all the way and become conversational or fluent? Employers won't be very impressed if you can say "please" and "thank you" in Russian, but they'll take notice if you can speak fluently. And they'll be especially impressed if you're fluent in another country's terminology related to the field you hope to enter, such as business, politics, or the arts. This shows brains, hard work, and commitment to a goal.

If you're thinking about studying abroad:

If you're a current student or recent grad considering spending time abroad, here is the most important thing you need to know when it comes to using your overseas experience to help you get a job in the future: having fun isn't enough.

I'm not saying that you shouldn't have fun, go to a lot of museums, make friends with the locals, and party till dawn, but I am saying that studying abroad can be a big factor in your postcollege planning . . . if you apply a little bit of strategy.

Choose your country wisely. If you are interested in theater, you may choose London so you can go to plays in the West End. If you're interested in business, you may opt for a country with a fast-growing economy, such as India or China. If you're considering a career in the nonprofit world, you may choose a developing country where you can see issues of poverty in a new way. Even if you choose a country for its nightlife or luscious beaches, you can still find a connection to your potential career interests. For example, you are likely to find chapters of various industry associations in foreign countries and may be able to attend meetings or involve yourself in volunteer projects.

Keep a journal. This is a great thing to do in general, but it can be particularly helpful when it comes to applying your study abroad experience to your career planning. Keep notes of experiences that you might be able to talk about in an internship or job interview—challenges you faced and overcame, communications issues you dealt with, diverse kinds of people you never would have met at home or on campus. Millions of things happen every day while you're traveling, so a journal will help jog your memory when you get back stateside.

Blog. Why not turn your international adventure into a piece of writing you can share with potential employers someday? Free tools like Tumblr and Blogger make it easy to share photos, videos, and your written observations. Just be sure to keep your blog appropriate and professional enough to help your career prospects and not hurt them. Done the right way, a blog can serve as proof that you used your study abroad adventure as a learning and growth experience. (See Tip #61 for more suggestions on how blogging can help you land a job.)

If you're an international student wanting to work in the U.S.:

I've focused a lot here on American students studying abroad, but you may be reading this book as a student from another country who is studying here in the United States. If you are studying here and looking to land an internship or job here, you have a lot to offer, but will face some unique challenges.

According to Trudy Steinfeld, assistant vice president and executive director of the Wasserman Center for Career Development at New York University, "Finding a job in the U.S. can be very tough for international students, but there are always opportunities for students with some skill sets that are in demand. Students should be prepared to have done some of the legal homework, such as Optional Practical Training (OPT) and visa conversions. Being an international student also means that you have to have a powerful skill set to market. You will have to conduct a job search that is highly effective and involves intense networking. You also need to identify companies and organizations that have a history of hiring international students."

Jean-Marc Dedeyne, CEO and founder of U in the USA, a company he created to assist international students with their career goals, offers these tips to international students looking for jobs here:

- Become an expert on U.S. immigration laws.
- Master soft skills, such as the ability to listen well, communicate effectively, be positive, handle conflict, accept

responsibility, show respect, build trust, work well with others, manage time effectively, accept criticism, work under pressure, be likable, and demonstrate good manners.

- Attend workshops or lectures on working or doing business in the United States.
- Find publications, websites, and television programs that give you a cross-cultural view of what's going on in the world and in the United States.
- Find mentors, such as individuals currently working in your field, and ask them for help and guidance.
- Always believe in yourself and have a stubborn insistence on pursuing your dreams.

Your university career services office can help with many of the tips given by Trudy and Jean-Marc, but as an international student you'll have to be proactive every step of the way.

52. FAIL

I admit that I had a lot of success when I was younger. I got good grades in school, I was accepted into a good college, I had friends, I didn't do anything too terribly embarrassing in public. There were ups and downs, but for the most part I never experienced any massive failures.

Unfortunately, this meant that when I finally had some biggies, they were completely devastating. In college I auditioned for an a capella singing group and was rejected two years in a row. I was deeply ashamed and, not knowing what to do, I completely quit singing for the next ten years. Years later, after my first coauthored book was published, I submitted a proposal for another book. It was flat-out rejected by fifteen publishers. It took me three more years to even think about writing another proposal. Because I had so little experience with failure, I didn't know how to deal with it and move on. I let it incapacitate me. I let it beat me. I let it stop me from taking new risks.

This is why I wish I had failed earlier and more often in my life. And why I recommend that to you.

Failures will happen to you, and probably already have. Some employers you pursue will reject you. Some "dream" internships will turn into nightmares. You might blow a big presentation. You might completely freeze on an interview. You might start a business and go broke. You might get laid off at some point. And my response is: Congratulations. Get the help you need to get through the pain and disappointment (talking to friends or family, writing in a journal, seeking counseling if necessary) and move on. Now you've got some certified failure experience, and you'll be better at knowing how to recover the next time it happens.

Failure stinks. But make no mistake about it: real failure comes from never trying something in the first place.

Reality Check

"It's great to have ambition to ultimately succeed in a chosen field, but don't let that make your vision too narrow too soon. Don't shut out the larger picture: that there will be dozens of ways to fail, succeed, and grow."

Heike Currie,
program coordinator,
communications, The
Juilliard School

Chapter 6

GIVE YOURSELF AN EDGE

If the previous section offered suggestions for "required" experience, then this section offers "elective" experience—the kind that just might put you over the top in a competitive job market.

This section offers you a comprehensive and creative list of ways to get additional experiences under your belt that could make the difference between the yes and no interview piles. These are the extras that can help you figure out your best career path, learn great new skills, make interesting connections, build your confidence, and, of course, get real job leads and experience. Some of the experiences will take five minutes, and some will require a year or more. Some are fun, some are a bit out there, and some may prove to be much more beneficial than you could ever imagine.

Regardless of which experiences you choose to pursue, I strongly encourage you to read through every tip in this section, as some may spark ideas that lead you to even more diverse, fulfilling, and marketable experiences that help you stand out from the crowd.

53. MINOR IN SOMETHING MAJORLY HELPFUL

I'm a big fan of liberal arts education (because I had one, of course). I think that college is a wonderful time to lose oneself in the study of Shakespeare, Nietzsche, Rembrandt, Rachmaninoff, Elizabeth I, Copernicus, or anything else that interests you or helps you learn how to think and reason and communicate. I wouldn't trade taking that fascinating and not-remotely-related-to-my-major course on the Ming dynasty for anything in the world.

But.

Four years of college offers many opportunities to take courses outside of your major, whatever it may be, and it's a pretty smart idea to learn about some subjects that may position you for an easier postcollege job search. Every school has different requirements when it comes to double majors, minors, and course loads, but I think every student should consider some vocationally focused classes.

If you plan to be a professor, art critic, or philosopher, you may be tempted to ignore this advice. Or if you are currently majoring in accounting or business, you may check off this chapter and think you're all set. But I strongly urge you to consider how helpful it can be for anyone—regardless of career plans—to expand his or her horizons.

There is no time like college to explore new things in

> **Reality Check**
>
> "I wish that I had taken a more diverse set of classes instead of focusing on courses in my major and adjacent subjects. I have learned that breadth of learning is as important as the depth of your knowledge in a specific area in helping you advance and grow in your chosen occupation."
>
> Loren Woo, director, product management, large software company

a safe environment. You can ask as many questions as you'd like without fear of losing a boss's respect or irritating your colleagues. You can try something like macroeconomics or computer science, realize you don't like it or you're not very good at it, and the class is over a few months later. Or if you try something and realize you do like it, you can pursue that skill as far as you can go. In the workplace, you'd be stuck either way.

If you're a liberal arts major, consider a minor or some coursework in accounting, business, information technology, finance, economics, or something else that is vocational.

If you're in a vocational major, such as any of the fields listed above, or an industry-specific major like physical therapy or hotel management, consider a minor or some coursework in a topic that might give you a unique specialty—such as a foreign language (extra points for a language that's particularly in demand today, such as Arabic or Mandarin). In today's ultracompetitive job market, every edge helps.

Double majors are another option that can benefit you during the transition from college to career. Pursuing multiple degrees isn't for everyone, but it is certainly impressive and makes a candidate stand out. It shows that you are not afraid to work hard (usually a double major means a double workload) and you're passionate about different types of academic study. What it also says is that you're not afraid to take on more than the norm, to go the extra mile. And that's a quality that employers love, particularly in uncertain economic times when many companies are asking employees to do more with less.

Doing a little bit extra can give you a lot of advantages.

54. KEEP LEARNING

What's the last thing you probably want to do after attending school for the past eighteen or so years of your life? Go back to school, right? Well, that's exactly what I'm about to recommend. By taking a few more classes or attending some educational events, you can give yourself an advantage in the entry-level job market.

Additional education is a great way to add new or more advanced skills to those you can already offer to potential employers. Continuous learning is also something you can do while pursuing other types of experience: after hours, over the summer, or between paid gigs.

Look to local colleges, university summer programs, online learning programs such as LearningAnnex.com and iTunesU for courses on any subjects that interest you or where you feel you need training. Classes on such topics as public speaking, Excel, HTML5, or negotiation could be just the boost you need to convince an employer that you could hit the ground running as a new employee.

This is an especially good idea if you fear you are lacking certain knowledge required for the job or industry you're pursuing. For instance, if you are a liberal arts major applying to investment banks, you might take an evening or summer course in financial modeling. If you want to work in IT support, you might improve your knowledge of the latest Mac operating system. Such an experience can give you additional skills that will be useful on the job, introduce you to industry buzzwords that may come up during an interview, and demonstrate to a potential employer that you are a self-starter who goes the extra mile to achieve your goals. Plus, if you don't like the class, you may decide that a related career is not actually the right choice for you.

If you are a student at a liberal arts college and you want to pursue a career in business, you might also consider a more in-depth precareer educational experience. A variety of top-notch graduate business schools offer intensive summer programs for college students and recent grads that teach the fundamentals of business—including accounting, marketing, management, leadership, and more. Check out the Tuck Business Bridge program at Dartmouth College, the McIntire Business Institute at the University of Virginia, the Stern Advantage Program at New York University, and the Stanford Graduate School of Business Summer Institutes, among others. Such programs are pricey, but financial aid is often available.

On a totally different note, consider taking a class or workshop on a random topic that you find fascinating or have always wanted to try, even if it doesn't directly connect to your career planning. You never know what talents you might discover in your Saturday afternoon fashion design class, what career opportunities you might learn about through your Introduction to Photoshop night course, or what confidence you will build by learning CPR.

As a bonus, you'll expose yourself to additional networking opportunities no matter what you choose to study. Introduce yourself to fellow classmates and especially to your instructor. Be open about the fact that you're job hunting, and demonstrate your hireability by always being prepared for class and making comments during discussion. As a current college student or recent grad, the classroom is your native habitat, so use your comfort to your advantage!

55. BECOME BRIC SAVVY

In Tip #51, "Go Global," we talked about the importance of studying abroad and having an international perspective in today's global economy. When it comes to the topic of international

awareness, certain countries have emerged as particularly significant to the current and future world economy and, therefore, to
your future career. These countries—Brazil, Russia, India, and
China—are collectively referred to as "BRIC," a term coined in
2001, and they represent the biggest and fastest growing emerging
markets in the world. You will increase your marketability if you
educate yourself about these countries and their cultures. According to Trudy Steinfeld, assistant vice president and executive director of the Wasserman Center for Career Development at New York
University, "Students who understand these cultures and have
language skills are being sourced heavily. Especially if you want
to work in Asia, being a native speaker of English and having an
understanding of the culture can be a tremendous asset."

Even if you don't want to live and work in another country,
knowledge of these emerging markets will be an asset. Says Jean-
Marc Dedeyne, founder and CEO of U in the USA, "Whatever job
or business venture they choose, today's students are likely to have
global careers and deal regularly with collaborators or competitors
who see the world differently."

Below are some ways that you can familiarize yourself with
the BRIC countries, or any country or culture you'd like to work
with someday:

- **Follow international news.** Subscribe to the e-newsletters,
  websites, or Twitter feeds of such media outlets as CNN
  International, the BBC, the *Financial Times*, and *The
  Economist.*
- **Consider language study.** Take classes or download
  language-learning software such as Rosetta Stone for Mandarin, Russian, Portuguese, or languages from other emerging economies. While English is the primary language of
  business in many foreign cultures, you'll get much further
  if you can converse in a colleague's or client's native tongue.

- **Complete international coursework.** If you are still in school, consider taking some classes in international relations, Russian literature, Chinese history, international economics, or anything else that will help you build a global perspective. Professors who teach these courses almost always have experience and connections in the countries about which they teach, so be sure to ask them for advice on finding a job or living in the country of their specialty.

- **Build your cross-cultural soft skills.** This tip comes from Lingfang Chen, a graduate student from China who is pursuing a master's degree in international business at Hult International Business School in San Francisco. Lingfang says, "Soft skills, such as cultural sensitivity, cross-cultural communication skills, the ability to apply knowledge to new situations, and the ability to work in team settings, especially with people from diverse backgrounds, are more readily available to people with international experiences." You can learn such skills through studying abroad, by joining international student clubs on campus or professional associations such as the Asia Pacific–USA Chamber of Commerce (APUCC), and, of course, through friendships with students on your campus who grew up outside the United States.

A final reminder comes from Laura Lee Williams, an entrepreneur who spent many years working as an executive in Hong Kong. Her tip is specific to China, but applies to any cross-cultural situation: "Whether you are visiting China or learning from a Chinese tutor or teacher, you are a guest in their country and guest to their culture. Respect is the highest form of flattery you can provide."

56. BE A WINNER

There's a reason why any person who wins an Academy Award is forever titled "Academy Award Winner." People love winners and feel confident investing in them. When you receive any award, honor, or prize, this acts as a third-party endorsement and makes other people want to jump on your successful bandwagon.

The big secret is that there are tons of awards, honors, and prizes out there, so lots of people, including you, have multiple opportunities to win something. All you need to do is conduct some research and you're bound to find some opportunities to win. Employers love to see these types of honors on student and recent grad résumés, both to show that you've been recognized and to show that you've taken the time to apply for recognition of your achievements. In a competitive working world, companies like to hire established winners.

Here is just a partial list of the types of awards that exist:

- Prizes and awards for general academic achievement
- Prizes for college papers or projects, by department or university-wide
- Writing-contest prizes for works of poetry, essays, fiction, nonfiction, memoirs, and more
- Awards for scientific research in a variety of specialties
- Awards for filmmakers, musicians, web designers, programmers, and artists participating in festivals and exhibits
- Grants and awards for starting a business as a student (check out the Global Student Entrepreneur Awards at www.gsea.org)
- Awards for achievement by minorities and women
- Community service awards
- Awards for fraternity and sorority leadership

- Awards given by professional associations for students aspiring to work in their industries

There are thousands upon thousands of awards across the country waiting to be won. And many of these awards grant scholarship money to winners, so you'll not only be impressing future employers, but also saving money on your tuition or expenses. But you can't win if you don't apply. Go for it—you have nothing to lose and everything to gain.

Make This Work for You

Research and apply for awards and honors at your school, in your community, or on the national level. You can find opportunities on your university's website, professional association websites, or by typing "awards for college students" into a general search engine.

And if (or should I say when!) you do win an award or prize, make the most of it. List it on your résumé, include it in your online profiles, and send an announcement about your award to your social networks, your college newspaper or alumni magazine, and your hometown newspaper. If a news outlet writes a story about you, it will appear online (thus making you more Google-able) and will make a great clipping to include in your brag book (which you will learn about in Tip #66).

☐ Done!

57. TAKE A PHYSICAL CHALLENGE

My friend Dave was stressed. He graduated from college, decided late in the game that he wanted to go to medical school, got a job to pay his student loans, and then studied for the MCATs while working full-time.

Oh yeah, and he also trained for a triathlon.

Dave was not superhuman, but he was supersmart. Finding himself in a highly stressful situation—working full-time and studying for an extremely difficult exam—he took his strong work ethic and discipline and applied it in another area: his physical health. In turn, he excelled in all activities in his busy life because he found some balance. While the MCATs and triathlon training are both very intense, Dave was able to enjoy them both because neither effort became all-consuming.

Some of the country's most successful people—including our two most recent U.S. presidents—take serious time to stay in good physical health. If you're smart enough to achieve big things in your career, you're smart enough to know that you have to let off some of your stress with physical activity.

Plus, exercise of any kind adds another dimension to your image as a job candidate and in the workplace. Being a runner may bond you to a boss who also loves to bring her running shoes on business trips. Running clubs in cities and towns can be enjoyable and productive networking opportunities. Likewise, playing on a city softball team may offer great networking with a wide variety of people, in addition to fun games and postgame barbecues. If you love biking, you may help coordinate a charity bikeathon in your first year as a junior employee of a big corporation. Or your knowledge of yoga poses may come in handy when a colleague is particularly stressed—you'll win kudos for calming him down before a big presentation.

Any sort of physical exertion keeps your mind fresh and helps you be as creative as possible. You often hear business gurus talk about "thinking outside the box." Well, I believe in thinking outside the office as well. Sometimes a hike up a mountain can be more productive than a meeting.

Your commitment to completing a challenging event like a marathon or a triathlon stands out to recruiters as well. Lauren E. Smith, partner with a major executive search firm, told me the story of a vice president of engineering she worked with who was seeking to hire a very results-oriented employee. "He ended up hiring an avid runner who had completed multiple marathons," Lauren reports. "The VP saw that this was someone who was very goal driven."

Triathlon training may not be for everyone, but I think it helped Dave get accepted to medical school. And it definitely kept off the pounds from those late-night pizza study breaks.

58. PRESENT

Which would you rather do: deliver a speech to a roomful of strangers or eat a bowlful of cockroaches?

I wouldn't be surprised if most would choose the latter. Public speaking is one of the biggest human fears, and most people would do pretty much anything to avoid it. It's also one of the best skills you can develop for a successful job search and career, and a great way to stand out from your peers. Being articulate and confident will get you very, very far. Public speaking is not just for politicians—it's a skill that transfers to virtually every career path. No matter what career you choose, you're going to have to talk.

Public speaking skills are particularly important at this stage of your life. Kim Dower, coauthor of *Life Is a Series of Presentations,* says, "College students and recent grads don't have a lot of experience, so their résumés can't really speak for themselves. For those of us who are older and have been out there in the workforce, we can simply e-mail a résumé or list our accomplishments, and a lot of how we sell ourselves can be on paper. Younger people don't have that to fall back on and must make solid and important in-person impressions. College students and recent grads need to connect and impress mainly through their speaking skills."

According to Kim, one of the easiest ways for students to become more comfortable speaking is simply to speak up in class. "People who dread public speaking or feel nervous or self-conscious about getting up in front of a group of people will forgo speaking up in class. They'll sit in the back of the room and look down when a question is asked and do anything they can to avoid having to speak up. Forget that! Now is your chance to learn how to do it. Force yourself! Like everything, including fear of flying, the more you do it, the less afraid you become and the more comfortable you learn to be."

Another tip is to speak up during student club meetings or in your extracurricular activities. "Get involved in something you love and talk a lot while you're there!" encourages Kim. "It's easier to be verbal and to speak articulately and passionately when you *feel* passionate. Get a sense of what it's like to go on about something that excites you. Join a club where you can get up and speak and feel the power of talking to a group about something that turns you on."

Kim is very clear that you don't have to be a born presenter. Anyone can learn how to be better. "Learning is all about practicing," she asserts. "Often, when we're in college we get stuck in certain behaviors. If public speaking is difficult for us, we find ways to not have to do it, and when we're out in the world going on job interviews it becomes very painful. We've decided we're no good at it because we have no experience. That's why we have to force ourselves in college to try and to know how important the skill is. We'll learn later on that good speaking skills are key to getting what we want and we can have them with us all the time! They can just become part of who we are.

"And it's almost guaranteed that when you feel self-assured and look someone in the eyes and smile, you get a great reaction back."

Make This Work for You

Presenting to a student club or for a class are both good opportunities to develop your presentation skills. Another suggestion is to join a group of professionals that meets exclusively to work on public speaking skills. Consider joining a local Toastmasters International chapter.

Toastmasters International (www.toastmasters.org) is an educational nonprofit with clubs worldwide, where people develop communication and leadership skills in a supportive environment. During regular club meetings, members learn to give speeches, evaluate one another's communications, speak off the cuff, and conduct meetings (all important workplace skills). Check out a meeting near you to pick up a few tips, or consider joining a chapter to further develop your presentation skills.

☐ Done!

----

59. PERFORM FIVE MINUTES OF STAND-UP

If you've ever tried it, you know that this might be the scariest assignment of all. As you just read, public speaking consistently ranks among the top national fears, and I would argue that stand-up comedy is the most frightening of all public speaking.

This is why you have to do it.

Being a strong public speaker is a skill that will serve you well throughout your career, and the sooner you learn the skill, the better. Being a strong public speaker *and* being able to tell a joke or two, well, that's golden. Any kind of acting training can help you to learn "soft" skills like poise, storytelling, and connecting with an audience—all of which will help in professional situations like sales or marketing pitches. If you can make an audience laugh, you can probably make them buy something from you.

Can anyone really try this? Yes, says Mark Malkoff, who is profiled below and has worked for a variety of comedy shows, such as the *Late Show with David Letterman*. Mark trained professionally at New York University and at Chicago's famous Second City Training Center (alumni include Bill Murray, Tina Fey, Halle Berry, Sean Hayes, and many other producers, directors, writers, and actors). And comedy is not only for aspiring performers: Ron Shaw, the retired longtime president and CEO of Pilot Pen, started his career as a comedian.

To try your hand at comedy, Mark recommends taking an improvisation (improv) class or diving right into stand-up at an open mike night at a comedy club. Based on his experience, Mark identifies several career-related benefits anyone, even those who feel they lack a funny bone, can get from trying stand-up or improv—remember that any of these outcomes are great to mention in a job interview or networking encounter if you decide to talk about this experience.

- Learning how to be present in the moment helps you think on your feet.
- Entertaining people and hearing them laugh at your jokes builds your confidence.
- Being attentive to your audience helps you build important listening skills and learn how to read the reactions of other people.

If nothing else, performing five minutes of stand-up comedy will show you that nothing is really that scary once you actually do it. Many formal public speaking and acting classes even require this assignment. My sister had to do this for a comedy writing class she took at a New York University summer program. All of the students had to perform at an open mike night in New York City. Even though not every student was hilarious, they all won applause for having the guts to get up there in the spotlight.

So do your five minutes. Even if it feels like five hundred.

Proof It's Possible

Perhaps you'll love comedy so much that you'll want to make it a career. Or maybe you're interested in the entertainment industry in general. If so, Mark Malkoff is a great role model.

Mark is an actor, comedian, and writer who is successfully working his way up the ladder of the entertainment industry. In addition to *Late Night*, he has worked for *The Colbert Report*, the Michael J. Fox sitcom *Spin City*, and many other TV shows. In my opinion, Mark possesses an amazing combination of major guts, a major work ethic, and major commitment to his dreams. Here is his story:

LP: How did you get into the entertainment business?

MM: I knew pretty early that I wanted to go into TV and comedy. I was pen pals with some of the *Saturday Night Live* [*SNL*] guys, like Adam Sandler, before they made it big. I grew up in Pennsylvania and started driving up to New York City when I was sixteen. I started going up to the *SNL* set and got hooked. I snuck into the set in a suit and slipped into after-parties.

I went to NYU and fell in love with the city and the glamour. I got "found out" sneaking into *SNL* my freshman year, so I thought, "Maybe I should actually get serious." I did internships starting my freshman year. My first internship was with a comedy manager for upcoming comics, and many of those clients are now famous. That's why the most important thing is to hold on to your relationships—you just never know where people will end up. It's all about relationships.

And—this is important—you can be a nice person and still succeed in entertainment. You can be cutthroat and backstabbing, but you'll kill your relationships, and it just doesn't have to be like that. Some of the most successful people at the top of their game are genuinely nice people.

LP: How did you get your internships, and what were they like?

MM: I got all of my TV show internships from the internship coordinator at NYU. Most shows won't take you unless you're getting college credit. I interned at all types of shows to see different processes and personalities. Nothing can prepare you until you jump into it. Internships are the most important thing.

LP: Do you have to go to college in New York or LA to get a good entertainment internship?

MM: I think you can come from anywhere, and there are some unique opportunities depending on where you're from. For instance, the guys who run the *Onion* [a satirical newspaper] are from Wisconsin, so they hook up people from there. Alumni from your school can be helpful if you contact them. Just come to New York for the summer if you can and get in that way.

LP: What's your advice to students and recent grads about internships?

MM: You have to maximize internship opportunities. Don't be pushy, but let people know you're interested in getting a job eventually. Some interns I've worked with were too passive about making it known they were looking for work. Don't be afraid to knock on people's doors and ask them about their careers. You have to get to know people on a personal basis. Take initiative and stay later than all the other interns.

LP: How true is the starving artist stereotype?

MM: Different people take all different amounts of time to get to where they want to be career-wise. Getting in is the most important thing. The money was a joke at the beginning—I had to have a weekend job just to keep up with the bills. Eventually the money will trickle. The money will come.

60. HAVE A HOBBY

There's nothing better than finding out your newest contact shares your passion for hang gliding, stamp collecting, or fine food. Here are two proven career-advancing hobbies you might want to check out, if you haven't already:

- **Tee off.** You're probably familiar with the stereotype of big-time moguls hatching and closing multimillion-dollar deals on the golf course. Well, like most stereotypes, it's often true. Many businesspeople do play golf, and they find the sport to be a huge asset in their careers. Executives bond with clients on golf outings, companies take employees away on golf retreats, and many sales organizations offer golf trips as incentive programs. The funny thing about golf is that you don't have to be that good at the sport in order to reap the business networking benefits. A few lessons can teach you the basic mechanics and etiquette and allow you to get out on the links pretty quickly.

  If you're a student, take lessons on campus. Most colleges have great student discounts at local golf courses, which make it a cost-effective time of life to pick up the game. At some schools, taking golf lessons can even fulfill a phys ed course requirement. Even if you're not yet ready to hold a club in your hands, you can attend a golf tournament, watch some golf on TV, read through a golf magazine, or subscribe to a golf e-newsletter (such as the free one offered by LearnAboutGolf.com) to become familiar with the terminology and basics of the game.

- **Make a move.** Join the chess club? Geek alert! Next thing you know I'll be telling you to wear a pocket protector, right? Not at all. Chess has outgrown its nerdy image and is widely recognized as a smart way to build some career-boosting skills—particularly if you plan to go into any sort of business environment.

What are the career benefits of learning and playing chess? It builds strategic thinking, logic, and concentration, just to name a few. And you may find a nice connection to a fellow chess player you meet networking or interviewing for a job. I've certainly seen chess boards in the offices or homes of some very successful people.

You don't even have to find a live opponent or join a live chess club to try the game—you can learn and play on your computer, phone, or iPad (PlayChess.com is the most popular site) with other players from around the world.

Not interested in golf or chess? Lots of other hobbies, pastimes, sports, and games can give you a competitive advantage over your less active peers. Sports like ultimate Frisbee, soccer, softball, basketball, squash, and touch football are popular ways to network in the working world. Card games, especially poker, are good to know if you're ever invited to play with colleagues or networking acquaintances. Singing in a choir, performing in an orchestra, or acting in community theater are great possibilities as well.

Pretty much any group activity can provide networking, leadership, and learning opportunities that will help you stand out in your job search and once you begin working. By all means mention your hobbies in job interviews and networking situations—they make great conversation starters and help people remember you. You can also list a few pastimes in an "Interests" section on your résumé; however, don't count on generic hobbies like travel, jogging, reading, camping, or movies to make much of an impression. Recruiters tell me that they're really impressed only when an interest listed on a résumé is extraordinarily unusual (flamenco dancing, bobsledding) or you've reached an impressive level of achievement (sailing around the world, performing on Broadway).

61. BLOG

For the past three years I've been writing a career advice blog (www.lindseypollak.com/blog) and it's been an amazing experience. According to the Nielsen Company, there were over 156 million public blogs in existence as of February 2011, so writing a blog is also an amazingly popular thing to do. But can writing a blog lead to career opportunities? The answer is, increasingly, yes.

When done in a professional way, writing a blog can lead to many advantages in your postcollege job search, including real internship and job opportunities. Here are a few of the benefits of blogging:

- Enhancing your online personal brand and Google-ability
- Demonstrating skills such as writing, design, photography, and analytical thinking
- Showing your ability to take initiative and commit to a project
- Connecting you to a whole new network of other bloggers and commenters

Because the barrier to entry is so low, blogging is also something you can try for a while to see if you like it. If you do decide to join the blogosphere, here are some tips for getting started:

- **Guest blog first.** One way to dip your toe into the blogging waters is to write a few posts for other people's blogs.

Check with friends, your university's career center or campus newspaper, professional associations you belong to, and college-student-focused websites such as Her Campus (www.HerCampus.com) and *USA Today* Education (www.usatodayeducate.com) to inquire about guest blogging opportunities.

- **Sign up for a blogging service.** When you're ready to blog on your own, you'll need to set yourself up with a blogging tool. Although my blog is a little snazzier now, I originally set it up using the free site Blogger.com, and it took about 10 minutes (and most of that time was spent choosing what color scheme I wanted). I now blog on the WordPress platform and would recommend both services. Tumblr.com is another popular choice, especially for artists and photographers. These services will set you up with a URL that includes their name, like "lindseyblog.wordpress.com." To give yourself a more professional image, purchase a domain name for your blog (e.g., "lindseyblog.com") using a site such as Register.com, 1and1.com, or GoDaddy.com. Domain name registration is very inexpensive, starting at about seven dollars a year.

- **Write for the career you want.** While it's nice to blog about any topic that interests you, the only way your blog will help your job search is if you write about your career interests. If a recruiter checks out your blog, he or she must know immediately what you're interested in. One of my favorite blog posts by tech evangelist Robert Scoble (www.scobleizer.com) puts it this way: "Post something that teaches me something about what you want to do every day. If you want to drive a cab, you better go out and take pictures of cabs. Think about cabs. Put suggestions for cabbies up. Interview cabbies. You better have a blog that is nothing but cabs. Cabs. Cabs. Cabs all the time."

- **Be very careful what you post.** The major reason most job seekers don't blog is because they're afraid that blogging might hurt their chances more than help them. This is a very real concern. If your blog is filled with photos of cats playing the piano, rants about parking tickets, or sad tales of relationships gone bad, you're not going to impress any employers. As Scoble has written, "Your blog is your résumé. [It] needs to have 100 posts on it about what you want to be known for." Think of your blog as a purely professional forum and you should be just fine.

- **Be consistent.** Although I said that you can give blogging a try before you commit entirely, once you do commit to being a blogger, you have to post consistently. (And if you decide you don't like blogging, delete the entire blog from the web so it doesn't look as if you abandoned the project. You can share your favorite past posts on Facebook or elsewhere.) It's up to you whether you want to post once a day, once a week, every two weeks, etc., as long as you post consistently. If your posts are sporadic, it will appear that you're not fully committed, which does not impress employers.

- **Respond to comments.** Besides employers, your blog may attract comments from other readers, including fellow bloggers and others who are interested in your subject matter. (And your mom, of course!) When people take time to comment on your words, it's not just polite but also good networking to respond. Anyone paying attention to your blog could become a new contact and supporter.

- **Drive people to your blog.** The downside of being one blogger among 156 million is that people may have a hard time finding you. This means you have to be proactive about guiding people—especially potential employers—to your blog. As long as your blog is 100 percent professional, you should list it on your résumé, your business cards, your LinkedIn profile, your e-mail signature line, your Facebook contact information, your Twitter profile, and anywhere else you can think of.

- **Drive blog readers to your credentials.** On the flip side, you want to make sure anyone who comes across your blog is aware that you are a great job candidate. On the "About" page and/or on the list of links you can display on your blog, be sure to include links to your LinkedIn profile and a PDF download of your résumé.

Proof It's Possible

I met Alex Priest when he attended a speech I gave at American University. At the time, Alex was a student at the Washington, D.C.–based school, and he instantly impressed me with his knowledge of social media and his follow-up skills after my presentation. Alex, who hails from rural Kentucky and majored in marketing and public communications, began his blog in college and has used it—along with a strong social media presence—to successfully build his postcollege career prospects.

Here is some insight and insider advice from Alex:

LP: Why did you start your blog as a student?

AP: I actually started way back in high school, inspired by my much-older sister, an author, who got her first book published after being discovered on her blog. I first started writing regularly in my junior year, documenting my college search process. By the time I traveled abroad to Japan the summer after graduation, blogging my experience the whole way, I was totally hooked.

LP: Has your blog helped you careerwise?

AP: Absolutely. Between my blog and my presence on social media, I've received some fantastic benefits, including internships and, recently, job offers. And perhaps most important, it's led to other amazing opportunities, including the chance to write for larger publications like *USA Today* and Technorati.com. My blog has acted as a hub for my online life, and it's connected me with amazing professionals and fellow bloggers all over the world.

LP: Do you recommend that other college students and recent grads start blogs to help build their online presence and career plans?

AP: Yes! Blogging not only helps you get your name out there and build a brand for yourself, but it's a great stress reliever and thought inducer as well. And in today's world it's easier than ever to build an incredible network online. Having a blog is essential to give people a place where they can get a full picture of who you are, how you write, and what you want to make of yourself.

LP: What tips do you have for blogging in a professionally appropriate way?

AP: A few:

- First, buy your own domain name (preferably your real name) and use that for your blog to secure your brand and ensure that when people look for you, they find you.

- Second, unless you want to go into politics or relationship counseling, don't talk too much about politics or relationships; that can be a big turnoff for readers.

- And finally, don't be afraid to be yourself and be an adult

on your blog. You have a sense of humor, so show it. If
you're passionate—even angry—about something, don't
be afraid to show it. Just be reasonable and keep it under
control.

Check out Alex's blog at www.AlexPriest.com.

62. OPEN YOUR MOUTH AND SAY, "OM"

If meditating is something you've never considered (or thought
was a little bit out there), I totally understand. And I think you
should try it anyway.

The reason I recommend the experience of meditation is this:
the working world can get pretty stressful, so it's important to
learn ways to cope with that stress. You need a reliable method
for removing yourself mentally and physically from high stress
moments and calming yourself down. The sooner you learn how
to do this, the better off you'll be in your job search and your career.

For some people, taking a walk around the block clears their
mind and releases stress; for others, it might be a phone call to a
friend, a long run, a yoga class, or playing hours of video games.
These are all great, and I encourage you to use whatever stress
management tool works for you. But you can't do many of them
in a cubicle, in your car before a job interview, or on the train
home from work. Besides all of its other benefits, meditation is
convenient.

What exactly does it mean to meditate? At the most basic
level, it means clearing your mind. While many meditation practices consist of focusing your mind on a mantra (a syllable, usually
in Sanskrit), you can also meditate simply by focusing on your
breath.

Meditation, or any form of stress relief you choose, is a huge asset to a budding career. Many employers will ask you in a job interview how you deal with stress, particularly if you're applying to work in a stressful environment, such as a trading floor, an inner-city classroom, or a hospital. It's also important if you've had any anger problems in your life and you're worried (rightly so) that your temper will not be an asset to your career. While it's okay to be human in the workplace, it's not okay to explode at a coworker, throw a coffee mug across the room, or make a rash decision out of annoyance at a client or customer.

Make This Work for You

Elizabeth Scott, the stress management guide on About .com, recommends this simple karate meditation for beginners. According to Elizabeth, this meditation is fast but powerful. It combines breathing—which has been shown to have significant effects on the mind, the body, and one's moods—with simple meditation, to help you become more physically relaxed and mentally centered.

1. Sit in a comfortable position. The seiza ("say-zah") position, where you sit folding your legs beneath you so you're resting on your feet with your knees directly in front, is recommended. However, you may also sit cross-legged or in another position that's more comfortable.

2. Close your eyes but keep your head up, your eyes (behind your lids) focused on the horizon.

3. Take one deep, cleansing breath, and hold it in for the count of six. Then breathe normally and focus your

attention on your breathing. As you breathe, inhale through your nose and exhale through your mouth.

4. If your thoughts drift toward the stresses of the day ahead or of the day behind you, gently refocus on your breathing. Feel the air move in, and feel the air move out. That's it.

5. Continue this for three to ten minutes, and you should notice that your body is more relaxed and your mind is more calm. Enjoy the rest of your day!

For more stress management tips and resources, check out Elizabeth Scott's About.com Stress Management website at http://stress.about.com.

☐ Done!

Chapter 7

MARKET YOURSELF
ON PAPER AND ONLINE

Now that you have some experiences and accomplishments to show potential employers, you have to think about how these achievements appear on paper and on the web. Your résumé, cover letters, and online profiles are the marketing materials that represent you in the professional world. No matter how whiz-bang fabulous you are in person, you must have these other elements in order to get hired.

First, let's put the résumé into perspective: a résumé is one tool in a comprehensive, multifaceted job search. Just because it's an "official" document, don't panic and give the résumé more power than it actually has. It's a tool. A marketing piece. A necessity. It is not going to single-handedly get you a job, but you need it to get your foot in the door and eventually get hired. All of that said, you should also be aware that a résumé can *lose* an opportunity—if it's messy, unprofessional, unpersuasive, or has errors or typos.

As we've discussed a lot already, your online image is just as important. According to a recent Microsoft survey, 70 percent of employers have rejected a job candidate because of information they found about that person online. On the positive side, the same Microsoft study found that 85 percent of employers say that a positive online reputation influences their hiring decisions.

If I haven't completely freaked you out by this point, let's get started making sure your résumé, cover letter, and online reputation are as stellar as you are.

63. MAKE OVER YOUR RÉSUMÉ

I am not going to tell you how to write a résumé. My experience with college students and recent graduates is that you already have one that you wrote from a book or with help from the career services office, and it's sitting in a file or hidden under a pile of old exams, and that you probably hated writing it and get bored whenever you attempt to work on it.

Or maybe that was just me.

If I'm wrong and you can't think of anything more exciting than spending a Saturday night sitting at home working on your résumé, then I truly apologize. If I'm right and you disliked the résumé-writing process as much as I did in college, then I have some good news and some bad news for you.

The bad news is that your résumé is really important and I strongly recommend that you spend time making it the very best it can be.

The good news is that I'm going to tell you how to breathe new life into even the most run-of-the-mill, even-my-mother-falls-asleep-halfway-down-the-page résumé.

Here are my favorite résumé tips, from my own experience writing and reading them, and from résumé experts I've tapped for their best advice:

Be careful with contact info. Every phone number or e-mail address you put on your résumé could be used by a potential employer. Make sure you frequently check any communication method you list. And as mentioned earlier, you need to have a professional-sounding voice mail message on every number you list and an email address that is 100 percent professional.

Include an objective statement. The biggest problem with entry-level résumés is lack of focus. Because college students often major in one subject, gain experience in two or three additional areas, and participate in volunteer work and extracurriculars in yet other fields, employers can't tell what kind of job a student actually wants. Do not expect potential employers to sift through your résumé to figure out what job would best fit you. That's your job. You need an objective statement to direct people how to read your résumé and know what kind of job you want. (If you don't want to include an objective statement, then I recommend briefly summarizing your skills and experience in a one-sentence profile statement at the top of your résumé.)

I know it's challenging to decide what your objective should be (which is why the following tip encourages you to create a résumé for each opportunity you're exploring), but I strongly recommend it. Even if your cover letter clearly states what kind of opportunity you're seeking, your résumé still needs to include this information. Why? Because you can never guarantee that anyone will read your cover letter.

The best entry-level objective statements relate to a job function, an industry, or both. They also focus on what you can contribute to an employer, not what skills or experience you hope to learn or develop from the position. (Recruiters roll their eyes at objectives stating, "I would like to find a position in which I can learn." They are paying you to do a job, not to learn!) And they are not vague. Avoid the generic "Seeking a challenging position" at all costs.

According to the helpful advice website QuintCareers.com, "The objective statement can be as simple and straightforward as the title of the position you're applying for, which can be adjusted for every job you apply for. Or you can embellish the objective statement with language telling how you'll benefit the employer. Something like: 'Objective: To contribute strong _____ skills and experience to your firm in a _____ capacity.'

For loads of examples of effective objective statements for a wide variety of industries (which you should customize and not simply copy, of course), check out QuintCareers.com or other career advice websites such as Vault.com and Monster.com.

Tweak your résumé for different jobs and industries. It is very likely that you will be applying for jobs in a variety of different companies and even different industries. Employers can tell when they are seeing a generic résumé that is being blasted out to anyone and everyone. It's fine to have such a résumé as a template, but then you need to customize that résumé with a different objective statement and different keywords that fit with the individual companies to which you're sending it. For instance, if you are applying for positions in both investment banking and consulting, you should have one résumé for each, with "an investment banking position" included in your objective on one résumé and "a consulting position" on the other.

Another smart way to customize your objective is for the type of company. If you are applying for engineering jobs at government agencies and corporations, one résumé objective may highlight your desire to work in public service, while the other might refer to your desire to increase a corporation's bottom line. Note that most online job sites allow you to store multiple versions of your résumé online.

One major warning: if you are sending your résumé to a large corporation or posting on the recruiting website of such an organization, you will have to choose just one version. Recruiters have told me that it's irritating and confusing for one company to have several versions of a candidate's résumé. If you are thinking about applying to a few different departments within a single corporation, I'd advise choosing departments that are closely related (such as marketing and public relations) so you don't appear scattered and directionless.

List your GPA only if it's 3.0 or higher. If your overall GPA is lower than 3.0, but your GPA in your major is over 3.0, then list "major GPA" on your résumé. Feel free to list both, of course, if they both qualify. I know that not listing a GPA at all implies that you had a low one, but that's okay. Just be prepared to discuss why your grades were less than stellar if the subject comes up in a job interview. And if you're still a student, try to boost your grades up above that 3.0 mark—it can make a big difference in your job search.

Include key words. Not only will online job sites search for key words on your résumé, but so will potential employers. Employers' eyes are natually drawn to the words they're looking for—the brand names, skills, and experience they need. This is particularly important in technical fields, such as computer programming. So make sure you give them what they want. You can have the exact experience an employer is seeking, but if it's not presented on your résumé in the words they're looking for, your résumé will never show up in their searches.

The best way to find the right words to use is to look at online job listings for the kinds of positions you're interested in and the LinkedIn profiles of people who have the positions you want. Then use some of the prominent words and phrases in those job listings and profiles on your résumé—in your objective statement and in your experience section, if they are relevant and true. For instance, instead of "Basic Accounting," the more descriptive "Balance Sheet

Accounting" is better. "Experience with Photoshop, Illustrator, and InDesign" is much stronger than "Design Experience."

Quantify everything. Make sure your résumé is as specific as possible about numbers as well. "Managed a team of camp counselors" is less impressive than "Managed a staff of 12 camp counselors and 5 counselors-in-training." This can also give life to menial administrative tasks: "Receptionist at a 4-doctor medical practice handling over 100 clients per day." If your work helped to raise money or profits, that's superimportant as well. Employers love to see résumés with phrases like, "Improved sporting equipment sales in my department by 50% in six months" or "Raised $2,000 through solicitation of alumni donations." This shows your specific results and also demonstrates that you are a person who understands the importance of measuring those results.

Prioritize. When you list bullet points under each job, internship, or volunteer experience you've had, be sure to list the most important task, accomplishment, or responsibility first. It's highly unlikely that a potential employer is going to read every bullet point under every item on your résumé, but most people will read the first or second bullet point on each list. You don't have to list accomplishments chronologically; list the most impressive first. Also note that more challenging jobs should have more bullet points than less challenging work experiences.

Diversify. You've probably heard that it's important to describe your accomplishments with action words: managed, directed, founded, led, coordinated, etc. This is absolutely true, but a common mistake is to use the same action words over and over again. Show recruiters that you have a strong vocabulary (or at least a thesaurus) by varying the words and phrases.

List internships, volunteer work, and unpaid summer jobs. Just because you didn't get paid for something doesn't mean it doesn't count as real experience. Be honest about what each situation entailed (duties, responsibilities, and time commitment), but definitely include them.

Note anything notable. Be sure to list anything about you that is unique and uncommon. According to the website CollegeGrad .com, "These notables are what set you apart from the crowd. They are what I look for in deciding whom to interview. And they are the basis for many of the compelling stories told in interviews which lead to eventual offers." Some examples include, "Founding president of first-ever entrepreneurial club at XYZ University," "Winner of the Anita Lawrence Scholarship for Excellence in Social Studies, awarded annually to the top junior history student," or "Youngest person ever promoted to assistant manager at this local high-end jewelry store."

Don't highlight something on your résumé that you despised doing. As you can see, there are many ways to draw a reader's eye to what you want that person to see on your résumé, so avoid these strategies when you *don't* want to promote something. In fact, if you've had a task or responsibility that you hated and never want to do again as long as you live (like selling vacuums door-to-door or cleaning animal cages), then don't include it on your résumé. You can even leave off an entire job if it's not relevant to your current job search.

Don't lie, exaggerate, or stretch the truth. This happens way too often, and it's never a good idea. There are so many reasons not to lie on a résumé. First of all, if your lie or truth stretching gets discovered, you'll lose a job opportunity with that company forever. Second, if you exaggerate your skills, such as being fluent in

Spanish when you really just studied it in high school, or you say you know C++ when you don't, your lie will become extremely obvious the day you start your job and you lack the skills you said you had. And finally, any little white lies you put on your résumé now can cost you big later in your career. Even if the lie is discovered twenty years in the future (as has been the unfortunate case with some prominent CEOs and politicians), your early career mistake can ruin your entire professional reputation. I definitely encourage you to cast your skills and experience in the most positive light, but never, ever take it too far.

Keep it to one page. Some people will fight me on this, but I've seen senior executives with one-page résumés, so I don't see any reason why a college student or recent grad's résumé needs more than that. Remember that your résumé is a marketing tool and not a transcript or a laundry list of everything you've ever done. By keeping your résumé short and sweet, you're demonstrating that you can edit yourself and sell yourself clearly and concisely— both important skills in the professional world, especially if you want a job related to writing, sales, or marketing. To make sure you've formatted your résumé to be only one page, e-mail copies to a few friends, and ask them to view it on their computer screens (including both Macs and PCs) and print out a copy on their printers.

Curb your creativity. In the vast majority of circumstances, it is totally and completely inappropriate to present your résumé in any other format than a simple black font (Times New Roman, Arial, etc.) on a white background. If you have to present your résumé as a hard copy, as opposed to electronically, it's a nice touch to use the highest quality white or cream paper you can afford. It is not okay to use colored paper, scented paper (seriously—some people, and not just Elle Woods from *Legally Blonde,* have sprayed perfume on their résumés), colorful or creative fonts, or anything else to jazz up your résumé. Recruiters, especially those in the corporate world, laugh at these attempts to stand out and immediately throw such résumés away.

The only exception to this advice is for those of you applying for highly creative jobs, such as graphic design, where you might want to do a touch of design or graphic embellishment to your résumé. Before you do this, however, I strongly recommend that you check with your career services office and anyone you know in the industry to make sure this type of résumé would be well received.

Extra Credit

An interesting trend I've come across recently is the use of QR codes on résumés. QR—"quick response"—codes are those small, square bar codes that can be scanned by mobile phones and other devices. As you've probably noticed in magazines, on billboards, and elsewhere, QR codes are becoming more and more popular for marketing. When you see a QR code, you simply take a picture of it with your phone's camera (you'll need to download an app to do this) and you'll be directed to the embedded information in that code, such as a website or text message.

Why could this be relevant for job seekers and other professionals? Because of the crucial importance of standing out from the crowd. Adding a QR code to your résumé, business card, portfolio, or any other personal marketing tool could be the detail that helps you get noticed by an employer, particularly if you want to work in an industry in which QR code savvy is important, such as marketing, real estate, or technology.

How do you create a QR code?

It takes about two minutes to set up a QR code using Google or a variety of other free online tools. Ryan Rancatore of the Personal Branding 101 blog suggests that you monitor the results of your QR code placements by using bitly to shorten your link before creating the code. Then, use bitly's analytic tools to track visits to your link. This is a great way to see if your QR code is catching on and to know which employers are potentially interested in you.

Where should your QR code send people?

There are many options here. Depending on what you feel best represents you, your QR code might send people to your LinkedIn profile, your blog (as long as it's professional), a downloadable vCard with your contact information, or an online portfolio of your work.

Will people get it?

Afraid that people won't know what that little black-and-white box is? Not to worry, according to John Heaney of the Job Shopper blog: "Even if the individuals reading your résumé don't know how to act on the QR code, including it on your résumé can still position you as someone who is technically proficient, stays up to date on business trends and technology, and is an early adopter of powerful and creative ideas."

Leave off references. Potential employers will request a list of references if they want one. Don't waste precious space on your résumé with something unnecessary at this point.

Following the above tips should improve your résumé to the point where it represents you in the strongest way possible and differentiates you from other entry-level job seekers. Remember, too, that a résumé is a constant work in progress, so update it whenever you gain new experience or skills, and keep your eyes and ears open for additional tips and tactics to make your résumé a document you're proud to send as the paper version of you.

Make This Work for You

Circle any tips above that you have not yet applied to your résumé, and make the changes immediately. Get the editing over with right now, while it's on your mind.

☐ Done!

---

64. PUT YOUR RÉSUMÉ THROUGH THE WRINGER

Before you show or send your newly made-over résumé to any potential employer, you have to test it first. You may already have done this at various informational interviews, or with your school's career services office, or with your parents, which are all great. But there are a few more tests your résumé needs to pass before I feel comfortable giving you the go-ahead to send it out into the Real World.

First, give it the one-minute scan test. I picked up this tip from Allison Hemming's job search book, *Work It!*, and I use it with every résumé I see. Hemming recommends that before you send your résumé to potential employers, you ask a few friends or trusted advisers to take an initial sixty-second peek at it. Then, she says, "Once the minute is up, ask them a few pointed questions about what they learned about you and your work experience. Your goal is to see how much they were able to glean. Really listen to what they have to say, and if your key points aren't sticking in their heads, you need to rework your résumé." As I like to think of it, if a ten-year-old looked at your résumé, he or she should be able to describe the kind of job you want.

Next, make sure your résumé will pass muster in the industry you want to join. As you learned earlier, you need eyewitnesses to give you advice about job searching in a particular industry, and these people are also important advisers on your résumé. What is impressive on a legal résumé is different from what is required on an artist's résumé, which is different from what's necessary on an engineer's résumé. If you haven't already, show your résumé to anyone you know in your desired field(s) and get their opinion before you apply for jobs.

Finally, check, double-check, triple-check, quadruple-check for any typos or spelling and grammar mistakes. Sometimes the worst offenders in this area are English majors, because they assume they're smart enough not to make any errors. Typos happen to the best of us, so be careful. A typo can absolutely lose you a job opportunity. According to *Entrepreneur* magazine, 84 percent of executives say just one or two typographical errors in a résumé removes a candidate from consideration; 47 percent need only one error to decide. There is zero excuse for an error on a résumé. To me that screams carelessness and inattention to detail. Show your résumé to anyone you know who has excellent grammar and spelling skills. You can never have too many proofreaders.

- - - - - - - - - - - - - - - -

Make This Work for You

A great proofing strategy is to read your résumé aloud a few

times, and ask others to do this as well. Grammar mistakes
or awkward sentence construction are often easier to spot
when you hear them instead of read them. You'll also notice
any missing words or weird syntax. Remember, if it sounds
weird to you, it will sound weird to the recruiter reading it.

☐ Done!

65. CRAFT IMPRESSIVE COVER LETTERS

Different recruiters will tell you different things about cover letters. For some recruiters, the cover letter is more important than
the résumé—it shows your personality, your attention to detail,
and, of course, your written communication skills. For other
employers, it's just a formality and they want to get right to the
experience and skills listed on your résumé. The thing is, you never
know which type of reader you're going to get, so you have to have
an excellent cover letter no matter what.

Your cover letter is a form of marketing—you need to show
that you know your market (the employer), you've got the skills
and experience they need, you know what they do, and you really
want to work for them.

For expertise on writing dazzling cover letters, I turned to my
friend Nicole Williams, who is the founder of WORKS by Nicole
Williams, a company that assists young professionals in building
the careers of their dreams.

According to Nicole, "They're called cover *letters* for a reason: they are, in fact, letters. While the basic format of a cover letter is pretty standard, the essence of the letter must be unique to
both you and the person to whom you are writing the letter. Most

people underestimate the power of the cover letter, and it's actually one of the most effective ways to make a personal impact and differentiate yourself."

Here is an outline of how to do just that:

First paragraph: Start with your reader

The most effective way of capturing the reader's attention, says Nicole, is to make it all about that person. The worst thing you can do in a cover letter is address it "To Whom It May Concern." Just think how you feel when you receive a letter addressed to "Occupant." Find an actual person to address your letter to. If you don't have a name, call the company and talk with HR or search LinkedIn to find the director of whatever department you are applying to. If at all possible, personalize.

You also want to find something specific about the person or organization you are writing to that you can reference. Your industry research skills will come in handy here. Do a Google search of the individual's name and cross-reference his or her company name and industry—something to ensure you have the right person. You should also scour the general news, the company's website, LinkedIn, Twitter, and any press releases related to the specific department you are applying to so you can explain why this company appeals to you. If you are being recommended by someone in common, make reference to the person and the positive things he or she had to say about the employer. In short, do anything you can to make sure your letter is not generic. And yes, this means you need a unique cover letter for each opportunity you pursue.

Second paragraph: What do you want?

Be very specific about why you're writing. The majority of people are busy, and the quicker you are able to identify what specific opportunity you are looking for, the longer that person will keep reading. This is generally your shortest paragraph and in some cases is only a sentence or two. Clearly state the department, function, or specific job title (if you know it) that you are seeking.

Third paragraph: Why your reader should give you a job

In this paragraph, it's your turn to shine. Nicole advises that you very succinctly highlight exactly how you are going to make this person's job or life easier. Make an explicit connection between who you are and how you are going to contribute to this business—not how you are going to contribute to *any* company (that's a big mistake!), but to *this* company in particular. Don't just explain why you are great; explain why you are a great fit for this particular organization and this particular position. Along with your general research, pay attention to the style of the company's website and echo the terminology, tone, and essence of the company's brand in your letter. Translate yourself and your skills into a perfect fit for their business. You want the reader to leave this paragraph thinking, "This person really knows herself, and this company is such a great fit for her. I want to meet this young person."

Remember as well to focus on what you can do for them, not what's in this for you. Companies don't want to hear how much you want to learn or how you want to try something different. They want to know what you will contribute. A quick way to know if your cover letter is too focused on you? Count the number of times you use the word "I."

Fourth and final paragraph: Next steps

Nicole recommends that you finish quickly with a reminder of what you want to result from this letter—usually a meeting or interview. Indicate that you are going to follow up with a call or e-mail within a specific time frame (usually within a week if this is a specific posting, two weeks if this is about an opportunity/meeting you'd like that isn't officially "out there"). Do not write that you "look forward to hearing from" the organization or that they should "feel comfortable reaching out to you." These are too presumptuous. Finally, thank the person for his or her time.

As with your résumé, be sure to "test" any cover letter with a few trusted advisers, professors, coaches, or family members before sending. Check for style, spelling, grammar, factual correctness of whatever you say about the company, and overall tone.

66. CREATE A BRAG BOOK

My friend Joan K. Snyder is one of the most successful, impressive twentysomethings I know. I give her 100 percent credit for this tip because it's a strategy I had never considered before, and the minute I heard it I knew it would be a huge differentiator for anyone who tried it. Case in point: I immediately did it myself.

Joan credits her great postcollege job at a major pharmaceutical company and her subsequent promotions in large part to her creation of what she calls a "brag book." The brag book is a three-ring binder that presents all of Joan's accomplishments in an organized, impressive visual fashion. Think of it as a more detailed, in-depth, three-dimensional version of a résumé. It takes some time to put together, but once you have the book it can be an invaluable tool to update and use throughout your career.

"My mother taught me to be obsessed with organized binders," Joan tells me. "The brag book evolved because my mom collects every little thing, from programs to every concert to the award saying I was the sixth-grade valedictorian. She sent me all of my files, my résumés—starting in high school—and certificated everything else so I didn't forget anything I'd done."

By her freshman year in college, Joan had quite a collection of impressive documents. She continued to collect them, such as acceptance into the University of Pittsburgh's prestigious Blue and Gold Society and programs from conferences in which she participated. According to Joan, the brag book always presented both activities and academics.

Joan says she began to use her brag book "officially" when it came time to interview for jobs the summer after her junior year at Pitt. The brag book proved to be a secret weapon in the interview process. Joan used it to show prospective employers who she was, what she'd accomplished, and why she was the right fit for a particular job. Needless to say, employers were impressed with not only the accomplishments featured in the book, but also the fact that she'd gone to the extensive effort to create such a sales tool for herself.

Here is a list of what Joan includes in her brag book, along with her great tips for making your book the very best it can be. You can start a brag book at any time—from middle school to midway into your career—so don't worry that it might be too early or too late for you to benefit from this tip.

And don't worry if you don't have as many impressive accomplishments or documents as Joan. Everyone has things they can include. Think of classes you've taken, sports you've played. As you begin, include anything and everything and then edit later. After you've read through Joan's instructions for creating a brag book, you'll find more tips on how best to use the book to help you get a job.

Joan K. Snyder's Brilliant Brag Book Instructions

Your brag book should include the following sections, ideally marked with page separators:

1. Personal statement

Buy a binder with a clear plastic sheet on the cover so you can insert a cover page of your own design. To create a generic brag book, this can be a cover with your name and contact information. If you are creative, you can design a more artistic cover. If you are using the brag book to bring to an interview for a specific job, Joan recommends making the cover a "personal statement"—a short paragraph outlining your talents, skills, and experience and why you are a good fit for the particular job. "This introduces what you plan to do with the rest of the book," explains Joan. If you prefer a binder without a plastic cover, then simply include the personal statement as the first page of your book.

2. Résumé

3. Academic accomplishments

Include any or all of the following:

- College transcript, if you have a strong GPA

- Copies of any awards you've won: academic honors (such as dean's list), scholarships, grants—include a color photocopy of the actual award certificate or a photo of you accepting the award with a caption about what the recognition means

- Copies of outstanding papers you've written, if they seem relevant to your job search, such as a business plan if you are applying to corporate jobs, or press releases if you are applying for jobs in PR

- Information from courses you took or conferences attended outside of the school curriculum

- Information or course work from study abroad programs or special degrees

- A list of your five most inspiring books—this is Joan's unique idea. She includes a list of the business books that most inspired her to pursue a business career, along with a paragraph about why these are her favorites. (If you're curious, here's a brief sample: Stephen Covey's *Seven Habits of Highly Effective People;* Daniel Goleman's *Emotional Intelligence;* Robin Gerber's *Leadership the Eleanor Roosevelt Way.*)

4. Leadership experience

Next, provide a summary of any leadership positions you've held, with examples. This could include:

- Certificates or letters of acceptance from any leadership training programs you've attended

- Flyers, programs, Web page printouts, or other documents listing you as the president of a school club or the leader of a committee or volunteer effort

- Flyer or program from any event where you spoke on a panel or gave a presentation

5. Work experience

Here you are giving detailed examples of the work experience listed on your résumé; this is what makes that

document really come alive. In this section you'll want
to include any examples of work you completed in various positions and feedback you received. Your goal is to
show how the work you've accomplished is transferable
to the work you want to do in your career. Include any
of the following:

- A blurb about each company you worked or interned
  for, along with a list of your major accomplishments
  (more detailed than the bullet points appearing on
  your résumé)

- Feedback reports

- Special assignments you completed (spreadsheets,
  press releases, newsletter articles, reports, etc.)

- Recommendation letters (addressed "To whom it
  may concern" is okay for these), from summer jobs,
  part-time jobs, internships, etc.

- Visuals from any job—photographs of work you completed, pie charts, PowerPoint slides, etc. According
  to Joan, "People love visuals! And it breaks up the
  book if you include color."

6. Community service/volunteer experience
According to Joan, this section "demonstrates a
community-minded commitment and will emphasize
your values, self-motivation, and social consciousness."
As with the above categories, you can include reference letters, feedback reports, lists of transferable skills
you developed through your volunteer work, flyers or
brochures from events in which you participated, work
examples from special assignments, and photos from
events.

7. PR

Have you received any press—a school newspaper story about your winning touchdown? A local newspaper article about a scholarship you won or a community service project you spearheaded? School websites with your photo or a quote? This is the place for any media coverage you've received, no matter how small it may seem to you. Show that you are "known" in your community, whether it's your hometown, your school, or the web.

This is a great section in which to include printouts of any impressive online content you created in Tip #15, "Shine Online."

8. Conclusion

In this final, optional section of your brag book, Joan recommends concluding with a statement that positions you in relationship to whatever job you are applying for. This means that you'll change this last page every time you show the book to a different company or networking contact. Joan calls this "The Why"—why you are the right person for the job or company in question. This should be in the format of a paragraph or two, perhaps with a few bullet points outlining the top reasons why you should be hired.

— — — — — — — — — — —

Again, don't worry if you don't have everything listed above. Your brag book is unique to you, and no one will have every item Joan suggests. Even if your book is quite thin, it's helpful to have all of your experience and accomplishments organized in one place. Here is how Joan recommends making use of your brag book once you compile it:

- **Only use your book in person.** A brag book is not a résumé that can be e-mailed around—it's a sales document that you need to present. Some people may find the book overwhelming if it's not accompanied by a real, live person. Be judicious with the ways and times you pull out the book. It's not an everyday tool, but a secret weapon for your biggest and most desired opportunities. "This is your closer," says Joan.

- **Save everything.** Your brag book is a work in progress. Continue to add to it throughout your career. Joan recently used her book to win a big promotion.

- **Create a table of contents.** Write down the order you put things in so you don't reinvent the wheel every time you want to create a new brag book.

- **Make professional copies.** "Go to Kinko's and make this look phenomenal!" advises Joan. If any documents or clippings are frayed or difficult to read, take the time to make nice color photocopies. You can even consider binding your brag book instead of using a three-ring binder. The more professional the opportunities you're applying for, the more professional your book should be.

- **Put your brag book online.** If you want, you can even scan every document and make your book into a website or a PowerPoint document you can present on an iPad—the possibilities are endless.

I know that putting together a brag book sounds like a lot of work, but once you have it, it's an incredible sales tool that you can use for the rest of your career. So, don't be shy—go ahead and show your stuff!

67. BECOME PROFESSIONAL FRIENDS
WITH FACEBOOK

One of the key tenets of sales and marketing is that you never know where a customer might be looking for your product, so you want it to be available everywhere. The same goes for your personal brand. You want to be visible and promoting yourself professionally in as many places as possible because you never know where and when an opportunity might arise.

I admit that I hesitated to talk about Facebook in this section because, as we covered in Tip #14, "Clean Up Your Internet Image," Facebook has gotten a lot of job seekers into trouble because of unprofessional photos or wall posts. But the reality is that hundreds of millions of people, including potential employers and other networking contacts, are on the site, so it could be an asset to your job search as long as you're careful and always make sure that your profile is appropriate. I know this might not be the most fun use of Facebook, but it's crucial if you want to use the site to help, not hurt, your job search.

For advice on this topic I asked Miriam Salpeter, author of *Social Networking for Career Success: Using Online Tools to Create a Personal Brand*, to share her wisdom. Here are some of her top tips for marketing yourself professionally on the world's largest social network:

- **Make certain areas of your profile open to the public.** Use the "just friends" privacy setting for everything except for "About Me," "Education and Work," and "Contact Info." For "About Me," write a bio to emphasize your skills and any important accomplishments (this can be the same as the bio you use on LinkedIn). For "Education and Work," list whatever information is relevant to your career goals.

For example, if you're seeking a childcare position, include any Red Cross CPR training or certificates in this section. "Contact Info" should include your professional e-mail address and links to your LinkedIn profile and your blog or Twitter feed if you have them.

- **Find, visit, and "like" Facebook fan pages for any company that interests you.** Don't use a company's fan page just to ask about internships or summer jobs. Do a Google search about the company, read the latest news, and ask something specific or comment on something the organization has posted on its page. For example, if the organization has a new product, you may want to comment on it or mention that you've tried it. Showing you can contribute in an online community is one way to demonstrate you have what it takes to get a job done—and you never know who might take notice of your contributions.

- **Use Facebook status updates to show what you know.** For example, if you want to work in retail, follow your favorite stores and write about how excited you are that a particular celebrity is representing them, or how great it is that a particular line of clothing will be available. Commenting on the news in your target industry helps alert your friends and contacts about your interests without your needing to constantly post "I'm looking for a job" notices. Every once in a while, add an update asking if anyone knows anyone at a specific company, but networking works better when you don't look needy.

Chapter 8

FIND OPPORTUNITIES

All right, readers. We've reached a big moment in our time together. You're organized. You're professional. You're clearer about what you want. You're networked. You're experienced. You've got an extra edge. You're résuméd. You're raring to go.

It's time to find Real Opportunities in the Real World. Let's do it. You're ready.

68. FOLLOW EVERY RAINBOW

Just as every person has a different ideal career dream, each person has a different path to find it. The next, and crucially important, stage of getting from college to career is clarifying how and where you're going to get hired.

When I was a little girl I used to love watching *The Sound of Music* once a year when it was broadcast on TV (yes, the world before DVR and DVDs). I also had the record album (yes, record album!), so I knew the words to every single song from the movie. "Sixteen Going on Seventeen" was my favorite, of course.

As corny as it is, when I think about career planning, I think about the Mother Abbess's big number, "Climb Ev'ry Mountain," where she reminds us to follow every rainbow until we find our dream.

And the Mother Abbess proved right in the film: if Fräulein Maria (played by Julie Andrews in her pre–*Princess Diaries* days) could go from junior nun to governess to stay-at-home mother of seven children, then any path really is possible. Jokes aside, there is a major lesson here: it is not necessarily easy to find your dream (your dream career in this case), and it may take a lot of searching to find it. But don't give up, because it's out there. And you never know if it's the mountain, stream, rainbow, website, or friend of a friend that will turn out to be the right path—so you have to explore them all.

To bring this analogy back to reality, here is some more wisdom from the survey I conducted. I asked responders how they came to find their first jobs, and I got as many different responses as there were responders. Note the very, very wide variety of ways you can get your foot in the door to get your first job and, hopefully, start on the path to your dreams. Some of these strategies may seem like climbing mountains, but others are as easy as asking a friend for help or making a simple phone call.

- "A family friend encouraged me to call the district director in the office of my local congressman to get advice on how to get a job in politics. I did, and although he wasn't very helpful, I sent him a thank-you note with my résumé in it. He ended up leaving that job very shortly thereafter, but his replacement found my note and résumé in her new desk, and called me for an interview."
- "Through the parents of a college friend."
- "I went to an employment agency, was sent for an interview, and was hired on the spot."

- "Campus recruiting. I was interviewed by an HR employee on campus."
- "I got my first job after school through a website, but I interviewed like crazy that spring—found things through websites, campus listings, a head hunter, etc. But the one I finally took was just a résumé I sent cold with a really enthusiastic cover letter."
- "Perusing the classifieds."
- "Networking with family friends and contacts from summer internships."
- "Job fair through school."
- "I applied to every job I could find on Monster.com that stated 'entry-level position.'"
- "I found it through a newspaper ad."
- "Networking—my father's best friend from college worked there and put in a good word."
- "Through a summer rental housemate of my oldest brother."
- "Referral from professors."
- "A friend I'd just met the summer after graduation at a journalism program told me about the job. She worked there."
- "I went to the college career counseling office to ask what you do with a history major. The head of the office said, 'Hey, we need a pre-law advising counselor to assist the head of pre-law advising, who is only here part-time. Would you like the job?' and I took it!"

What is the takeaway from this lengthy list? You never know where an amazing job opportunity might exist, so you have to pursue every angle and be open to any possible avenue. This means that using *only* campus recruiting, or *only* an online job site, or *only* your parents, or *only* the classifieds, or *only* cold calling is putting yourself at a disadvantage. E x p a n d your search as far and wide as you're willing to go.

Make This Work for You

Go through the above list and circle, underline, or highlight
all of the job-getting possibilities you've never considered.
Then add these strategies to your tool kit of potential job
search ideas.

☐ Done!

69. TAKE CANDY FROM STRANGERS

The reason to attend job fairs and recruiting events is not just
for the overflowing candy dishes inevitably found at every booth
(have I mentioned I have quite a sweet tooth?). The truth is that
formal recruiting events have a lot of real value for a lot of reasons.
Here are some success tips for working the job fair circuit:

1. **Know your prospects.** Always do your homework and know
   which employers will have booths at any job fair you attend.
   It is a huge mistake to arrive at a job fair and walk through
   the aisles hoping to find an opportunity that looks interesting. And nothing irks recruiters more than students who walk
   up to their booths and say, "What does your company do?"
   It's your job to know the answer to that and to know what
   kinds of opportunities are listed as available on their websites,
   what they are sharing on their Facebook fan pages, what they
   are saying on Twitter, and what company news and statistics
   appear on their LinkedIn company pages (www.linkedin.com/

companies). The majority of job fairs post all of their exhibitors on a website, so there is no excuse for being unprepared. When a recruiter asks what kind of job you are interested in, you should be prepared with a very specific response, based on your research: "I'm interested in the rotational program in your energy division," or "I've read a lot about sales assistant jobs and would love to learn more about how these jobs differ depending on the product category." Saying the dreaded "I'll take anything" is basically saying, "I didn't do my homework."

2. **Use that introduction.** Think back to the work you did in Tip #29, "Be Able to Introduce Yourself." Now is the time to show off your brilliant sales pitch about yourself. Who are you, what are your major skills and experiences, and what are you looking for? You will have a very short amount of time at a job fair to sell yourself, so practice several times before you attend.

3. **Combine #1 and #2.** The real trick is to introduce yourself *and* talk about why you want to work for the particular company you're talking to. Why should they remember you out of all the candidates they will speak to that day?

Reality Check

"I think a lot of students view career fairs as occasions for them to see who is hiring and what jobs are out there, rather than times to make lasting impressions on current employees and HR reps. I wish I had known sooner to sell myself and secure contacts at career fairs, rather than moseying around in a suit contemplating which company I might like to work for."

Katrina Stroup, marketing and sales manager, Medieval Times

Here is a very specific plan of action from Nu Huynh, campus relations manager for the Principal Financial Group: "During a job fair or recruiting event, the Principal looks for candidates who present themselves well—people that are outgoing, professional, assertive, and motivated. Having tangible experience and qualifications makes all the difference. Candidates can stand out from the crowd by being confident in what they want and why they want to be part of our team. Within sixty seconds, candidates should be able to articulate highlights of their experience, how it's relevant, and how they could add value to our company." Follow that advice carefully, and your résumé should end up at the top of the pile.

4. **Show your knowledge.** Because recruiters are so impressed by candidates who really know about their companies, prepare a few specific, insightful questions that you might ask if you are granted a few extra minutes with a recruiter. Ask about a recent product launch, a new senior executive announced in the week's news, a new division of the company, or a management training program that several alums of your school have raved about. Show that you are up on the news and that you are in the know about your industry and their company. (Of course, don't bring up negative press!)

5. **Arrive early.** This shows enthusiasm, focus, and professionalism. And it's just human nature that the recruiters will have more energy in the morning. One warning: don't carry a coffee cup, no matter how early it is. That's just a big, embarrassing spill waiting to happen!

6. **Bring résumés customized to the companies you'll be meeting.** Refer back to Tip #63, and make sure you have a different résumé for different job functions and industries. To keep all

of them straight, I strongly advise that you keep each résumé in clearly marked folders, preferably of different colors, so you're sure not to make a mistake and hand the wrong résumé to a recruiter.

7. **Be on your best behavior at all times.** Be very aware that recruiters are watching everything out of the corners of their eyes. They will notice if you are meeting with every recruiter at every booth—this makes your targeted pitch seem a lot less genuine. They will notice if you are chatting on your cell phone, popping your gum, or texting while waiting in line, rather than standing quietly, reviewing your résumé, or chatting politely with other candidates. They will notice if you walk up with a smile and give a strong, confident handshake. These people are standing on their feet in a big room all day—a little kindness and good manners can go a long way.

8. **Ask about next steps.** Before you leave a company's booth, be sure to ask what the next step might be, and if it would be appropriate for you to follow up with that particular recruiter or another person on their HR staff. Request a business card, and if the recruiter agrees to give it to you, take a few minutes to jot down some reminders to yourself on the back of the card—any specifics of the conversation so you can remember to mention them in your follow-up. If the recruiter gives you advice or instructions (such as posting your résumé in the company's database, following up with a particular department, or signing up for a campus interview), do exactly what that person recommends, and send the person an e-mail to say you've taken the advice. Showing that you listened and took directions is much more effective than just sending a follow-up e-mail that says, "Nice to meet you."

9. **Build on your interaction with a company.** The most important fact about job fairs is that they are only one aspect of an effective job search. If you find a company or two that you really want to work for, make a point of showing up at any event related to that company. Make sure the job fair is just your introduction to that organization and not a one-off interaction. You want to increase your visibility. "Don't depend solely on a job fair or career event," says Nu Huynh of the Principal Financial Group. "At any given time, our organization has hundreds of job opportunities. So job seekers should apply online and continue to watch for available openings via the company's website. Candidates who attend job fairs can show additional interest in the Principal by attending other company-related campus events, including information sessions, presentations, sponsored organization meetings, and more. Make an effort to connect with a recruiter or representative of the company at each event."

10. **Don't eat the candy.** I was just kidding about the candy thing. Grabbing a handful of candy or taking too much interest in any little giveaways can distract from your core mission of impressing the employer and getting a foot in the door. If necessary, go to the candy shop after the job fair to celebrate a successful day.

70. START SMALL

Did you know that, according to the U.S. Small Business Administration, small businesses represent 99.7 percent of all employer firms in the United States and employ just over half of all private sector employees? How about the fact that small businesses hire a larger proportion of employees who are younger workers, older workers, and part-time workers? What you probably do know is the fact that many small businesses often don't recruit through formal campus recruiting programs.

These statistics are really just the tip of the iceberg when it comes to all of the job opportunities that exist outside of the big-name corporations that do offer college recruiting programs. Corporate programs are excellent and have a place in many entry-level job searches (as you can see from the number of corporate recruiting experts I've quoted in this book), but they are only one avenue of job opportunities.

Part of casting a wide net and following "every rainbow" in your job search includes considering opportunities with diverse types of employers. Small-business employers, and women- and minority-owned businesses and start-ups in particular, are an untapped mine of entry-level job opportunities. Any smart job search strategy should explore this diverse and growing community of companies.

Where can you find these opportunities? Most small-business owners I know rely on referrals from their personal and professional networks when they're hiring. If they post job opportunities online, it's usually on LinkedIn, Craigslist, or association job boards, not on the big national sites. This is just one more example of how networking and association membership can really pay off for a young person. Be sure to check out the job boards on any associations you belong to, job postings in any LinkedIn groups you've joined, or any other organizations in the area where you are looking for a job, to find such "hidden" opportunities.

For help finding a job at a start-up, which is admittedly easier if you have technical skills like web design or programming, some job sites have popped up, such as Startuply.com, VentureLoop.com, Jobs.Mashable.com, and Jobs.37signals.com.

Here are some great national women's, minority, and small-business organizations to check out as well. Not all of these groups have official job postings, but they all have websites and events that can facilitate networking with members who may be looking for young employees.

Women's Business Organizations	Web Site Addresses
Downtown Womens' Club	www.downtownwomensclub.com
National Association for Female Executives	www.nafe.com
National Association of Women Business Owners	www.nawbo.org
Women Presidents' Organization	www.womenpresidentsorg.com
Women's Business Enterprise National Council	www.wbenc.org

Minority Business Organizations	Web Site Addresses
The National Black Chamber of Commerce	www.nationalbcc.org
National Minority Supplier Development Council, Inc.	www.nmsdcus.org
U.S. Hispanic Chamber of Commerce	www.ushcc.com
U.S. Pan Asian American Chamber of Commerce	www.uspaacc.com

Small-Business Organizations	Web Site Addresses
U.S. Small Business Administration	www.sba.gov
Any local chamber of commerce	www.uschamber.com/chambers/directory

When it comes to looking for jobs with smaller companies, you may need to look in different places, but you shouldn't alter your get-hired plan at all. Even though most small companies don't have human resources departments, they can be just as picky, just as thorough, and just as impressed by professionalism as large corporations. When applying to work at a small company, you still need to be on top of your game. And rest assured that working for a smaller company can give you the skills and hands-on experience that will make you marketable to larger organizations you may want to work for in the future.

━ ━ ━ ━   ━ ━ ━ ━   ━ ━ ━ ━

Proof It's Possible

Brittany Albright is a 2006 graduate of Northeastern University in Boston. She initially got a job as a marketing assistant with a small woman-owned business as a six-month internship in January 2003. She continued to work at the company part-time for several more years, including two more full-time internships for six months each. Here is Brittany's story and her advice for those considering working for a small business:

LP: How did you get your job?

BA: I got the job through a mutual connection. My aunt worked for one of the company's clients, so she and Nancy [the CEO] knew each other. She asked Nancy if she was hiring. It turned out Nancy was looking for an assistant and had employed interns in the past. We got in touch with each other, and Nancy asked me to meet her the following morning at eight at a speaking engagement. I later found out that this was a test—whether or not I would show up at 8:00 a.m. on such short notice. Of course I did. I got

to see Nancy speak; we talked a little and connected well
personality-wise, which I have found to be extremely important. She offered me the job and I accepted it (including
the three-hour round-trip commute on public transportation
that came with it, but it was worth it).

**LP: What are the advantages and disadvantages of working for
a small business?**

BA: Advantages:

- Responsibility

- More challenging/interesting work

- Ability to really impact the business

- Work closely with high-level, successful businesspeople

- More casual, relaxed office environment

- Flexible work hours and the potential to telecommute

- Great learning potential

- Wonderful opportunity to add experience to your résumé
  and to get referrals, testimonials, and other help from a
  supportive boss in taking the next step in your career

Disadvantages:

- While I enjoy having a lot of responsibility, it can be
  stressful, especially for someone who prefers to have
  a real routine with specific responsibilities. In a small
  business, things are constantly changing, and you
  tend to be involved in everything on some level, so you
  have to be ready and willing to do what's needed and
  to be held accountable.

- You probably won't be working as a team as much as independently. In some respects, a small business is very team oriented, because everyone is so critical, but because it's small and there are fewer resources, a lot of projects need to be fully handled independently.

- May not get benefits

- Pay is often lower, because budgets are smaller

- You don't get to put an impressive big name corporation on your résumé

LP: What advice would you give students and recent grads who are considering working for a small business?

BA: Small businesses that are going through a growth phase tend to be hiring a lot of new employees. If the company seems to have strong potential, but the salary is not as high as you'd like, I'd ask about stock options. They could pay off big-time.

Depending on the size of the business, you may be doing a lot of work independently, which I personally like, but it's not for everyone. You will get to take on more challenging projects and will have more responsibility at a small business, often with little to no training, which can be scary but never boring. You have to be okay with that. It's also important to be very flexible, since you may have to take on extra projects, work under a tight deadline, or help out with someone else's work. Being willing to do anything is key.

Last, but not least, take advantage of your boss or the business owner as a mentor, teacher, and friend.

71. LOOK UP THE BEST

If you strongly identify with a certain ethnic group, gender, cause, or lifestyle, you may want to pursue opportunities in companies that are particularly noted for advancing employees like you. Having worked for Working Mother Media, an organization that produces three lists of such employers, I know that it is a source of pride for companies to be listed, and they are often pleased to attract employees because of appearing on these "Best of" lists. Here is a sampling of national lists, and I encourage you to seek out local lists, from the top diversity hiring companies to the top companies by industry or revenue.

- *Black Enterprise* magazine's 40 Best Companies for Diversity
- *Business Ethics'* 100 Best Corporate Citizens
- DiversityInc's Top 50 Companies for Diversity
- *Fortune* magazine's Best Companies to Work For
- Global 100 Most Sustainable Corporations in the World
- Human Rights Campaign's Corporate Equality Index, for gay, lesbian, bisexual, and transgender (GLBT) employees
- National Association for Female Executives' Top 50 Companies for Executive Women
- *Working Mother* magazine's Best Companies for Multicultural Women

If you'd like to work for a company that has been named to a list like the ones mentioned above, I encourage you to read every piece of information provided about the company in the list where it is mentioned. Then, when you apply for a job, you can mention the company's achievement (and some specific pieces of information that interested you, such as its women's mentoring programs, its environmental sustainability initiative, or its minority affinity groups) in your cover letter, to acknowledge that you are aware of it and that you are applying to the company in part because of it. This shows that you have done your homework and that you plan on being the kind of employee who contributes to the company's place on such lists in the future (i.e., you'll make them proud).

You should also try to attend events and visit websites related to such lists. Many companies use these lists as a form of recruiting, and many of the organizations that produce such lists host events, such as job fairs, conferences, and trade shows, for the winning companies to attend. They also create websites that often link to special job boards that feature only winning companies. This is a phenomenal, targeted networking and job search opportunity.

After all, who doesn't want to work for the best?

72. CONSIDER YOU.GOV

Another employer that often gets overlooked is not small but gigantic: our own U.S. government. Although the recession of 2008 has led to cuts in many government agencies, current students and recent grads are in a unique position when it comes to getting jobs in this sector: according to the federal government's Office of Personnel Management, nearly half of all government employees will be eligible for retirement over the next several years. The office's website, www.usajobs.gov, even has a dedicated area for students and recent grads.

What kinds of jobs does the government offer? Pretty much anything you can think of, from engineers to scientists to editors to administrators to diplomats to park rangers to social workers to federal agents. And government jobs provide excellent benefits and job security. Uncle Sam even helps you find your place by listing government jobs by academic major.

To give you a taste of what types of civil service opportunities are growing, here is a list of the occupational categories where twenty-four major federal agencies plan to do the most hiring over the next several years, according to a recent report, *Where the Jobs Are: The Continuing Growth of Federal Job Opportunities*:

1. Security, enforcement, and compliance
2. Medical and public health
3. Engineering and sciences
4. Program management/administrative
5. Accounting, budget, and business

Don't forget local and state governments as well. Again, budgets have been cut, but many positions are often available, especially on the entry level. FederalJobSearch.com lists federal, state, and local government jobs and contains helpful information about the number and type of government jobs available state by state.

73. WORK TO CHANGE THE WORLD

"Take a year to change lives. Take a year to change your life."

This is the motto of City Year, a program of the national organization AmeriCorps that brings together seventeen- to twenty-four-year-olds in a Youth Service Corps for a year of "full-time, rigorous community service, leadership development, and civic engagement."

In addition to City Year, AmeriCorps also coordinates the VISTA program, which places volunteers in rural communities. Many other national and international service programs last one, two, or multiple years, such as Teach for America, the Peace Corps, and Habitat for Humanity's International Volunteer Program. (Note that although these programs generally pay lower salaries than comparable work in the private sector, some of the government-sponsored programs offer loan repayment assistance plans when you commit to a year or two of service.)

Working as a full-time volunteer is a terrific choice for anyone interested in getting paid (albeit a small amount) to do community service for a year or two. I encourage everyone to consider these programs. Life is long, and it's hard to work full-time on community service when you have a family or when you're older and less energetic. It's obviously a great first job for those considering a lifelong career in social change. And it's also a wise choice for college students and recent grads who aren't sure where to start their careers. In fact, when I asked Evan Hochberg, national director, Community Involvement, for Deloitte & Touche USA LLP, for his best advice to college students and recent grads who have absolutely no idea what they want to do with their lives, he replied:

"Tell them to give back. Tell them to volunteer, because of the skills they will learn. Volunteering doesn't have to stop at altruism; it can be a valuable skill-building and professional development opportunity."

Wise advice, indeed. If you're not sure what job you want to get (or even if you are), do consider a volunteer year.

Completing a service year in your late teens or early twenties can set you on a positive path for the rest of your life. You'll meet a wide variety of people, learn teamwork, expand your skill set, and change a corner of the world in the process. A service year will also look great on your résumé no matter what you decide to do after the year is over. And you'll have a multitude of unique experiences to draw from when you're selling yourself in job interviews.

Some organizations even allow you to defer a job offer for a year or two to give back through a program such as Teach for America or City Year. So this is an option you can consider along with, not instead of, applying for full-time jobs.

One caveat: Service programs increased significantly in popularity during the recent recession as private sector job opportunities became more scarce. In 2010, for instance, 46,000 college students applied for Teach for America and less than 10 percent were accepted. Because these programs often require a lengthy application process, be sure to check with your career services office to learn about requirements and deadlines.

━━━━━━━━━━━━━━━━━━━━━━━━━━━━

Proof It's Possible

Here are the stories of two City Year participants, sharing what they learned from the experience and describing how giving back affected their career plans and their lives in general:

Matthew Little
College attended: University of Memphis
Job after completing City Year: Coordinator of K–12
    programs for Nashville State Community College

As I neared my graduation from high school, I desperately wanted to go to college, but neither my family nor I had the financial wherewithal to make that a possibility. During my spring break I visited my aunt in Boston and told her about my situation. She mentioned City Year, and as luck would have it there was a corps member in the aisle next to us in the CVS. After talking to him about the program and the chance for a college education while serving the community, I decided to apply.

Beyond providing me with the ability to go to college, City Year helped focus my career plans. I knew I wanted to work with children, but I didn't know how. When I joined City Year I was placed in an inner-city elementary school in classrooms where a student having a parent who wasn't in jail was rare, with a team that was different to me in every way. I began to worry: Would I be able to help? Would I even be able to relate to my teammates?

Those worries were replaced by opportunities: opportunities to create a prereading curriculum for kindergarteners, a chance to provide a remediation for second- and third-graders in a homework club, and a chance to codirect seven free vacation camps that served over two thousand students in the Boston area. Through it all, I was given inspiration: inspiration that came from my students, students who came to me with Fs and left my homework club with As. I was inspired by my kindergarteners, who couldn't even read all the letters on the board, but by the end of the year were reading me stories. This experience led me to realize I wanted to spend my life helping students.

Chris Brown

College attended: Valparaiso University

Job after completing City Year: NYU Reynolds Graduate Fellow in Social Entrepreneurship (and formerly the program director for the National Foundation for Teaching Entrepreneurship—NFTE)

My father, who is a retired fighter pilot, sat next to a City Year corps member on a flight out west. He was so impressed by what this young woman shared that he called me at school and asked that I look into it. Before I agreed to anything, I spent some time reading about the organization and visiting them during their annual conference, entitled cyzygy, in Washington, D.C. I was struck by the flurry of red jackets and the stomp of Timberland boots as they ran through the campus of Howard University. There was such a sense of purpose and discipline, not to mention a common call to service and spirit of togetherness that was palpable.

Plus, I couldn't help but notice that the people carrying walkie-talkies, making executive decisions, and mobilizing thousands of people in service projects were all about my age and were from every walk of life. While so many of my friends at that time were delving into start-ups in the technology boom, I had found my own entrepreneurial endeavor to make my mark.

What proved to be most useful for me professionally, in addition to the insights provided to me by these leaders who are still mentors of mine, were the practical tools for building teams, managing projects, conducting research and systematic evaluation, while meeting with students, principals, sponsors, and governmental champions. City Year taught me some of the best models of managing my time and resources plus leveraging scarce resources in a competitive public sector.

For three years I directed programs for an organization that combines my two great passions: youth development and entrepreneurship/business building. In New York, I oversaw approximately 100 school- and community-based partnerships who work with roughly 4,500 young people who have the desire to start up their own businesses. Each day I worked with private sector partners, board members, principals, community leaders, and young entrepreneurs. Not a day went by when I didn't rely on a tool or resource I was given during my year of service.

This has certainly been the case for me in my most recent transition from NFTE to my current endeavors as an NYU Reynolds Graduate Fellow in Social Entrepreneurship. The program is designed to attract and cultivate the next generation of leaders in public service. On countless occasions, I pull on the intellectual and operational assets that I developed as a City Year corps member. I feel uniquely positioned now, more than ever, to use these skills and leverage this academic opportunity as I explore my own vision for social change on a much broader scale.

74. TACKLE A PROJECT

Sometimes job hunters have to get a little bit creative. If you're having trouble finding a full-time job in the industry you want to join, but you've been successful in your networking efforts, it may be a good strategy for you to offer to do some project work—unpaid (freelancers refer to this as working "on spec," in the hope that more business will come) or for an hourly rate—for one of the professionals you know. This is a great way to build experience, learn skills, get feedback, and possibly even impress people enough to hire you full-time at some point in the future.

Winning project work is just a matter of asking, "I'd like to build my experience in your field while I look for a full-time position. Do you have any small projects I could help with?" Most often this strategy works best when you approach a small business, nonprofit organization, or entrepreneur, particularly one for whom you have already interned or worked. Project work is also listed online at such websites as Craigslist.org, elance.com, and UrbanInterns.com. I've seen project work listed through university departments as well. When I was in graduate school I got a freelance gig writing a newsletter for a cosmetics company, which was a great way to build my writing and interviewing experience. My mother has hired students to work in her small business as well, and most of the students come as referrals from teachers at a local school. Ask some of your favorite professors if they've heard of any such opportunities. You never know when a small project, executed well, can lead to a big opportunity.

Proof It's Possible

Karlin Sloan, now the owner of her own leadership consulting firm, Karlin Sloan & Company, decided in her twenties that she wanted to work in consulting. "I knew I wanted to do this stuff, but I had no idea how to break into it," she shares. "So I offered to do a project for free for a friend's mother who ran a consulting boutique firm. She wanted someone to draw a model for a training program. I took the outline she provided, I drew a model, and made materials out of it."

"She was so excited about it that she actually hired me full-time! I didn't think there was a job available. I had just wanted experience and her feedback to know if I was doing the right thing. I think she offered me a job because I didn't just do what I volunteered to do; instead I did much more. This woman became my mentor and has made a huge difference in my life."

75. LOOK ONLINE

Many people, and especially younger workers, make the mistake of spending way too much time looking for jobs online. In reality, your chances of finding a job through networking are much, much higher. As I mentioned earlier, experts estimate that 70 to 80 percent of jobs are found through networking, so 70 to 80 percent of your job-hunting efforts should take place through networking. This means that approximately 20 to 30 percent of your job search energy should be spent searching online job sites.

Job hunting online *is* a great way to research what kinds of opportunities are available, and it certainly works for some people. The trick is to be smart and strategic about where you look and how you apply for those positions once you've found them.

Where to look:

Here is a brief overview of some of the best places to look for entry-level jobs online:

- **Job sites targeted to college students and recent grads.** This is a way to narrow your search and not have to sift through lots of jobs that require more experience than you have. Check out CollegeGrad.com, CollegeRecruiter. com, Experience.com, LinkedIn's student jobs portal (www .linkedin.com/studentjobs), and Monster College (www .college.monster.com). On these sites (as well as others), you can set up job search alerts that will e-mail job listings directly to you so you don't have to spend all day searching. Many of these sites have apps and mobile alerts as well, so you can look for jobs anytime, anywhere.

- **Professional association websites.** Most industry associations host their own job boards, which generally include
  opportunities with both large and small companies. Many
  post available positions to their LinkedIn groups and Facebook fan pages as well.
- **Individual company websites.** As you learn about various
  companies whose ranks you might like to join, look at their
  websites for job listings. This is a great way to target your
  search—and you'll be doing valuable background research
  on the company at the same time.
- **Craigslist.org.** You've seen me mention this resource a few
  times already. This community website is the preferred job-
  recruiting tool for lots of smaller businesses that don't have
  the bucks or the time to list their open positions on the
  bigger, national websites.
- **Local and regional job boards.** Although these sites
  don't focus on entry-level positions, they are beneficial
  if you know where you want to work. Examples include
  DenverJobs.com, FloridaJobs.com, and MountainJobs.com.
- **Aggregators.** Job aggregators are essentially search engines
  for jobs, where job postings are aggregated from a wide
  variety of online job boards, classified ads, and company
  websites (i.e., virtually all of the kinds of websites I've just
  mentioned). Results of the searches you type into their
  search engines often appear accompanied by links to salary
  information and a way to check the LinkedIn.com community to see if you know anyone already working at the
  company. SimplyHired.com and Indeed.com are the two
  major players in this space.

Keep in mind that the jobs listed online represent only a frac-
tion of all the jobs available in the world. Never, ever, ever limit
your job search just to your computer screen.

Make This Work for You

How can you maximize your chances of landing a job from an online posting? My recommended strategy treats the online posting simply as a jumping-off point. It is only the first step in a more comprehensive process of research and networking. Here's why this is so important. A recruiter friend once told me that he always has two stacks of résumés on his desk: one huge stack of résumés that have arrived from anyone and everyone who submitted an application on the Internet and one small stack of résumés that have been sent or handed to him by people he knows personally. Clearly, you want to be in that smaller, more elite stack. Here is how to get there:

1. Find a job online that sounds like a good fit. Commit to applying as quickly as possible because opportunities disappear very quickly. Ideally, you'll want to submit your application within a few days, so you have to work fast.

2. Look up the company that posted the position on LinkedIn using LinkedIn's advanced search, a free feature of the site. (Obviously you can't do this if the job listing doesn't post a company name, but in my experience, vague job postings with no company or contact name are often long-shot opportunities anyway.) Use LinkedIn to:

   - Find out if the job is cross-posted on LinkedIn under the Jobs tab. If it is, you can often see the exact name of the person who posted the position (and his or her LinkedIn profile), which enables you to customize your cover letter as opposed to writing the dreaded "To Whom It May Concern." Do not automatically send your résumé to this person on LinkedIn, though. That may be too intrusive. Continue with the following steps.

- Discover if you have anyone in your personal network who works, or has worked, for the company. You'll be surprised how often you have some connection to an organization through your broader network.

3. If you do discover that you have a friend of a friend who works for the company, ask your mutual connection to introduce you. Or send a gracious e-mail or direct LinkedIn message asking that person if he or she would be willing to chat with you briefly about the company. At first, you just want to ask for information and advice (What do they look for in employees? What are the company's biggest priorities at the moment?). Then, when the person has helped you a bit, you can politely ask him or her to pass along your résumé and cover letter. Don't be shy about doing this. Remember that if you are a great job candidate (which I know you are!), you will make your contact look good for recommending you. Just remember to be very polite, modest, and thankful every step of the way.

4. Immediately begin to follow the company that posted the job listing on LinkedIn and Twitter, and fan the company's Facebook page. This will ensure that you know as much as possible about the organization and can include relevant keywords or information in your cover letter and, hopefully, future interview. (On the company's LinkedIn page, you can also look to see if the organization has any other open positions that might be a good or better fit for

you. LinkedIn company pages also have a cool feature that enables you to see where people at that company worked before and after joining. Check out those other companies—often competitors, vendors, or clients—to see if *they* have any open positions that could be a good fit as well. Remember, you never want to put all of your eggs in one basket and not apply for enough jobs.)

5. Write a cover letter that includes any new knowledge you learn about the company from your research and anyone you've been able to speak to. Even if you don't have any "in" to a company, a customized cover letter will stand out.

6. Incorporate any relevant and truthful key words from the job description into your résumé and LinkedIn profile. If the job posting mentions very specific skills that you have, make sure your résumé clearly points that out. Recruiters specifically look for such matches.

7. If your contact is willing, ask him or her to submit your cover letter and résumé for you. Sometimes the person will say no, but it's worth asking. If you submit the application yourself, at least you'll have a real name to address it to based on your LinkedIn research.

8. Once your application has been submitted, keep everyone you've spoken with in the loop. Even if you don't land the job, people will appreciate being informed about how everything turned out.

Does all of this take a ton more work than simply shooting off your résumé in response to an online job posting? Absolutely. But that's why it's a ton more effective.

76. THINK "AND," NOT "OR"

Hopefully, the past few tips have opened your mind to some new possibilities for finding real job opportunities, but I suspect you may be thinking, "Great, Lindsey, now you've made me think about even more options. How will I ever decide what I want to do, find opportunities, and actually get a job that makes me happy?"

Fear not. It is good—no, it's great—to have options.

I was reminded of this recently when a senior at Smith College asked me if she should apply for a postgrad public relations internship program in New York, an international graduate school scholarship, or a job with a company owned by an alumna of her school.

My answer was "Yes."

Whether you're in college, graduating tomorrow, sure of your direction or completely clueless, hoping to pursue a creative passion but not sure now is the time, one thing is certain: there is no reason *not* to keep all of your options open at this stage of your life. While it certainly takes time to pursue several opportunities, you have absolutely nothing to lose by keeping several doors open. As long as you have the time to follow a variety of leads, do it.

Many people worry about the potential dilemma of having several offers, but I can't think of a better outcome. Eventually you will have to make a choice, but there is no reason to cut off any options until that decision time comes. Here are some reasons why:

- If you're like most everyone else in the world, you probably have more than one passion. At this early stage of your life, there's no reason to force yourself into pursuing only one area of interest until it's time to make a decision. While you're still in the exploratory phase of gaining experience, building your contacts, and looking for opportunities, it's smart to cast a wide net.

- You will be a different person tomorrow than you are today. Some jobs, internship programs, and study abroad opportunities have very long lead times—you must apply up to a year in advance—and you may feel differently about such options when the letter comes with an acceptance or rejection. Don't lock yourself into (or out of) a program months before a decision needs to be reached.

- All opportunities are networking opportunities. Every job you research, interview you attend, and program you apply for is a chance to connect with the people on the other end. While you certainly don't want to apply to programs that don't interest you (it's a waste of your time and the time of the program organizers), there's no need to limit your options unnecessarily. Remember that a job offer this year may lead to another one in the future, as long as you keep in touch.

- You never know how the cookie—or job offer—may crumble. Unfortunately, some offers do fall through at the last minute, so it's always good to have a backup plan (or two or three or four).

Think of this principle as similar to when you applied to colleges: no one would ever dream of applying to just one school. Your career is no different. Think broadly, and don't force yourself to make a choice too early in the process.

When it is time to choose—and my hope is that this book results in many job opportunities for you—remember that you have a support network to help you decide which path to select: your family, friends, college advisers, professional networking contacts, coaches, career services staff, mentors, association leaders, and, of course, your own gut instincts. You are never alone, and your career path will be long and varied. Don't be afraid of having too many options. Instead, embrace this exciting time in your life, and access all of the help and guidance available to you.

Chapter 9

OVERPREPARE FOR INTERVIEWS

And now we've reached the moment you've been waiting for: preparing for a real interview with a real human being who can get you a real job at a real company with a real, honest-to-goodness *paycheck*.

(I will pause for a moment to allow that to sink in.)

Luckily, if you've followed the tips to this point, you've already had lots of interactions with professionals in your desired industry, so this shouldn't feel too intimidating. And in even more good news, people have been interviewing for jobs for centuries, so there's a ton of information available on how to prepare and how to turn an interview

> ## Reality Check
>
> "What impresses me most are candidates who have researched the company both online and/or in person to gain familiarity and share feedback with me. I look for candidates who present themselves well, have a sense of confidence, and are comfortable in their own skin."
>
> Barbara, HR director, fashion company

into an offer. I encourage you to read other books and online advice on this topic to get as much information as you can stand about interviews and how to ace them. What I'm going to offer is insight into what hiring managers tell me matters most.

77. CONDUCT COMPANY RESEARCH

Every tip in this section encourages you to overprepare for each aspect of interviewing, starting with company research. You know the old Boy Scouts motto, Be prepared? Today, in the information age, this translates to: don't do anything before searching the Internet first.

Karen Bochner, organizational psychologist for a major lifestyle media company, puts it best: "I want you to have done as much as possible on your side." Don't waste an interview opportunity asking questions about a company that you can learn from its website, its Facebook fan page, its LinkedIn company page, its Twitter feed, or the myriad other ways that exist today to gather information.

This is the number one pet peeve of interviewers: when candidates know nothing about their companies. As soon as you land an interview with an organization, immediately follow that company on all social media and set up a Google alert so you'll be up on current news. Next, spend at least an hour or two on the website of the organization before you interview. I know a small-business owner whose first question to job candidates is, "Have you had a chance to look at our website?" If the answer is no, she ends the interview right there.

"Be prepared," echoes Nu Huynh, campus relations manager at the Principal Financial Group. "Come to the interview with a sense of direction and goals. Take the time to visit a company's website to learn about their business, interview process, career tracks, available openings, and more. Candidates who do their homework—research our company and have a general understanding of our business—have an edge by demonstrating initiative."

How do you go about getting this edge? What exactly should you look for on a company website? Executive recruiter Don Leon, managing director at Stephen-Bradford Search, recommends this strategy:

1. **Research the management team.** This is important for two reasons: (1) When talking to people at an organization you need to know key names and facts about the company's leaders. Any unique details are important, too; perhaps the company has a new CEO or a woman CEO or a foreign CEO. All of this affects the company, the culture, and the employees. (2) Management bios contain key information that might help you find a point of discussion or networking opportunity. For instance, you may learn that the chief marketing officer graduated from your university, which could make it easier for you to score an internship there. Or the executive director of a nonprofit you're researching may have started her career at Dress for Success, where you have volunteered every summer. You never know what you'll find once you start looking. You may even find, particularly at smaller organizations, that members of the management team tweet or blog. If they do, follow them immediately for additional insight into the organization and potential topics to discuss during the interview process.

2. **Read all recent press releases.** What could be more helpful than reading exactly what information the company wants the public to know? Company press releases (sometimes found

under a link called "News," "Press," or "Media") will inform you about new product launches, mergers, newly hired senior employees, recent media campaigns, earnings statements (for public companies), community efforts, and much more. You'll learn a lot about an organization's priorities and whether it's a place you'd be proud to represent. Be careful, though: press releases are designed to put a positive spin on the news, so don't necessarily take all of the information at face value.

3. **Research the company generally (in other words, Google 'em).** Simply type the company's name into Google or any other search engine and see what pops up besides the organization's own site. This will give you a more balanced view of the company. You may find media articles, particularly not-so-positive ones, reviews of the company's stock performance or products and services, and information about former employees. Again, all of this is helpful in deciding whether you want to work there and will give you great info to know at interviews or informational meetings.

I once received the advice to spend at least an hour researching each of the following four areas before showing up for a job interview:

1. The industry to which the company belongs

2. The company itself (following all of Don's helpful tips above)

3. The major competitors of that company (for large corporations you can find this information at Hoovers.com or on the company's LinkedIn page)

4. The particular job function for which you are applying

This is a great strategy for organizing pre-interview company research and determining whether a particular opening really is a good fit for you.

Additionally, some websites have cropped up that offer an "inside" view of various companies and jobs, based on anonymous posts from current and former employees, such as Glassdoor.com and Jobitorial.com. Of course the type of information found on these sites, particularly because it's posted anonymously, is for your knowledge only and should not be referenced during a job interview or any other interaction with a potential employer.

And—I know this may shock you—some company research can be done offline, in person. If you want to work for a retail bank, check out that institution's branch in your neighborhood. If you want to work as a junior buyer for a retail chain, shop at their stores. If you want to work in marketing for a consumer electronics company, try that company's gadgets. If you want to work for a TV station, watch that network's shows and be able to talk about which are your favorites. All of the information you gather from these personal experiences will help you decide whether a company's mission matches your interests and values and will provide you with information and observations to share during your interview.

Make This Work for You

Following the suggestions in this tip, research one organization you would like to work for. Be sure to review the bios of the management team, read press releases, and check out the competition (heck, you might end up adding them to your Really Big List!). See how you feel after about thirty minutes: Are you more excited or less excited about the idea of joining this company?

When you mock interview in preparation for a real interview (see Tip #82), print out a few pages of the company's website and have your mock interviewer quiz you on a few key points, such as the CEO's name, the company's major products, any recent news, and the name of the department(s) where you'd like to work.

☐ Done!

78. KNOW YOUR VALUE

One of the biggest anxieties surrounding the job hunt relates to the inevitable salary negotiation. As you carry out your research and preparation for interviews, it can be easy to feel like you're in a David-and-Goliath situation. It's true that entry-level job seekers don't have a ton of clout, especially because companies often have to invest a lot of training in you, but you do have value and employers do need you. Don't ever lose sight of this. Part of interview preparation is becoming aware, albeit humbly, of that value and developing the confidence to discuss compensation.

Some entry-level job seekers don't even think about building their negotiation skills because they feel they'll be fortunate to get any job and salary offer at all. According to Carol Frohlinger, a lawyer and cofounder of Negotiating Women, Inc. (www .negotiatingwomen.com, which offers e-learning negotiation courses specifically designed for women), and my own trusted negotiation expert, this is a mistake.

According to Carol, recent college graduates have value in the marketplace and do have the ability to negotiate for what they want, at least a little bit. Perhaps more important, you have the ability to turn down offers that you don't want even during tough economic times. But you have to believe in yourself and know your value to do this.

According to Carol, way before you even get a job offer and formal negotiations begin, your ability to negotiate for yourself matters. But if you are getting in your own way by undervaluing the worth of your knowledge, skills, and talent, you are limiting the negotiating power you have. For example, you may:

- Pass up opportunities to interview for positions for which you may be qualified
- Settle for a job that isn't a good fit
- Accept a compensation package that is less than what you deserve

True, you are new to the Real World of work. But it is also true that the promise you offer, coupled with your education and experience, is in demand. The catch is that *you* must believe that it is before you'll be able to convince anyone else.

How to prepare for a salary negotiation

Here are some tips to help you feel confident and comfortable when the inevitable question, "What are your salary requirements?" arises. It's wise to become a strong negotiator now, as this will be the first of many more compensation conversations in your future. As my friend Manisha Thakor, an author and personal finance expert, says, "Remember that no one will ever care about your career path or your salary progression as much as you do."

1. **Start with research.** It's hard to pick a salary requirement out of thin air, so start by finding out what is a realistic sal-

ary based on the industry, type of company, and region of the country or world to which you are applying. Online resources like Salary.com and Glassdoor.com are helpful for getting a ballpark estimate, as is talking to your career services office or any professional associations you belong to. The very best way to get an accurate assessment is to talk to someone who actually works in the type of job you want. Tap your personal and alumni networks for recent grads in your field who might be willing to share some numbers with you. You also need to do the math to figure out what you'll require to cover your expenses while you're working. There's nothing wrong with having six roommates or moving back home because your first job salary is low, but you want to make sure you can cover your student loans and essential living expenses.

2. **Know what's nonnegotiable.** Note that in some situations, such as large companies that hire an entry-level "class" of employees, there is no possibility of negotiating because everyone receives the exact same compensation package. You'll need to know this going in (you can ask your career services office) so you don't appear unaware of this policy. You can certainly try to negotiate in any circumstance, but if an employer says, "The salary is absolutely not negotiable," stop right there.

3. **Determine if you offer anything truly special.** Do you have a very rare and in-demand coding skill? Do you speak an obscure language that is exactly what a company needs? Have you been working part-time in the employer's field for years and therefore have significantly more experience than other entry-level candidates? In these cases, you can make a strong case for receiving a higher salary than may first be offered.

4. **Aim for a range.** When asking people for salary advice and communicating it yourself to a potential employer, always give a range of $5,000 to $10,000. However, be aware that the low number is what the employer is going to hear. I remember going into my first salary negotiation assuming I would get the middle of the range I asked for—not realistic! So, if necessary, bump up your range a bit, knowing that you will need to be happy with the lowest salary you say you will accept.

5. **Say the number(s) out loud.** This may sound silly, but it is incredibly important. It can be scary to talk about money, so you have to practice, practice, practice saying the salary you want. Otherwise when you open your mouth to speak in the actual interview you may not be able to get the words out.

6. **Convert your skills, character traits, accomplishments, and "lessons learned" into a currency that counts in the field of your choice.** This is another tip from Carol Frohlinger. The idea is to make a business case for the salary you are requesting. "I need to earn forty thousand dollars to pay my rent and bills" is not a good argument. You have to speak about what you will be providing the employer. Says Carol, "If you know that the culture of the company where you'd like to work is one where they expect you to figure things out without a lot of guidance, you might highlight a summer internship where you had to make things up as you went along." If you can demonstrate that you will hit the ground running and require less training than other candidates, you might be able to nudge up an offer.

7. **Avoid negotiating with yourself.** I've seen too many job seekers talk down their salary requests before they even hear a

response from the employer. For instance, "I am looking for a salary of $30,000 to $35,000, but . . . um . . . I know budgets are tight so . . . um . . . a little bit lower would be okay . . ." This is another reason to practice saying your number. State it confidently and then *stop talking*.

8. **Don't forget benefits and other nonmonetary compensation.** In addition to negotiating your financial compensation, do some thinking about what other benefits would be valuable to you. This can come in handy if your employer simply won't pay you the salary you want. You might be able to negotiate for a six-month review at which you can revisit the salary question or for a perk like schedule flexibility, additional vacation time, or relocation expenses. Depending on your industry and the size and type of company, you never know what might be possible.

9. **Be respectful at all times.** Remember that you have not gotten the job yet, and more than a few candidates have lost opportunities because they have been too arrogant or pushy during the salary negotiation phase. Again, keep in mind that many entry-level salaries are nonnegotiable or minimally negotiable.

10. **Know that you can say no.** If an employer simply can't offer you the compensation you need to live or the compensation you believe you deserve, it's okay to turn down the offer.

If you need any more incentive to be a good negotiator, check out this fact from Manisha Thakor: "The money you earn and save early on in your career is the most valuable, because it has the most time to grow and compound. If you can negotiate a salary or a bonus that enables you to save an extra $5,000 a year, and you save and invest that extra $5,000 a year every year for forty years and earn 7 percent on it—you'll have $1 million more in savings than if you had not had that conversation." Sounds pretty great to me!

79. FIGURE IN WORK-LIFE FIT

Another piece of "internal" research to carry out during your interview prep is to think about what kind of cultural fit you're seeking. In particular, what level of work-life balance? One of my biggest surprises when I first started speaking about career issues on college campuses was the number of students who asked me questions about work-life balance. College women (and more than a few men) as early as their freshman year were asking me about how to build a career that would enable them to have flexibility for child rearing, service projects, travel, or other pursuits.

But here's the thing: If work-life balance is important to you—because you eventually want to get married and have children, because you want the opportunity to take classes at night, because you want to take a sabbatical in the near future, or because you just plain want personal time in your life—then you have to plan for it. Don't assume that every employer will be happy to give you extra days off or let you work from home once in a while, even with today's multitude of technologies to enable this. And though it probably seems a little early in your life to worry about balancing family with your job, many of the professionals I interviewed for this book told me they wished they'd paid attention to the balance issue sooner. Think about work-life balance issues before you enter an interview situation, not once you're on the job.

The good news is that work-life balance is a much more prominent issue today than it used to be. There are more moms in the workforce, more workers who want flexible lifestyles, and more awareness of the dangers of stress and workaholism on people's health. This means that many companies actively promote their work-life balance policies and openly discuss them during recruiting sessions and job interviews, and even on their websites and social media posts.

Of course, not all companies support flexibility and alternative work arrangements. If this issue is important to you, then add "work-life fit" to your Really Big List and start learning more about it, talking to people who have experience with it, and incorporating it as a factor in your pre-interview company research. If you want a flexible work environment in your first job, it's a mistake to believe that it will all just work out. A little bit of research and planning will go a long way to making sure you find a working environment that works for you.

Perhaps you're wondering, "Can I really get a flexible job as an entry-level employee?" The answer is: it's definitely possible. Cali Williams Yost, work-life strategy expert and author of *Work + Life: Finding the Fit That's Right for You,* and the blog www.work lifefit.com/blog shares this example:

"A manager in his early fifties recently told me the story of a young man who worked for him for two years out of college, as a junior-level consultant at a big accounting firm. One day, the young man came into his office because he was a long-distance runner and he wasn't getting enough time to train for his marathons. He presented a detailed plan, whereby he would come in at 11:00 a.m. every Friday, and he had thoughtfully figured out what he was going to do to get everything done to take those few hours off every week. The manager said his first thought was, 'You've got to be kidding!' But then he realized the young employee had been so thoughtful about this and it was so important to him and he'd probably quit if the manager said no. So the manager agreed. Six months later, it's been successful."

Note that the young employee waited until he had a track record with his manager; he didn't ask for flexibility from day one. If you do know that flexibility is crucially important to you, then you can subtly ask about it when you interview with potential employers. Here is what Cali recommends:

"Try to figure out companies where you know they think about these issues. If you ask too soon, they might think you don't want to work hard. There are a lot of old-time managers out there, who believe you have to be at work for face time. What I would do is say, 'How does the company feel about remote working?' instead of saying, 'I want to work less.' Ask about the parameters for flexible hours or working from home. Ask if the employer has any examples of people who work nontraditional hours. Just get a sense for whether people work all the time or if there's some lee-way. You want to see that there is space for flexibility. You probably shouldn't ask for it as a brand-new employee, but you'll know that it's a potential conversation."

If this issue is important to you, then do exactly what Cali advises: figure out companies where you know they think about these issues. Look at lists such as *Fortune* magazine's 100 Best Companies to Work For, or *Working Mother* magazine's 100 Best Companies for Working Mothers. Understand at which companies a conversation about work-life fit can take place, and research and assess an organization's culture as part of your interview prep.

If you're a young professional wanting a career with balance, here are some specific suggestions:

1. **Understand the possible compromises.** While I want you to have it all, I also have enough experience to know that compromises are often necessary, especially when you're just starting out. For instance, when I first launched my own business, I

had a ton of flexibility and freedom, but I was also making less
money and had to pay for my own health insurance. That was
a compromise I was willing to make because independence
was my number one priority.

2. **Be realistic.** A major complaint I hear from entry-level recruiters is that Gen Ys feel entitled to flexibility and vacation time
from day one of a new job. This isn't always reasonable. Most
jobs really do need you to be there all day, every day, at least
during the first several months, when you are learning the
ropes. You can certainly ask about flexible hours or time off
when interviewing for a job, but be realistic about how soon
you might be able to take advantage of such policies.

3. **Do your homework.** There are still many industries where balance is just not part of the culture (investment banking and
law being the prime examples). While there has been some
movement in these industries (for example, law firms considering a project-fee model rather than billable hours), the reality is that an entire industry is not going to change its culture
overnight. Do your research to find out whether a particular
industry is known for a lack of balance and consider staying
away if balance is at the top of your list of career priorities.

4. **Create pockets of balance.** Finally, remember that balance
doesn't have to be "given" to you. Even if you're working
hard and have a demanding boss, you can find ways to inte-
grate your personal needs with your professional ambition.
Even small moments can add up to more happiness. For
instance, you can take a gym class during your lunch break,
go for a brief walk around the block each afternoon and listen to your favorite music, walk over and chat with a friendly
colleague, or join an internal community service group that

does charity work. These types of activities will give you a respite in a busy day and may end up boosting your career prospects as well.

5. **Make your decisions based on your current realities.** This is a final tip from Cali: "You don't have to create a fit today that will fit your life in twenty years. Just be where you are today, and know that managing your work-life fit will change many times over the course of your life. Right now when you're young, you may want to go for it—kick it! Build your base, travel, build up that goodwill of high performance. Then, when your realities change, draw on that goodwill and present a plan. You will be shocked at how often employers will accommodate you."

80. BUY A DARK SUIT

I am constantly amazed at the horror stories I hear about what young people wear to job interviews. According to a survey by the National Association of Colleges and Employers, nearly three-quarters of employers surveyed said that an entry-level job candidate's grooming would have a strong influence on their opinion of the candidate. Appearance counts. A lot.

So, what is appropriate professional dress for a college student or recent grad going on an interview? I'm going to give you the professional, fail-safe, careful choice: always err on the side of formality and wear a dark suit as the base of your outfit. Then, as you'll see below, depending on the industry, type of organization, and region of the country, you can make adjustments accordingly.

The following guidelines should be followed for any professional, career-related situation in which you find yourself—job shadowing, informational interviewing, attending association events, attending career fairs, and, above all, formal job interviews:

- **Ask.** It is perfectly fine to call a company's main phone number or an administrative assistant in the HR department and ask what is appropriate to wear before you attend a job interview. Just say, "I'm coming in for an interview, and I'm not sure what dress would be appropriate. Can you please tell me?" (There's no need to give your name, and usually no one will ask.) You may learn that it's not appropriate to wear a suit if you'll be interviewing in a drug rehab facility or a kindergarten, or you'll be told that everyone at the firm in question wears a suit every day. You can never go wrong if you call and ask.

- **It's always better to be overdressed than underdressed.** When in doubt, wear a suit. Even if the office dress code is corporate casual. Even if it's the hottest, most humid day of summer. Even if it's the coldest, most blustery day of winter. Even if you just broke your leg. This is particularly important if you have a young-looking face (trust me on this one; I have dimples). Diane K. Danielson, CEO and founder of DowntownWomensClub.com puts it this way: "If you are young and you dress young, you'll be thought of as an intern for the rest of your life." This goes for women and men. If you discover at your job interview that you're overdressed in a suit, you can always remove your suit jacket and tie or formal jewelry. (Women should avoid wearing sleeveless tops underneath a suit so you won't be underdressed if you do decide to remove your jacket.) The only time I personally have deviated from the "always err on the side of formality" rule was on October 28, 2004, the day after my dad's favorite baseball team, the Boston Red Sox, won their first World Series since 1918. I had an important client meeting that day, and I wore a Red Sox cap along with my conservative pantsuit. Actually, come to think of it, that's a good addendum to the "Always wear a suit" rule: you are permitted to break it once every eighty-six years.

- **You can't go wrong with basic black.** The fail-safe choice in any situation, for women or men, is a black suit. Black is always professional (even in the summertime). It's not a disaster if you accidentally spill something on it, and you're more likely to blend in with the crowd if for some reason you're a bit overdressed or underdressed. Every young professional should own at least one simple black suit. If you're on a limited budget, the extra bonus of a black suit is that less expensive fabrics (such as polyester) look better in black than in lighter colors. If you absolutely hate to wear black, then go with navy, brown, or dark gray.

- **Iron.** Nothing will make you look more like a young, inexperienced kid than wrinkles. Make sure that all of your clothes are freshly pressed in professional situations. If you don't know how to iron, I'm sure your mom or dad would be more than happy to give you a lesson.

- **The less skin, the better.** Want to guarantee you're dressed inappropriately in any professional situation? Show too much skin. Women, it's never, ever okay to wear a top that shows your midriff, and most work environments even frown on open-toed shoes. Before you wear any shirt to work, raise your arms to see if the shirt stays tucked or is long enough to cover your stomach. If not, save it for the weekend. In many offices, women also need to wear pantyhose or stockings with a skirt. If you learn on your first day that bare legs or sandals are okay at your office (and they may be, particularly in warmer climates), then you can remove your hose in the bathroom. But I'd strongly advise against bare legs or visible toes in any corporate interview situation. Guys, I hope I don't have to tell you not to bare your midriff. But I do want to remind you to wear high socks so you don't flash any skin if you end up crossing your legs during an interview. I know this sounds conservative, but you want an employer paying attention to your words, not your body.

- **Understand the meaning of "business casual."** Many offices today have a business casual dress code, but sometimes dressing for this vague criteria can be challenging. In a Silicon Valley start-up this could mean shorts. In a Boston bank, this could mean khakis and a button-down. If you are told to dress business casual for an interview, try to dig a little deeper and find out, for instance, if jeans are acceptable. If you're not sure, play it safe with nice pants, closed-toe shoes (no sneakers and definitely no flip-flops), and a button-down shirt for men or women or a cardigan set or nice sweater, or a knee-length dress or skirt, for women.

- **Accessorize cautiously.** I think it's great for a guy to wear a unique (but appropriate—no *Family Guy* characters!) tie to interview at an Internet start-up or trendy advertising agency, but I recommend the most conservative tie possible (and a white shirt) if you're interviewing at IBM or Morgan Stanley. The same goes for women when it comes to necklaces, earrings, scarves, or pins—these are great ways to show a bit of spunk, but be very careful when interviewing at more traditional companies.

     Here are a few additional accessorizing tips for each sex, with a focus on formality. Again, always research the environment of a company to determine what's appropriate. By the way, these instructions do not come from out of the blue. They are all real mistakes that entry-level interviewees have made in the Real World:

Men:

- Wear dress shoes, and get them shined before an interview. Don't ruin a professional suit and tie with clunky rubber-soled shoes.
- Shave the morning of an interview, and make sure your fingernails are clean and short.
- Baseball caps are a definite don't.

Women:

- Beware of distracting jewelry—dangly earrings, jingly bracelets, or oversize rings that bruise people's fingers when you shake hands.
- Makeup is perfectly fine, but be careful not to overdo it.

Both sexes:

- If you're interviewing at a conservative company, it's a smart idea to cover up tattoos and remove multiple piercings.
- Remove your sunglasses from the perch on top of your head or the front of your collar.
- No flip-flops, ever!
- Don't carry any food or drinks in to the interview. You'll likely be offered water or coffee, so don't weigh yourself down by carrying a water bottle or a takeout coffee cup.
- Don't overdo it on the scent. I've heard one too many interviewers refer to someone as "Cologne Guy" or "Perfume Girl."
- As flight attendants say, turn off and stow all electronic devices. Don't even leave them on vibrate mode—even

that little buzzing sound can be distracting during an interview.

- **Don't arrive with baggage.** If you've flown in for the interview, of course, it's fine to have a suitcase, but if you're just coming from across town it's not a good idea to come to an interview loaded down with shopping bags, a gym bag, or other "stuff."
- **Beware outerwear.** Don't do all the right things with your interview outfit and then cap off your look with a grungy raincoat or a threadbare overcoat from a thrift store. If your interview happens to take place on a rainy or cold day, make sure your coat, hat, scarf, or whatever else you need fits with the professional image you want to project.
- **Carry a pocket mirror.** Even if your outfit is perfect, you'll want to double-check for food in your teeth, a blob of gel in your hair, pen marks in weird places, or any other last-minute visual glitches. There are few feelings worse than going into the bathroom after a job interview and realizing you had a big lipstick mark on your cheek from where your mom kissed you good luck that morning.
- **Ignore this advice if you must.** Perhaps some readers are feeling irritated right now. "How dare you make me wear a suit!" "My piercings express my individuality, and I refuse to remove them!" My response is this: Okay. No problem. If you want to wear jeans every day or dye your hair different colors, then you'll have to work in an environment where that's acceptable—and there are plenty of them. But don't expect to get a job in corporate America.

Ultimately, in any professional interaction, the goal is for your clothes to be in the background. Avoid any situation where any element of your appearance makes a bigger first impression than you do. When you look at yourself in the mirror and you worry that an item of clothing might be too casual or too wrinkled or too low-cut for a professional opportunity, then it probably is. Your best bet is to have one or two reliable outfits that you know are appropriate for a job interview or professional event—and keep them freshly dry-cleaned or washed and ironed at all times.

It's hard enough to get a job. Never, ever lose an opportunity because of what you're wearing.

81. TAKE YOUR ELBOWS OFF THE TABLE

I'm so sorry, but I have to relate another "Kids today!" moment. I recently read an article in which a professor criticized young people as the "fast-food generation" and commented, "What kind of table manners can you expect when the most formal restaurant they've been to is Applebee's?"

There's nothing wrong with Applebee's, or with other casual restaurants for that matter, but in the professional world you're likely to face some occasions where you'll have a job interview over a formal meal. By formal, I basically mean that you'll sit at a table with a table covering and cloth napkins. And make no mistake about it, if you are invited to a business meal with potential employers, they are watching your manners and how you interact in a social setting.

Before you find yourself in this situation, you need to have the experience of dining in such an environment and knowing how to handle yourself. I hate to say it, but what you learned at home dining with your family might not be proper etiquette. Luckily, dining etiquette "rules" are well defined, and you can practice anywhere—in the dorm, at home, or even at Applebee's.

Here are my top etiquette rules for job-interview-related meals. Some of these are common sense and some are a little more complicated, so review them carefully.

1. Always use basic good manners. Say please and thank you, keep your elbows off the table, and don't speak with your mouth full. A good tip is to take small bites so you'll never have a big chunk of food in your mouth when an interviewer asks you a question.

2. Thank your food server as often as necessary. This common courtesy makes a good impression on your tablemates (many interviewers admit to paying close attention to how job candidates treat waitstaff), and since you or your friends have probably waited tables at some point, you know this is greatly appreciated.

3. Do not start to eat until everyone at the table has been served. However, if the person who has not yet been served insists that you begin, it's okay to start. Just go slowly so you don't finish way before your tablemate.

4. When it comes to utensils, eat from the outside in. For example, use the outermost fork (which is usually smaller) for the appetizer course. If you see a spoon, fork, or both placed horizontally at the top of your plate, these are for coffee and dessert. Once you've used a utensil, note that it should never again touch the table. For instance, always rest your soup spoon and butter knife on the saucer or plate rather than directly on the table.

5. Be sure to sip from the correct glass and eat the right roll. Your place setting is arranged with your bread plate to the left of

your plate and your beverage to the right. My friend Diane K. Danielson taught me to remember this order by thinking "BMW," like the car: Bread, Meal, Water.

6. Pass shared items like bread baskets, butter, salad dressing, sauce, sugar, etc. to your right. If they're within your reach, pick them up and start them moving around the table. Do not help yourself first. If someone requests the salt or pepper separately, always pass both together as a set. Whenever you pass something with a handle, such as salad dressing or gravy, pass it with the handle facing the other person so he or she can grasp it easily.

7. Bread should be buttered by breaking off one piece at a time and buttering that piece. Don't cut your bread into lots of pieces or butter the whole slice or roll at once.

8. It's best to avoid drinking alcohol during the job interview process. Water, iced tea, and soda are all appropriate. If you're over 21 and you find yourself in a situation where a drink seems acceptable, be very careful about how much you consume. One glass of wine or beer is a safe bet.

9. When you're finished with your meal, place your utensils together diagonally across your plate. Place your napkin to the left of your plate, not directly on your plate. If you need to get up at any point during the meal, the correct place to put your napkin is on the seat of your chair.

10. I know that *everyone* has their phone on the table during meals these days, but this is not okay during a job interview when you are the candidate. Especially because you're a young professional (a demographic assumed to be obsessed with

being constantly connected), show your maturity and interest in the other person or people at the table by turning off and storing your cell phone, iPhone, BlackBerry, etc. in your jacket or bag. It is never okay to text, e-mail, or—gasp—answer a call (even if your host is checking his or her own device!).

If anything goes wrong—you drop your fork on the floor, you spill your water, etc., remember that good etiquette is about being discreet and making other people comfortable. In other words, don't make a scene! If you drop a utensil on the floor, politely get a server's attention and ask for a new utensil. If you have a pit or bone in your mouth, discreetly remove it with your fork or napkin (no toothpicks at the table). If you spill a beverage, apologize to the table and get a server's attention for help. The more comfortably you handle any snafu, the more quickly your tablemates will forget it ever happened.

In general, you don't want to stand out at the table. For instance, if you're a vegetarian and the only choice is steak, then move the meat around a bit on your plate and eat the side dishes. You also don't want to look picky, so if there's some food you don't like in a dish, such as broccoli in a salad, avoid pushing all of the broccoli to the side of your plate.

If you're not sure what to do in any dining situation, watch the people around you, and take clues from their behavior (and just pray they know what they're doing!).

In reality, perfect etiquette isn't as important as representing yourself as a mature, polite person. Potential employers are not necessarily looking for impeccable, Miss Manners–approved etiquette as much as they are looking to make sure you would represent a company with class and confidence.

Make This Work for You

This week, apply the above tips in any dining situation, no matter how casual. Get in the habit of good manners so they feel like second nature when you're in a professional situation. And if your school offers etiquette training (often held at a local restaurant, so free food is involved!), definitely sign up. Get as much experience and training in this area as possible.

Also note that the points in this section have focused on general American dining etiquette, but these are only the tip of the iceberg. Etiquette rules can vary based on the type of cuisine you're eating (think chopsticks), the region of the country you live in, and of course everything changes if you have the opportunity to dine overseas. If you're particularly interested in this topic, or you find yourself in a challenging dining situation (lobster, sushi, Ethiopian food, etc.), here are some additional resources to check out:

GENERAL RESOURCES

- *Emily Post's The Etiquette Advantage in Business: Personal Skills for Professional Success* by Peggy Post and Peter Post

- *Business Etiquette for Dummies* by Sue Fox

INTERNATIONAL ETIQUETTE GUIDES

- *Do's and Taboos Around the World* Edited by Roger E. Axtell

- *Kiss, Bow, or Shake Hands: The Bestselling Guide to Doing Business in More Than 60 Countries* by Terri Morrison and Wayne A. Conaway

☐ Done!

---

82. MOCK INTERVIEW

Now that you've done your research, determined your salary strategy, prepared what you're going to wear, and anticipated dining situations, it's time to talk about the core of the interview: the questions you'll be asked.

Every time I give a workshop or speak on a panel about job hunting, I receive countless questions about how to succeed in job interviews, and I always give the same advice: practice, practice, practice. You can anticipate the majority of questions you'll be asked, so the more experience you have answering those questions succinctly and successfully, and the more feedback you've gotten about your performance, the better you'll do on the Big Day. Never let your real interview be the first time you talk out loud about your experience and what you want in your career.

For expertise on this topic, I turned to the people who know best: recruiters and hiring managers who interview hundreds of candidates a year. I also strongly recommend that you read a book or blog or study a website that lists common interview questions and shares tips on the best answers. Be as prepared as you can possibly be so you walk into that interview with as much confidence as possible.

Here are some important tips on how you should prepare for a job interview:

- **Become a better listener.** Statistics show that the more the interviewer talks on a job interview, the more likely the candidate is to get the job. This doesn't mean being silent or answering questions with one-word grunts; it means being a good listener. Allow the interviewer to share his or her thoughts, and never interrupt. This is particularly important at the beginning of an interview. Let the interviewer set the tone. You can practice this by being a better listener in conversations with your friends and family.

- **Be able to explain why you made the choices you've made.** Employers are not just listening for what you did—they can learn that from your résumé anyway—but why you did certain things and how you felt about them. Executive recruiter Lauren E. Smith says, "I can tell a lot about individuals by what they choose to tell me and what they don't tell me. I can tell whether individuals just let life happen to them or whether they were proactive. I learn about their thinking process. I want to know why they chose the college they did, how they chose their major, why they took a particular job on their résumé. You can say it wasn't a good choice, but I want to know why. You have to have reasons."

- **Don't be wishy-washy.** Think about it: if you walk in and say you're interested in working for this manufacturing firm, but you're also looking into management consulting, and the next candidate says it's been her lifelong dream to work in manufacturing and this firm is her first choice, who do you think will get the job? Never say that you don't know what you want, even if that's the truth. This advice comes from Don Leon of Stephen-Bradford Search. "Your job on the interview is to get this job," he says. "Then you'll have the choice of whether or not to accept it. When you're in the interview, you have to treat this like it's the only job in the world for you." Remember, an interview is a pass/fail situation.

- **Think PAR.** Don also recommends talking about your experiences in the format of the Problem you encountered (such as raising funds for your string quartet to tour in Europe), the Action you took (hosting a fund-raiser and selling sponsorships to local music-related businesses), and the Result you achieved (raising enough money to tour for three weeks and pay for all four students' travel and accommodations). When you're mock interviewing, have your mock interviewer keep track of how well you answer questions in this key format. The goal here is to give examples to back up any general statements you make. For instance, "I'm a responsible leader," sounds nice but hollow unless you can back it up with a PAR example, such as "Junior year I was a resident adviser in my dorm, and one of the freshmen had an asthma attack and needed to go to the emergency room. This put all of her floor-mates into a panic. I asked one student to be my contact person, and I called her every thirty minutes by cell phone to keep the sick girl's friends updated on her situation. She recovered, and when we got back to the dorm, several students came up and thanked me for keeping them in the loop and allowing them to show their concern for their friend while not panicking. The dean of students learned of the situation from the asthmatic girl's parents and I was given a special award for leadership at the end of the school year."

- **Anticipate dreaded questions.** If you have a low GPA, a major totally unrelated to the job you are seeking, a gap in your education, or any other red flag on your résumé or in your professional or academic history, assume that the interviewer will ask you to explain it, so have a strong answer prepared. I recommend practicing a concise, positive response (e.g., "I struggled with core class requirements my first two years, but as you can see, my grades improved significantly as I started taking more courses in my major. That coursework fascinated me and most closely relates to the job I'm seeking"). Test your answers while mock interviewing to make sure you have a good response to any challenging questions and your tone is not defensive or apologetic. It's okay to have blemishes in your past as long as you can address them in a constructive way.

- **Learn how to talk about your weaknesses.** A commonly dreaded interview question for job seekers of all ages is, "What is your biggest weakness?" There are several schools of thought on this topic; for instance, some people feel the right answer is to describe a strength and hide it as a fault (e.g., "I just can't help being organized!" or "I'm a total workaholic and never leave a project undone"). I think this strategy is transparent to an interviewer. My advice on answering this question is to talk about a real weakness, to show that you are self-aware, and to use the question as an opportunity to show that you are someone who works on developing yourself and overcoming your flaws. For instance, "During my first internship I had a hard time communicating professionally, but I carefully observed my colleagues at work and took a business writing class this semester, and I feel I've really improved."

- **Prepare more questions than you could ever ask.** You never know what topics will be covered during the interview, so when the interviewer says, "Do you have any questions for me?" you always need to have some. This is important because you want to show your interest in learning more, and to show that you are prepared. Don't ask any questions to which you could have found the answers through the company's website or informational interviewing. Here are some tips for preparing good questions:

- Don Leon likes the question "How did you get into this business?" People love to talk about themselves, so let the interviewer share his or her story.

- In general, avoid "Why" questions, says Don, because they tend to put people on the defensive. "What are the reasons this job is available?" is better than "Why is this job available?" "How" and "What" questions are the best bet.

- Ask a question related to an initiative, project, or positive news item you've discovered through your company research that you find interesting. This is a good way to show you've done your homework: "Can you tell me a bit more about the company's new social media initiative and how that's going so far?"

- Show your ambition and desire to have an immediate impact: "What would you consider to be exceptional performance from someone in this position during the first three to six months on the job?"

- Ask about the culture of the organization and what type of person succeeds there. Remember that you want to make sure the job is a good fit for you. You might ask, "What are the traits and skills of people who are the most successful at this organization?"

- Ask for the job! At the end of the interview, it's absolutely encouraged to say, "I'm very interested in this job, and I would love to work for your company."

- **Inquire about next steps.** To mitigate the stress of waiting to know if you're getting another interview or being offered the job, ask at the end of your interview what the next steps of the process will be. Most interviewers will let you know if you'll hear back in a week or two, if there are several interviews in the process, or if you'll be hearing from HR directly or from the specific department to which you're applying. Don't be too pesky about it, but try to get some information about what will happen next.

When it comes to interview success, I'll say this one last time: practice, practice, practice. Ask anyone and everyone to mock interview you, just as you would ask lots of people to run lines with you if you were starring in a play. Most college career services offices will videotape mock interviews, which will also help you to improve any tics in your speech or bad habits like slouching or gesturing with your hands too much. And wear your planned interview outfit to give it a test run before real interviewing begins.

If you follow the above tips, when you walk into that room with a real interview for a real job, you will have the confidence of knowing deep, deep down in your gut that you are totally prepared to wow those interviewers as they've never been wowed before. Preparation is *everything*.

Make This Work for You

Mock interview with anyone you can! If you can't find someone to interview you in person, you can do this by Skype, iChat, or FaceTime. In addition, I recommend writing down your answers to the most common job interview questions so that you'll be familiar with them and will be able to recall experiences and stories you want to be sure to relate. Here are some questions to work with, and again, I recommend buying or borrowing an interview preparation book so you can look at an even larger variety of questions that might be asked:

- Tell me about yourself.

- Why did you choose to attend your college?

- What do you see yourself doing five years from now? Ten years from now?

- Why are you interested in this career?

- How well do you work with people? Do you prefer working alone or in teams?

- How would a good friend describe you?

- Tell me about your proudest achievement.

- What's been your biggest disappointment, and how did you handle it?

- Give me an example of a time when you had to think out of the box.

- What makes you qualified for this position?

- What do you think it takes to be successful in a company like ours?

- In what ways do you think you can make a contribution to our company?

- What's the most recent book you've read?

- What two or three accomplishments have given you the most satisfaction? Why?

- Why did you decide to seek a position in this company?

- What can you tell us about our company?

- What do you know about our competitors?

- What two or three things are most important to you in a job?

There are lots more questions—one book even offers 250—but this is a good start. Again, I encourage you to write out your answers, practice with your career services office or willing friends and family members, and ask eye-witnesses on your informational interviews about the most common interview questions and what answers are most impressive in the particular industries where you'd like to work.

☐ Done!

83. NEVER, EVER, EVER ARRIVE LATE TO A JOB INTERVIEW

There are unavoidable mistakes that can happen to the best of us, and then there are avoidable mistakes. Being late for a job interview falls squarely in the category of totally, massively, extremely avoidable mistakes. There is simply no excuse ever to be late for a job interview, yet according to every human resources person I speak to, this happens all the time.

Showing up late to a job interview is a red flag to an employer that you're either not that interested in the job or you're just not professional and respectful enough to show up on time. I know that life happens: traffic jams occur, public transportation runs late, security check-in lines at big office buildings can snake around the lobby. Take every precaution you can (e.g., do a dry run of the drive to the interview rather than trusting your GPS or MapQuest directions, bring spare pantyhose in case you get a run on the way), and then assume that whatever can go wrong on interview day will go wrong and give yourself gobs of time to get to the interview. Bring a magazine (newspapers may leave black ink on your fingers), iPad, or book to read if you arrive early and need to kill some time in the car or at a nearby cafe. Or just sit and listen to music in your car or take some deep breaths to calm any pre-interview nerves. Just don't get so distracted that you end up running in at the last minute! As the stern music director of my high school used to say when warning us about being punctual for rehearsals: to be early is to be on time, to be on time is to be late, and to be late is to be unforgivable!

Now on the flip side, don't be too early for an interview either. This can be equally harmful and downright irritating to employers who are expecting you at a later time. By all means, get to the company's building or parking lot as early as you'd like, but don't enter the actual office any more than 15 minutes before your scheduled interview time.

84. BE NICE TO RECEPTIONISTS

When I arrived at my interview for the Rotary scholarship (after sitting in the car for nearly an hour because I was so early!), I found an elderly man sitting outside the interview room. He was reading the newspaper.

I wasn't sure if he was even involved with the Rotary program, but I went up and introduced myself. He invited me to sit down next to him and told me he was a retired Rotary Club member and had volunteered to wait outside the interview room for the students who arrived. I told him my name was Lindsey Pollak, I was excited about the interview, and I asked him about his experience with Rotary. We chatted for about ten minutes before the interview room door opened and I was called in.

A few weeks later when I received the call saying that I had won the scholarship, the head of the interview committee told me that the elderly gentleman outside the interview room had an equal vote in deciding who would win the scholarship. They wanted to see how each candidate would interact with him: Would they ignore him because he was elderly? Avoid him because they didn't know why he was there? Say hello and then bury their heads in their notes? They liked the fact that I had engaged with him, and that I had not just talked about myself or pumped him for information, but that I had asked him questions about himself.

Lesson: The minute you walk into the building where you're interviewing for a job, or any time you call that office, you are being assessed. Be polite and kind to security guards, receptionists, assistants, everyone. Any interaction you have will likely be reported to the hiring manager—positive or negative. I know of many companies where hiring managers ask their assistants or receptionists for their impressions of a candidate. It makes sense: these people will see you and interact with you every day if you get the job, so they want to know what you'll be like. Show that you are the kind of person who will be nice and respectful to everyone, and you'll increase your chances of getting the job. Even if you're nervous, even if the elevator is taking forever, even if the person working at the front desk looks exactly like your ex-boyfriend or girlfriend, be on your best behavior at all times. Make no mistake about it: when you're interviewing for a job, all eyes are on you.

85. GO WITH THE FLOW

While most job interviews follow a pretty typical format, you never know what might happen when you arrive on interview day. People are quirky, interviewers have good and bad days like the rest of us, and in some cases, the interviewer may want to make a statement by *not* adhering to standard interview procedure. There is no way to predict what might happen when you walk into that room, so you have to be prepared—I mean overprepared—for anything.

If an interviewer throws you a curve ball (such as asking an unexpected question or talking about a job you hadn't known about previously), do your best to stay in the moment and go where the interviewer takes you (as long as it's appropriate and legal, of course). Listen carefully to what the interviewer is telling you or asking, and take time answering questions, especially if they are unanticipated. Feel free to ask for clarification on any questions you don't understand or for more information about anything that is new to you.

Going with the flow also means staying true to yourself. An interview that does not turn out to be what you expected is an enormously important piece of information about what working for that employer might be like. An interview is also a chance for you to determine if an opportunity is a good fit for you, so pay attention to any weird feelings in your gut or hints about what it might be like to work for the organization (for instance, if the interviewer takes three phone calls and checks her BlackBerry during your interview, it may be a highly stressful environment). Going with the flow might mean crossing that employer off your list and flowing toward something more suited to your expectations.

But I do encourage you to be open to the unexpected, the surprising, and the spontaneous in your interviews. Sometimes those are the best and most enjoyable opportunities of all. I once interviewed for a position with a woman who kept the door open while we were chatting. About halfway through the interview, a colleague stuck her head in the door and joined the conversation for a few minutes. She and I hit it off immediately and she asked me to stop by her office on the way out. As it happened, the first job wasn't a great fit, and the second woman offered me a job instead!

86. BE AVAILABLE

How often do you check your e-mail? How about your voice mail? Do you check messages when you're away on vacation? How long does it generally take you to return a phone call?

These are really important questions when you're involved in a job search. Once you start putting yourself out there and interviewing, you have to make sure you're available when all of your hard work starts to pay off. Check every e-mail account you have (including inboxes on social media sites like LinkedIn—better yet, set messages on these sites to forward to your regular e-mail inbox) and listen to every voice mail message as soon as possible, even if you think you recognize the number that called.

I was shocked to hear a story on this topic from Barbara Sucoff, founder and president of Focused Consulting, LLC. Barbara has a wide variety of experience training all levels of employees at some of the top corporations around the world. She recently told me that one of her corporate clients, a recruiter of candidates from college campuses, shared her exasperation one day during the spring hiring season. "Her biggest source of disappointment," Barbara told me, "occurs when a candidate who is about to receive an offer *never* returns a phone call to her or a senior vice president at her company." I was shocked enough, but Barbara added, "This has happened to me more than once as well."

It's one thing not to return a phone call from a geeky girl or guy who likes you, but not to return a call from someone who is offering you a job? That's insane! Especially when a job offer is at stake, you must return all calls within twenty-four hours (even better, on the same day when possible). More than a few breaks have been given to the first candidate who responds to an opportunity, and more than a few opportunities have been lost when someone takes too long to respond. Returning a phone call or e-mail message quickly is a sure sign of professionalism, respect, and competitiveness—all positive attributes in the job market.

Make This Work for You

It's perfectly fine not to be available 24/7 (and employers understand that if you're still in college you'll be spending a lot of time in class or at the library), but you must check your e-mail and voice mail regularly. One suggestion is to schedule a certain time of the day to return all important e-mails and voice mails. You won't struggle to find the time if you always spend about thirty minutes every day, say from 3:30 to 4:00 p.m., catching up on any messages. When you're heavily involved in a job hunt, you'll probably want to schedule this time twice a day to make sure you are appropriately responsive.

If you go away on vacation, it's finals week, or you're incapacitated in some way, set your e-mail with an out-of-office autoresponse explaining when you'll be able to return messages ("I will be unavailable until Thursday, November

30. I will respond to messages then. Thank you.") Any phone numbers you've given to potential employers or networking contacts should also have an out-of-office message. If you're actively involved in a job search and believe that an interview opportunity or job offer may be just around the corner, I'd add an alternate contact number, e-mail, or contact person to that message.

Finally, slap a sticky note on your computer screen reminding you to change your outgoing voice mail message and turn off your e-mail autoresponder when you return from any time away.

Don't miss an opportunity because of a missed message or delayed response. Ever.

☐ Done!

87. PERSIST (WITHOUT BEING A PEST)

Once you've had a job interview, it may take awhile before you know where you stand. This is a particularly difficult time, mostly because your time frame for a job offer (now) is often different from the employer's time frame (when they get to it). So, how do you remain on an employer's radar screen after the job interview without being a pest?

I learned a good strategy for this when I was quite young. My mother worked for herself and had a home office. When we were little, my brother, sister, and I used to pester her constantly for attention while she was working. One day when my brother was about five, he kept knocking on her door, walking in, making noise, and generally being a pain in the neck, and finally my mom came out of her office and yelled, "Robert! You have to stop! If you walk in one more time you're going to be in big, big trouble!"

"But, Mommy," Robert said, "I just wanted to tell you that I love you."

Of course she melted, hugged him, and let him play in her office the rest of the afternoon because he was so sweet and she felt terrible about yelling at him.

I, of course, was annoyed that I hadn't thought of this strategy myself.

Robert, who is now a lawyer (coincidence? I don't think so), had great instincts for smart persistence: if you persist in a meaningful, strategic way that brings value to the other person, you can often get what you want.

So, what's the professional version of saying, "Mommy, I love you"?

Here are some tips, and I urge you to keep in mind that every aspect of your follow-up is about what *you* can do for the company, *not* what the company can do for you. It's all about them, all the time.

- **Write a value-added thank-you note within twelve to twenty-four hours.** As you know, thank-you notes are positively essential for any people who interview you for a job (if there are four people in the room, then you should write four separate thank-you notes). In your thank-you note, which can be an e-mail, don't just express your gratitude for the interview; reiterate that you really want the job and that you are eager to contribute to the organization immediately:

  Hello, [Name],

  Thank you again for interviewing me for the _____ position last week. I wanted to check in and say again that

I'm very interested in the job and I would love to join your team. I'm particularly interested in contributing to _____. [Specifically mention an aspect of the job or a specific project to show that you were listening.]

Optional: After the interview I've thought more about the issues we discussed and I wanted to share some thoughts about how I can add value to the company. [List two to three ideas you've had based on what you learned about the job that the company needs to fill.]

I'm sure that you're very busy; I just wanted to check in, thank you again, and say that I look forward to hearing back from you about possible next steps.

Best regards,
[Your full name]

- **Wait at least a week to ten days before making any additional contact.** Be patient. Often it can take at least this long, and often longer, for a decision to be made, particularly at a large company.
- **If you don't hear from an employer in the time frame they've specified, try sending an e-mail.** Instead of picking up the phone, e-mail your main contact with a brief follow-up note. However, never criticize the employer for not getting back to you. Do not use phrases like, "Since I haven't heard from you . . ." or "You're probably not interested in me, but . . ." These are unnecessary and a big turn-off to employers who may just be busy. A great strategy is to do some additional research on the company and point out another fact you've learned that makes you eager to contribute to the organization's success, such as a new product,

an expansion to a new market, or a new development in the industry.

- **Leave a voice mail message.** If e-mail doesn't do the trick, try this tactic: call late at night or early in the morning when your contact is unlikely to pick up and you can leave a voice mail message. This is a nice way to reassert your interest, show your enthusiasm (make sure your tone is polite and friendly), and provide similar information to the e-mail above. If your contact does answer the phone, the best way to avoid being a pest is to ask this simple question before launching into your spiel: "Hello, this is Sofia Torres, the student you interviewed two weeks ago. Are you available for a few minutes?" This question shows respect for the employer, demonstrates your professionalism, and is likely to get you a much more sympathetic ear. The person will either say yes and then you can use the preceding suggestions, or he or she will give you a better time to call back.

- **Don't act desperate.** While you should be persistent and enthusiastic about working for a particular company, nobody likes the smell of desperation. If you're not sure how your persistence is coming across, have a friend listen in on your follow-up calls or test your e-mail message before you send.

- **Know when to let go.** You know the book *He's Just Not That Into You*? Sometimes this happens in the job search and you simply never hear back from a company that interviewed you. It stinks, but it happens. If you have politely and diligently followed up three times and haven't received a response, it's probably time to accept that the job isn't yours.

Finally, keep busy and keep looking. Even if you think an interview went extremely well, be aware that no job is a slam dunk and you never want all of your eggs in one basket. Do the appropriate follow-up work mentioned above, keep pursuing other options, and then let things happen. Take a break, watch some TV, set up a new informational interview, peruse a biography of someone who inspires you, attend a networking event, go for a jog. Do whatever you need to do to relax. Part of persistence is knowing when to let go and let the process happen.

Chapter 10

BEFORE YOU HEAD OFF INTO THE REAL WORLD . . .

I'm not ready to say good-bye just yet. Before you sail off into your fabulous future, I'd like to share a few parting points.

There are challenging days in any career, and these last three tips keep me going when I need a little pick-me-up or a check-in with my goals and dreams. This final section of the book is about being true to yourself and enjoying the journey of your working life, no matter where your path takes you. I hope you'll keep these thoughts in mind as you travel from college to career and make your mark in the Real World.

88. ASK FOR HELP WHEN YOU NEED IT

No one expects you to know everything.

There is no way that this book, or any career advice resource, can provide answers to absolutely all of the questions you'll face throughout your career planning and job search. And even if it could, with the speed of technology today, new situations and dilemmas are popping up all the time. Plus, every industry has different rules and protocols, and every region of the country has its own set of standard practices. With so much variation, how can you make sure you're doing the right thing in a given situation?

When in doubt, ask.

This is a foolproof strategy for a young person who is new to the workforce, and it works for established professionals as well. There is no situation too small that you can't ask a few trusted friends or advisers for guidance or reassurance. If you're not sure whether to call your new boss John or Mr. Smith, ask a few people in the office what's appropriate. Not sure whether that blouse you're planning to wear to a job interview is a little too low-cut? Try it on for a few people, and ask for their honest opinions. Concerned that a networking e-mail you're writing may not be properly worded? Send it to a few reliable friends or family members for approval and editing before you send it to your contact. For more general questions, such as what graduate programs are best in your field or what networking events are best to attend, post your questions to the people in your social networks.

Taking just a few minutes or hours to get more feedback and advice can mean the difference between winning and losing an opportunity. And you'll hear feedback from a friendly source rather than a potential employer.

During your career planning and job searching there will be lots of decisions you can't make on your own, and situations in which you can't know the right answer without asking someone with more experience.

Ask for help when you need it. We all need it sometimes.

89. BECOME A LIFELONG EXPERT ON FINDING YOUR OWN BLISS

Still want to do more self-exploration? The absolute truth is that figuring out what career will make you happiest is a life-long endeavor. While many coaches, counselors, assessment tests, books, blogs, and websites can help guide you in the right direction, the hard work of making decisions is up to you. The good news and the bad news is that you'll probably revisit this issue of "Who am I, and what was I put on this planet to do?" at several points in your life.

Personally, I try to see it as an exciting thing—that life changes, we change, and our careers can grow and morph and expand in infinite and varied directions. Just look at all the movie stars who started out as waiters, and the CEOs who started in the mailroom, and any entrepreneur who began as a company employee.

If your career is an important part of your life and you hope to express yourself through your job, then it's worth investing the time and effort to continue discovering your strengths and goals throughout your life. Luckily, bookstores and

Reality Check

"Instead of thinking of your career like a ladder and trying to go straight up to the top, think of your career like a smartphone. Your upbringing and your education are your basic operating system; from there, think about your career as a series of apps that you download. Some of the apps will be fun; some of the apps will be side projects and passions; some of the apps will be skills you're learning on the job."

Jenny Blake, blogger/speaker/life coach, author of *Life After College* the Internet are chock-full of content for you. Even better, many self-discovery books, blogs, and social media communities are geared toward particular segments of the population—minorities, liberal arts majors, adventurers, and career changers, just to name a few. You're likely to find a resource that suits your specific needs, so search until you find one (the Resources at the end of this book will give you a good start).

And the world contains an infinite number of people you can talk to—for advice, ideas, feedback, information, opportunities, and support. Talking and listening will serve you and your career well for the rest of your life.

If this issue of determining your ideal career path is exciting to you, then I strongly encourage you to do some further exploration at the library, a bookstore, online, and at in-person events. And, hey, there's a strong chance you'll find Yours Truly perusing the same self-development bookshelves, posting on the same social media sites, and attending some of the same conferences and events. As I'm sure you've guessed by now, I love this stuff.

90. *DON'T* CURB YOUR ENTHUSIASM

Every single tip in this book can help you achieve your career goals and dreams, and help you land a job you'll love. But there is one more element that I know from experience is the tactic that will put you over the top. And with this element, you will probably enjoy yourself a whole lot more in the process.

It's enthusiasm (also known as passion, excitement, a true love for what you're doing).

Think about it: people want to hire someone who will walk into the workplace every day with a smile, a real desire to be there, and a genuine wish to contribute. All things being equal, an employer will hire the person who appears to want the job most, who is passionate about the company's products, who can't help but read all of the industry journals and trade publications in his or her spare time. Be that person. Show that you want it.

In the end, I think achieving your greatest career dreams boils down to fear and overcoming it: Don't be afraid to show your passion, to say you really want the job, to introduce yourself to amazing people, to express that you have big goals. Don't be afraid to be a huge success. Everyone can achieve their wildest, most incredible career dreams. I see it happen every day.

You have nothing to be afraid of.

RESOURCES

ASSOCIATIONS, WEBSITES, AND ORGANIZATIONS FOR STUDENTS AND RECENT GRADS

Here are some organizations to check out for further information and opportunities. Descriptions are taken from the organizations' websites and, when available, provide Twitter handles. Note that listing here does not necessarily imply official endorsement by the author or publisher of this book.

AIESEC

Present in more than a hundred countries and territories and with more than fifty thousand members, AIESEC is the world's largest youth-run organization. It offers young people the opportunity to participate in international internships, experience leadership, and take part in a global learning environment. Each year, AIESEC provides more than ten thousand members the challenging opportunity to live and work in foreign countries in the areas of management, technology, education, and development.

www.aiesec.org

@AIESEC

AmeriCorps National Civilian Community Corps

AmeriCorps NCCC is a full-time, team-based residential program for men and women ages 18 to 24. The mission of AmeriCorps NCCC is to strengthen communities and develop leaders through direct, team-based national and community service.

www.americorps.gov/for_individuals/choose/nccc.asp

@americorps

Association of Young Journalists and Writers

AYJW is a nationwide network of persons younger than 35 who are working in the various media of the press. AYJW promotes and facilitates opportunities for the professional development and growth of journalists in their first decade in journalism.

www.ayjw.org

The Black Collegian Online

This is the electronic version of *The Black Collegian* magazine (a career and self-development magazine distributed on more than eight hundred campuses nationwide, primarily through career services offices). It is the first website dedicated to providing rich content and resources to black collegians and all people of color seeking career and self-development information.

www.blackcollegian.com

RESOURCES   313

Brazen Careerist

Brazen Careerist is a growing community of connectors, coaches, job seekers, recruiters, and entrepreneurs with a focus on Generation Y.
www.brazencareerist.com
@BrazenCareerist

Break Away: The Alternative Break Connection

Break Away: The Alternative Break Connection, is a national nonprofit organization that supports the development of alternative break programs by providing training and information primarily to colleges, universities, and nonprofit organizations interested in creating lifelong active citizens through these intensive service-learning programs.
www.alternativebreaks.org
@activecitizenHQ

City Year

City Year, a member program of AmeriCorps, unites a diverse group of 17- to 24-year-old people for a year of full-time, rigorous community service, leadership development, and civic engagement.
www.cityyear.org
@CityYear

Collegiate Entrepreneurs' Organization

The Collegiate Entrepreneurs' Organization (CEO) is a global entrepreneurship network serving more than four hundred colleges and universities. CEO provides student entrepreneurs with opportunities, events, chapter activities, and conferences to help start businesses.

www.c-e-o.org

Daily Endeavor

Daily Endeavor is a project to build the most comprehensive guide to jobs that's written by real people. The site's goal is to create a place where anyone can look up a type of job they have an interest in, or discover new jobs they never knew existed.

www.dailyendeavor.com

@dailyendeavor

Downtown Women's Club

Downtown Women's Club is a national online and in-person community designed for smart and sophisticated businesswomen. Its mission is to empower women through access to information and opportunities for collaboration.

www.downtownwomensclub.com

@DowntownWoman

Echoing Green

Echoing Green is an organization that provides start-up funds for projects that promote social change. In addition to funding, they offer a range of support services to social entrepreneurs, including training, networking opportunities, and consulting.

www.echoinggreen.org

@echoinggreen

Ed2010

Ed2010 is a community of "young, eager magazine editors and magazine-editor wannabes" who want to learn more about the industry and achieve their dream magazine jobs.
www.ed2010.com
@ed2010news

Forte Foundation

The Forte Foundation works to inspire young women to pursue leadership careers in business and to increase their access to business education and business networks.
www.fortefoundation.org
@fortefoundation

GenXPat.com

GenXPat is a resource site for the new generation of young, internationally mobile professionals. This is the place to learn more about living and working abroad, get support when the going gets tough, and connect with other GenXpats.
www.genxpat.com

GradView.com

GradView.com includes virtual tours of top graduate schools in the United States and Canada, graduate school financial-aid information and financial-aid resources, information and articles on careers and career planning as they relate to graduate school, information on graduate school admissions testing, and a library of articles.
www.gradview.com

INROADS

The missions of INROADS is to develop and place talented minority youth in business and industry and prepare them for corporate and community leadership. INROADS seeks high-performing black, Hispanic/Latino, and Native American students for internship opportunities with some of the nation's largest companies.
www.inroads.org
@INROADS

Institute of International Education

IIE administers two hundred international grant programs, including the Fulbright Program. Its mission is to increase the number of students, scholars, and professionals who have the opportunity to study, teach, and conduct research outside of their own country.
www.iie.org
@IIEglobal

InternationalStudent.com

InternationalStudent.com is an international student and study abroad online portal for those who are looking to further their education overseas. The site's goal is to enable students to pursue their dreams of seeing the world and improving their education experience.
www.internationalstudent.com
@intstudent

Jaycees: The United States Junior Chamber

The United States Junior Chamber (Jaycees) gives people ages 18 to 40 the tools they need in the areas of business development,

management, and community service, including access to individualized training and international connections.
www.usjaycees.org
@USJaycees

Management Leadership for Tomorrow

MLT's mission is to increase the presence of minorities in fast-track entry-level jobs and major graduate business schools as preparation for leadership positions in corporations, nonprofit organizations, and entrepreneurial ventures.
www.ml4t.org

National Urban League Young Professionals

NULYP's mission is to engage young professionals in the National Urban League's movement toward the achievement of social and economic equality. NULYP does this by providing an effective forum through which young professionals can support the Urban League's more than a hundred affiliates in 35 states and the District of Columbia.
www.nul.org

Negotiating Women

Negotiating Women, Inc., offers live training and online courses to provide practical advice for women at every stage of their careers. Their distinctive approach helps women claim their value and create conditions for success in business.
www.negotiatingwomen.com

Personal Branding Blog and Student Branding Blog

The Personal Branding Blog and the Student Branding Blog teach professionals how to position themselves for success so that they become known for their passion and expertise. The content includes videos, podcasts, interviews with experts, articles, research reports, games, and more.
www.personalbrandingblog.com
www.studentbranding.com
@DanSchawbel

QuintCareers.com

QuintCareers offers more than 4,500 pages of free content to empower people's success in college and career, including many templates and guides for the creation of résumés, cover letters, and portfolios.
www.quintcareers.com
@QuintCareers

Salary.com

Salary.com is a career-management portal that gives individuals access to industry-leading salary information and a unique set of career management tools. The site engages individuals at every step of their careers and offers advertisers unique opportunities to reach and influence them during key decision-making moments.
www.salary.com
@Salary

Teach for America

Teach for America is the national corps of outstanding recent college graduates of all academic majors who commit two years to teach in urban and rural public schools and become lifelong leaders in ensuring educational equity and excellence for all children.
www.teachforamerica.org
@TeachForAmerica

Toastmasters International

Toastmasters clubs are groups of people who meet for the purpose of improving their public speaking skills. At Toastmasters, members learn by speaking to groups and working with others in a supportive environment. The goal of the organization is to help its members become better speakers and leaders, and gain the confidence to succeed in whatever paths they've chosen in life.
www.toastmasters.org
@Toastmasters

Urban Interns

Urban Interns is a resource for finding part-time jobs, internships, and freelance positions—including virtual-work opportunities—and it is free to job seekers.
www.urbaninterns.com
@urbaninterns

Vault.com

Vault provides a mix of free and paid subscription content for job seekers, including job postings, anonymous employer reviews, career-advice articles, industry blogs, and digital career guidebooks. Vault also provides profiles of law schools and MBA programs.

www.vault.com

@VaultCareers

Young Entrepreneur Council

The Young Entrepreneur Council is a nonprofit led by the world's top young entrepreneurs. The YEC's mission is to take action against youth unemployment through programs that encourage aspiring entrepreneurs to start their own businesses. International initiatives include entrepreneurship education, advocacy, mentoring programs, events, and healthcare for young entrepreneurs.

www.youngentrepreneurcouncil.com

@theYEC

Young Nonprofit Professionals Network

YNPN engages and supports future nonprofit and community leaders through professional development, networking, and social opportunities designed for young people involved in the nonprofit community.

www.ynpn.org

@ynpn

Young Politicians of America

Young Politicians of America is a service-learning movement composed of young Americans ages 14 to 22 working together to revive political discourse and awareness by establishing nonpartisan civic clubs in high schools and colleges.

www.ypa.org

Your Success Network

YSN is an online community that offers young professionals ages 18 to 34 the Real World knowledge, tools, resources, and strategies critical to finding success at an early age. YSN includes online portfolios, discussion forums, industry Q&As, professional tools, resources, event listings, and career-related how-to guides.
www.ysn.com

Youth Service America

YSA is a resource center that partners with thousands of organizations committed to increasing the quality and quantity of volunteer opportunities for young people ages 5 to 25 to serve locally, nationally, and globally.
www.ysa.org
@youthservice

Youth Venture

Youth Venture helps to empower young people ages 12 to 20 by providing them all the tools necessary to create civic-minded organizations, clubs, or businesses. The organization provides access to a variety of resources, including a national network of like-minded young people, media opportunities, and up to $1,000 in seed capital.
www.youthventure.org
@AshokaGenV

AUTHOR'S NOTE

Dear Readers:

This book shared 90 tips that I hope will help you make a smooth and successful transition from college to career. But I'm sure there are tips I missed—this is where you come in! Is there any strategy you've used that worked like a charm? Anything I recommended that didn't pan out? Any tips you'd love to share with people in your situation? Connect with other job seekers and share your ideas on my Facebook page at www.Facebook.com/CollegetoCareer.

Thanks and good luck!

Lindsey

ACKNOWLEDGMENTS

So much has changed since the first edition of this book!

Thank you first to my enthusiastic new team at HarperCollins: Hollis Heimbouch, Colleen Lawrie, and Rohnda Barnes. Thank you to Knox Huston, Sarah Brown, and Matthew Inman for your early support. Thank you to Kaitlin Davis and Stephanie Michaan for your editing help, and to John Sansevere, Ben Salmon, and George Greenfield for your expertise.

Many thanks to the successful professionals, recruiters, and career-services professionals who have shared your experiences and insights with me—I couldn't have written this book without you. And thank you to all the college students and recent grads I've met over the years who inspire me every day. Keep those one-exclamation-point e-mails coming!

I am extremely lucky to have an amazing network of friends and supporters who have advised and encouraged me, especially those who championed this book project early on. Thank you to Laura Baird, Susan Phillips Bari, Gillian Baudo, Derek Billings, Mary Carlomagno, Meryl Weinsaft Cooper, Jason Criss, Sheila Curran, Diane Danielson, Cher Duffield, Carol Frohlinger, Jodi Glickman, Joanne Gordon, Christine Hassler, Natasha Hoehn, Cassandra Krause, Mignon Lawless, Alexandra Levit, the LinkedIn team, Jennifer Macaluso-Gilmore, Danielle Martin, Maggie Mistal, Solana Nolfo, Monaqui Porter-Young, the PwC team, Cari Sommer, Susan Stautberg and the women of TARA, Trudy Steinfeld, Barbara Sucoff, and Manisha Thakor.

Eternal thanks to my supportive and loving family: Mom, Dad, Rob, Anne, and Laura Pollak; Meredith Bernstein; the Rahos; and the Goodman/Ramsays. And to my loving and kind in-laws, Vivian, Georges, and Valerie Gotlib.

Finally, I dedicate this book to my husband, Evan, and our daughter, Chloe: I love you.